THE AFTERLIFE OF

Pitt Series in Russian and East European Studies
Jonathan Harris, Editor

THE AFTERLIFE OF AUSTRIA-HUNGARY

The Image of the Habsburg Monarchy in Interwar Europe

ADAM KOŻUCHOWSKI

UNIVERSITY OF PITTSBURGH PRESS

Published by the University of Pittsburgh Press, Pittsburgh, Pa. 15260
Copyright © 2013, University of Pittsburgh Press
All rights reserved
Manufactured in the United States of America
Printed on acid-free paper
10 9 8 7 6 5 4 3 2 1

Originally published as *Pośmiertne dzieje Austro-Węgier: Obraz monarchii habsburskiej w piśmiennictwie międzywojennym*
© Instytut Historii PAN and Wydawnictwo Neirton, 2009

Library of Congress Cataloging-in-Publication Data

Kożuchowski, Adam, 1979–
Posmiertne dzieje Austro-Wegier. English
The Afterlife of Austria-Hungary: The Image of the Habsburg Monarchy in Interwar Europe / Adam Kożuchowski.
    pages cm. — (Pitt Series in Russian and East European Studies)
Includes bibliographical references and index.
ISBN 978-0-8229-6265-6 (pbk.)
1. Austria—History—1867–1918—Historiography. 2. Hungary—History—1867–1918—Historiography. 3. Habsburg, House of. 4. Habsburg, House of—In literature. 5. Historiography—History—20th century. I. Title.
DB85.K68513 2013
943.6'04407204—dc23   2013033571

CONTENTS

PREFACE
vii

Introduction
1

CHAPTER ONE
Austria-Hungary in Historiography
23

CHAPTER TWO
Austria-Hungary in Essayism and Political Theory
66

CHAPTER THREE
Austria-Hungary in Literary Fiction
108

CHAPTER FOUR
The Empire Epitomized: Franz Joseph
149

Conclusion
166

NOTES
191

BIBLIOGRAPHY
205

INDEX
215

PREFACE

The present edition is based on the book published in Polish in 2009 by the Institute of History of the Polish Academy of Sciences and Neriton Press. While working on the English translation I have revisited the original edition, eliminated one chapter, reorganized and shortened many fragments, and added a number of new paragraphs. Some changes were inspired by my imperfect suppositions about the preferences and interests of Western readers. The majority of them, however, rose from my desire simply to improve the quality of the book and its argumentation and style and from my new reconsiderations on the issues discussed. Therefore, I humbly assume that the present edition is better than the original, even though I can still remember my delight when it was first published.

Unless otherwise noted, all translations are my own. And so are all mistakes.

I am deeply grateful to a number of people whose assistance, patience, and criticism helped me while I was working on the original edition. I profited most from the friendly but candid comments of my mentor at the Institute of History of the Academy of Sciences, Jerzy Jedlicki. I also discussed several fragments of the draft with my colleagues from the Section for the History of Intelligentsia: Wiktoria Śliwowska, Magdalena Micińska, Anna Brus, Magdalena Gawin, Maciej Janowski, and Grzegorz Krzywiec. Finally, the book owes a lot to remarks by the late István György Tóth, András Gerő, Hubert Orłowski, Maciej Koźmiński, Rafał Stobiecki, Philip Ther, and Grzegorz Krzymianowski. My work on the manuscript was only possible due to the support of my family, particularly my parents and Kamila. While preparing the English edition, I profited enormously from the help of Robin Krauze, Heidi Beck, and Lloyd Woodley. I am taking this opportunity to warmly thank them all again. I would also like to express my gratitude for Amberle Sherman, Alex Wolfe, and Peter Kracht from the University of Pittsburgh Press, who made this edition possible.

Finally, there is one thing I did not need to change: I dedicate this book to the lovable memory of my grandparents, Jadwiga and Wojciech Słomczyński, who first inspired my passion for history.

THE AFTERLIFE OF AUSTRIA-HUNGARY

INTRODUCTION

Austria-Hungary ceased to exist almost a hundred years ago. The oldest generation of Central Europeans can remember it from their parents' and grandparents' stories. The majority of them learned about it in high school and associates the monarchy with its few royals, particularly the late Franz Joseph and his eccentric wife Elisabeth. Those figures, already famous during their lifetime, entered the realm of popular culture and remain recognizable in most countries of Europe, providing a stable income for the souvenir industry in what used to be their empire and inspiration for screenwriters on both sides of the Atlantic. Naturally, the situation varies from country to country as far as history textbooks and historical monuments are concerned. Thus, Austrians and Hungarians are generally more familiar with the monarchy than are the Germans or Poles, not to mention the British and French, whereas Serbs, Italians, Czechs, and Romanians tend to be highly suspicious of it. The old monarchy also built quite well, so modern travelers who wish to see what is left of the Habsburg empire do not need to limit their curiosity to imperial residences, nor to the opera houses in cities such as Prague, Lviv, and Zagreb. In most cities of former Austria-Hungary, visitors can get acquainted with Habsburg architecture at the railway station. In this respect Vienna, heavily bombed by the Anglo-American air forces and the Soviet artillery during World War II, is merely a sad exception. Other traces of the imperial past can still be discovered in many private apartments, antique shops, and retro-style cafés, in cemeteries, and old photographs.

Those who wish to learn more about Austria-Hungary have to look for it in books. The monarchy is quite lucky in this respect, because many excellent authors have chosen it as their subject, or as a background for their narratives. A library dedicated to Austria-Hungary would consist of hundreds of volumes, and the bibliography to this book includes only those that I found most instructive. Before World War II the vast majority of authors dealing with the newly extinct monarchy were its former citizens. In the following decades a number of crucial studies on the subject were written in America, particularly by émigrés from Central Europe and their students. Even before the collapse of communism, studies on Austria-Hungary became popular again in Central Europe, and after 1989 this interest has only increased. Today, various aspects of its past and its legacy are researched at numerous academic centers on both sides of the Atlantic, and a valuable book is published nearly every year.

Still, those who have never plodded through a scholarly study on the monarchy, and know it only from one of the world literary classics—by Robert Musil, Hermann Broch, Franz Kafka, Elias Canetti, or Jaroslav Hašek—need not feel deprived. I also began my acquaintance with Austria-Hungary this way, and I can hardly imagine a better introduction. Indeed, one of the purposes of this book is to inquire why those popularly admired authors decided to write about this apparently bankrupt and almost forgotten country, why they have immortalized it. I argue that at the moment when the monarchy fell it was rather unlikely that future authors would find it fascinating, and that it owes its current reputation to a series of coincidences, one of which was its capacity to inspire the imaginations of some outstanding authors.

When it still existed, the Habsburg monarchy did have a few talented admirers. Most of them were shocked when Austria ceased to be a part of Germany after the Austro-Prussian War and the founding of Bismarck's German empire. They believed that Austria could have created a better version of this empire, more joyful, culture-oriented, and friendly toward its neighbors. The majority of European commentators, however, including Germans, were more than a little skeptical about the Habsburg monarchy. It was usually viewed as a country located at the peripheries of the civilized world, populated by a hodgepodge of half-anonymous nationalities and clumsily struggling against the fresh, ambitious, and apparently victorious idea of nationalism. It was rather peaceful, relatively civilized, but also irritatingly archaic in appearance, and being neither modern nor exotic before World War I meant being rather uninteresting.

Ironically, World War I was begun by Austro-Hungarian ministers with the approval of their peace-loving monarch, because of their astonishing belief that by crushing Serbia they would prove that their country was more vigorous and formidable than it actually was. Although millions fought bravely for the monarchy during the war, its dissolution in 1918 caused almost no protest, to say nothing of resistance. Most people considered it dead even before the successor states managed to agree—after considerable military and diplomatic clashes—upon their borders, organize their administration, and introduce their currencies, uniforms, and the new national colors. Nevertheless, soon after Austria-Hungary irrevocably disappeared from the map of Europe it started expanding in the realm of imagination. Consequently, the number of more or less talented authors who became obsessed or simply intrigued by it grew remarkably. Numerous public figures, essayists, and journalists commented on its fate; political writers and economists analyzed the causes for its weakness; historians described its decline and fall; poets and visionaries dreamt about an idea that should have arisen from its legacy; novelists resurrected it in the land of fiction. As long as Austria-Hungary actually existed, Austrian patriotism had been generally considered as nothing more than a superficial by-product of imperial pomp and a ridiculous dream of bureaucrats. Once the empire was gone, many found it an attractive, sublime, and profoundly humane idea, a solution to many problems of the present day. Of course, there were others who despised it wholeheartedly and ridiculed its memory. However, those who became nostalgic about Austria-Hungary, although their number was rather small, appeared remarkably—one could say disproportionately—successful. Their achievement was to change the image of the monarchy, and since its image was the only thing it had left, their impact has been immense.

In this book I will describe and analyze what may be called the discourse on Austria-Hungary in its formative years. I do not intend to compete with modern historians, nor do I question any modern study regarding Austria-Hungary as it actually was. It is my intention, however, to demonstrate how much modern historiography on Austria-Hungary owes to its interwar predecessors, particularly those who were not professional history writers. My analysis covers some three decades after the dissolution of the monarchy, until the outbreak of World War II in some places and the 1950s in others, particularly Austria. This was roughly the time when those who had witnessed the downfall of the Habsburg monarchy and could remember it from their own past dominated this discourse. It was their memory, their experience, and their passion that shaped it. In other words, this book is about a generation that took an ambiguous and unclear imperial legacy and transformed it into a coherent image of the past.

The situation they faced was unique. In 1914 the Austro-Hungarian monarchy was almost four hundred years old and its ruling dynasty, the Habsburgs, claimed to be the successor of the imperial title of Charlemagne.[1] Its size made it the second largest European state, after Russia, and its population put it third, after Russia and Germany. Its economy was doing well, its culture flourished, and its great power status in Europe had not been questioned for centuries. Technical innovations continued to flood into the country, officials were receiving their salaries and widows their pensions, and trains were generally running on time. To be sure, the dissolution of Austria-Hungary had many prophets—among them Napoleon, Karl Marx, and Adam Mickiewicz—and they had all pointed to the conflict of the monarchy's nationalities.[2] However, the dissatisfaction of the nationalists was remarkably peaceful; it manifested itself mostly in newspapers and in the speeches of the deputies to the Viennese parliament. Still, four years later Austria-Hungary was no more. Neither Austrians nor Hungarians (the formerly privileged nations) nor any political party wanted it back. History pronounced its verdict and then executed it immediately and irrevocably.

When the former Habsburg subjects sought a comparably spectacular change, they scarcely saw any examples in Europe's modern history. And yet they had to produce explanations, interpretations, and narrative formulas that would allow them to understand and organize their experience. Certainly the majority was too busy with everyday needs, and many were too enthusiastic about their newly established nation-states to care about such things. Thus, in this book I focus on those authors who, for many reasons, were still looking backwards, and who considered the breakdown of Austria-Hungary a major historical event.

In the first chapter I present an overview of the situation in the interwar successor states of the old monarchy, and attempt to contextualize the perspectives from which it was most frequently seen, giving special consideration to contemporary historical imagery and concepts. I also briefly discuss the main trends in post–World War II writing on Austria-Hungary, dividing them into three categories: history, journalism and essays, and literary fiction. Eventually, I consider this division as merely a useful fiction, and in the concluding chapter I emphasize that my sources are narratives that may be interpreted from a number of common perspectives. I also argue that as far as the transfer of concepts, ideas, and particular intellectual obsessions is concerned, the borders between genres mattered much less for the discourse on Austria-Hungary than ideological and national divisions. If I nonetheless respect those borders in my book, it is because I believe that crossing them consciously is more instructive and amusing than simply ignoring them or torturing readers with some new, artificial classification.

In the chapter on historiography I discuss, among other things, the problems in Austro-Hungarian and Austro-German relations, explanations of the causes of the monarchy's breakdown, and some counterfactual alternatives of its fate, as produced by interwar historians. In the chapter on journalism and essays I mainly concentrate on discussions about Austrian identity and the alleged Habsburg historical mission. In the chapter on literary fiction I analyze various literary images of the imperial past, and some historical interpretations provided by a number of excellent as well as some mediocre writers. Additionally, a short chapter covers the biographies of Franz Joseph and his image in other kinds of writings. His person provoked so much interest, controversy, and speculation among his contemporaries, and came to be so powerfully symbolic of the Empire, that I could not ascribe him to any other genre, but only to one of his own; evidently, he had been there before modern pop stars joined him. Finally, in my conclusion I summarize and evaluate the motifs, tendencies, and obsessions of the interwar authors, which appeared persistent and indisputably influenced postwar discourse on the monarchy.

The Habsburg Heritage between the Wars

Before we arrive at opinions, narratives, and images of Austria-Hungary let us first examine the situation caused by its rapid disappearance in light of some basic facts. It is true that actual changes do not necessarily determine our perception of the past; humans are able to see more than just the bare reality. The facts, however, should not be entirely ignored. Since they are all well known, I will emphasize those that seem to have influenced Central Europeans' attitudes toward the Habsburg monarchy.

Prospects for the monarchy seemed bright in 1914, even though it had many critics and malcontents. However, in order to realize how rapid its fall might appear to contemporaries, one needs to realize that by early 1918 its future, while not as bright after four years of war, still seemed firm. Three of its enemies—Russia, Serbia, and Romania—had been beaten. Italy was desperately fighting, but suffering losses. Although the Habsburg armies had already started fighting against their previously implicit enemies—the British and French, who landed in the Balkans—the Western Allies did not intend to dismember the monarchy at that point. Actually, they still did not care much about Central Europe, for they were too preoccupied by their struggle against Germany. On June 3 in Versailles, the Allies officially spoke in favor of the future independence of Poland. This meant returning Galicia to Poland, but that was supposed to be mainly an anti-German maneuver. As far as the Czechs, Slovaks, and the Southern Slavs were regarded, Western statesmen merely expressed their sympathy for the aspirations of these nations—and this implied no more than autonomy, democracy, and equality within the monarchy, a claim that US President Woodrow Wilson had already announced in his Fourteen Points. However, as early as June 26, Edvard Beneš, from the Czech National Council, obtained an official declaration from the French Minister of Foreign Affairs supporting the idea of a Czecho-Slovak state, and within weeks British and American officials joined him, consistently advocating the formation of Yugoslavia as well. In contrast to the next World War, the Allies kept their promises to Central European politicians.

Still, the Paris Peace Conference of 1919 left many Central Europeans bitterly disillusioned about the intentions of the peacemakers.

Actually, those expectations were mostly shaped by the idea of self-determination of nations, brilliantly advocated by President Wilson, who inspired much hope throughout Europe, varying from the enthusiasm of former enemies of the Central Powers to the naïve optimism of their supporters.[3] They all believed that Wilson could mitigate the mutual hatred and anger of the belligerent nations and their leaders, and that he would bring about a "just" peace settlement. This settlement, however, appeared to please the victorious powers—and their allies—exclusively. It was French diplomats who stubbornly advocated for Polish, Czech, Romanian, and Yugoslav claims at the peace conference, whereas the British and the Americans occasionally opposed them, although they often did not know where these disputed territories were located, not to mention the ethnic composition of their populations. In fact, some of the Allies' decisions were simply an acknowledgment of faits accomplis, such as the results of the Polish-Soviet War, the Czech occupation of Teschen (Cieszyn), or the Romanian invasion of the Hungarian Soviet Republic.[4]

The results of the conference were shocking for both Austrians and Hungarians; what was left within their new national frontiers was much less than they would ever imagine as acceptable. Hungarian delegates to Paris who had to sign the humiliating Treaty of Trianon resigned from their public functions because they considered their names to be too shameful for their compatriots. Indeed, it was scarcely possible to maintain that Trianon was based on the principle of self-determination, for it left some one-third of Hungarians, including vast Hungarian-populated territories, outside the country's borders. The basis for such a settlement was the "strategic" demands of Czechoslovakia, Romania, and Yugoslavia, as well as the fact that after the short-lived communist revolution, Hungary was bankrupt, occupied by its enemies, and totally defenseless.[5] As a consequence, as soon as Hungary recovered, it became a threat to all of its neighbors except Austria, for all the Hungarian parties and governments dreamt about revenge—indeed, some Hungarians still dream about it in the twenty-first century. Therefore, Czechoslovakia, Yugoslavia, and Romania soon formed an alliance, called the Little Entente, to oppose the Hungarian territorial claims; in other respects, however, these countries had little common interest, and the alliance soon proved unreliable.

The Austrians did not constitute a comparable threat to their neighbors. They did not even dare plan to regain the German-speaking territories they were forced to cede to Italy and Czechoslovakia. Instead, they dreamt of getting rid of Austria itself and incorporating it into Germany, and that was denied to them mainly because of French fears of an increase in the population of their "eternal" and still-mighty enemy. Deprived of their Slavic provinces, Austrians considered their country to be a part of Germany because of the common language and culture, and in light of the fact that Austria was bankrupt and cut off from its markets and its food supplies. Before the Allies forbade the Anschluss, plebiscites had been held in two provinces, Voralberg and Tirol, with the result of more than 90 percent positive votes. Forced to accept the decisions of the Treaty of Saint-Germain, Austrians formed the German Republic of Austria (Republik Deutschösterreich), which immediately faced a flood of veterans of the imperial army and bureaucracy, and a long economic crisis.[6]

In other words, the peace settlement did not solve most of the problems that had troubled Central Europe before the war and which were supposed to have contributed to the fall of the Habsburg monarchy. To be sure, Czechs, Poles, Romanians, and Serbs welcomed the changes on the political map with great joy and enthusiasm. However, the dissatisfied national minorities still numbered in the millions. Only the newly formed Austria and Hungary did not have any of them, except for the well-assimilated Jews. And it was exactly the former master-nations Germans and Hungarians, now forced to live under their neighbors' rule, who were the most frustrated. Their dissatisfaction was of a different kind than the sense of underrepresentation of the non-German and non-Magyar nationalities under the Habsburgs. They considered the new political status quo a fresh and inexplicable injustice, and they had their fatherlands to look up to for support and the League of Nations to appeal to. The Ukrainians of Galicia first lost the war against the Poles, and then were denied the autonomy promised to them by the Allies; in Czechoslovakia they had their own region, but its autonomy was an administrative illusion supervised by Czech officials. The Slovaks, Slovenians, and Croatians soon felt underprivileged in their new states of Czechoslovakia and Yugoslavia, which were supposed to satisfy the dreams of the oppressed Slavs of Austria-Hungary, but which actually resembled the monarchy in their multiethnic composition and ethnic policies. And there were the Central European Jews, who had special reasons to be afraid of the new settlement after the pogroms in Galicia during the Polish-Ukrainian conflict of 1919, and the anti-Semitic character of the "white terror" in Hungary after the collapse of the short-lived communist regime. Although anti-Semitism was omnipresent in Austria-Hungary, its revered emperor Franz Joseph was well known for his disgust for it, and Jews from the shtetls throughout the monarchy, as well as the rich and educated, simply adored Franz Joseph as their legendary protector. In comparison, the new rulers were considered either an enigma or the opposite. The so-called Little Treaty of Versailles regarding the protection of minorities, which the new states were forced to sign, was indeed proof of the persuasive power of Jewish public opinion in the West.[7] But Central European Jews had reasonable doubts about whether this treaty, imposed by foreign diplomats, could really protect them from their new governments and their Christian neighbors.

Furthermore, political arrangements regarding Central Europe seemed rather shaky from the beginning. New states emerged after a series of diplomatic and military clashes, which not only resulted in the Hungarian dream of revenge against almost all its neighbors but also in Polish-Czech, Romanian-Yugoslav, and Italian-Yugoslav animosities. Initially, France planned to make these new states its protégés and join their forces into what the French diplomats imagined as a bulwark against Germany, but they soon turned their eyes toward the Soviet heir of their reliable ally Russia. The promised peace did not seem to have a solid foundation.

Hopes for democracy quickly proved unrealistic. For Hungary the postwar era began first with the red terror of Béla Kun and then continued with the white equivalent of Admiral Miklós Horthy. The limited franchise and Horthy as the regent of the superficial kingdom remained until the next war, accompanied by anti-Semitic legislation copied from the Nazis in the late 1930s. In other countries democracy was crushed by popular dictators: Mussolini in Italy, Piłsudski in Poland, King Alexander in Yugoslavia, and Dollfuss in Austria. In Romania, the government managed to win all the elections without any constitutional changes, until Ion Antonescu installed his dictatorship in 1938. The Yugoslav king, the Austrian chancellor, the first Polish president, and a Romanian prime minister were all murdered by fanatical political opponents. The rise of authoritarianism in the region was in part a response to signals from Fascist Italy and Nazi Germany, which seemed fascinating and terrifying simultaneously. Finally, when Hitler felt strong enough to dictate his will to the region, only Poland and Yugoslavia dared to oppose him, although their determination was based on the false calculations that the Western Allies would keep their promises and help them to resist Germany militarily.

Czechoslovakia alone remained a stable, liberal democracy until it was first peacefully dismembered and then militarily occupied by Hitler. The Czechoslovak political consensus was, however, based on the personal reputation of the patriarchal President Tomáš Garrigue Masaryk, and the fear all Czech parties had of the largest, richest, and best-organized minority in the Central Europe: the Sudeten Germans. The other reason for Czechoslovak stability was that Bohemia was the most industrialized and economically prosperous country in the region that, cut into barely sustainable units by the new frontiers, suffered from an almost continuous economic crisis. The post–World War I and post-1929 depressions lasted longer and had more devastating results here than they did in the West. As in most of Europe, the interwar era brought unemployment, inflation, and impoverishment on a previously unknown scale. Some governments in the region introduced new legislation in favor of workers and peasants, but they were unable to provide them with jobs or a demand for their products. Social conflict was no longer limited to the anger of the poor against the rich, workers against capitalists, or peasants against landowners. After the Great War, which ruined many but brought fortunes to a few war speculators, the middle classes also felt frustrated. They could no longer expect that hard work, education, and tenacity would make them prosperous and secure. Moreover, most of the new governments of Central Europe and their bureaucracies were notorious for corruption, which was quite unlike the Habsburg epoch, when men of power had almost exclusively been aristocrats wealthy enough to not be suspected of abusing their positions. In Poland, for example, most of the anti-parliamentary campaign of Piłsudski in the 1920s was constructed upon accusations of corruption against the political class as a whole. Exaggerated as they were, they successfully undermined the nation's belief in democracy.

In other words, the interwar years brought enough poverty, disillusionment, and insecurity for the Central Europeans to make them look back at the "good old days of peace" with some deserved nostalgia. Of course, nostalgia did not necessarily mean dreams about the Habsburgs regaining their power. Outside of Austria and Hungary this idea simply seemed outrageous, since political independence was considered the most precious national achievement. The Austrians and Hungarians themselves did not consider it too seriously, although Hungary was officially a kingdom, and in Austria Chancellor Kurt Schuschnigg apparently attempted to recall some Habsburg patriotism to aid his desperate resistance to Hitler's pressure. Nostalgia, however, is not an active attitude toward the present; it does not need to seek a link between the past and present. It may all the more easily be fueled by the belief that what is gone is gone forever.[8]

Of course, the postwar era brought much more than social, political, and economic insecurity. Cinema, radio, jazz, phones, cars, and airplanes reached almost all corners of Central Europe, although they were available to a smaller number of people than in the West. Women could shorten their hair and dresses, and enter politics and professions requiring higher education, enjoying popular enfranchisement. Most young men shaved their beards and moustaches, and many made brilliant careers in the new national capitals, even though their social origins may have been very humble. In short, the realities of Austria-Hungary soon became anachronistic, not only because the Habsburg dynasty appeared to be politically bankrupt but because now progress and dynamism were enthusiastically expected to dominate all aspects of life. Because of enormous changes in everyday life during the Great War and its aftermath, time appeared accelerated. Hence, the last years of Austria-Hungary seemed to represent a past much more remote a decade after the monarchy's breakdown than, say, the turn of the century had represented in the spring of 1914.

I have emphasized conditions of the postwar status quo in Central Europe because the crucial fact for the attitudes toward Austria-Hungary at that time is that scarcely anyone claimed its legacy. For obvious reasons, nationally disposed public opinion in the successor states considered the Habsburgs foreign oppressors and their rule illegitimate. Indeed, such was the prevailing opinion not only among the Czechs, Poles, Romanians, and Yugoslavs but also among many Hungarians, although Hungary had been so much bigger and more powerful and prosperous within the dual monarchy. However, most patriotic, or indeed nationalist, Hungarians never forgot their defeat in 1849 and the uprisings of the seventeenth and eighteenth centuries, and regarded dualism as yet another form of oppression, insisting that a true patriot could approve of nothing but full and official independence. Furthermore, German nationalists also saw the Habsburgs as a major disaster in their country's history, for they had constituted the main obstacle against the unification of all Germans in one state throughout the nineteenth century. In Austria alone did the imperial legacy inspire popular sentiment. As far as the present and future were concerned, however, Austrians opted for unification with Germany. Some timid and desperate attempts by Schuschnigg, the last chancellor, to oppose German nationalism with the Habsburg one may best be illustrated with an anecdote. The chancellor, it says, asks an old Austrian about his opinion of his government. The old man responds that he is afraid of speaking, for the chancellor might report his words to the police—so the chancellor promises not to do that. The old man, however, is still afraid that the chancellor might report his words to the city mayor. When the chancellor promises not to do that, and not to report them to the local doctor, the teacher, the postmaster, the priest, and many others, the old man says, "Personally, I'm very happy with your government's policies."[9]

　The fact that Austria-Hungary already appeared remote just a relatively short time after its dissolution, and that it seemed perfectly dead as a political idea, shaped discourse on the monarchy in a special way. In short, the monarchy immediately became a historical subject par excellence. Moreover, people who had personal interests in interpreting the late history of Austria-Hungary were still there, and they influenced its image significantly. Many of them were actively involved in political life before 1914; some of them had even shaped the policies of the monarchy, and after it fell they wanted to prove that they had always been right and that others were to blame. Some of them sympathized with the monarchy and believed it deserved a better fate. In other words, emotions were certainly involved and the debates drew in a much wider audience than the purely academic disputes of specialists, and yet they were abstract and did not serve any practical purposes—except for, perhaps, saving some individuals' reputation and self-esteem, because their object had ceased to exist. The combination of these two features made interwar discourse on Austria-Hungary quite exceptional. It referred to the epoch that had recently ended and was still fresh in contemporaries' memories, and, on the other hand, it allowed for an intellectual detachment that normally requires a generation or more to pass away. One may argue that it matured faster than most modern historical discourses, full of national pride and complexes, militant ideologies and party lines, and yet it preserved much of their vigor and, last but not least, their ability to attract the public's attention.

Austria-Hungary and the Idea of History

Before moving to analyze particular interwar texts on Austria-Hungary, let us first consider some aspects of the monarchy that seemed obvious to contemporary authors, but which may not seem so today. They all profoundly influenced interwar discourse on the monarchy; however, contemporary authors did not necessarily comment on them explicitly. In short, they may be regarded as constituting the paradigm of knowledge on Austria-Hungary by the time it collapsed.

As I claimed, with World War I time relatively accelerated, and Austria-Hungary seemed to belong to a distinctively anachronistic past just a few years after its dissolution. Still, there were even more reasons to view it as such. First, Austria-Hungary had proudly appeared to be an old-fashioned country for a long time before it actually fell. The main pillars of the Habsburg political ideology were historical claims and historical splendor. The dynasty had claims to primacy among the European ruling families, it maintained special relations with the papacy, and obeyed a family code which drastically limited the number of potential marital partners. The emperor's titles included all territories that Habsburgs ruled from time immemorial; the most fantastic gem in this diadem was apparently Jerusalem, proudly reminding people about the time when the Holy Roman Emperors had led the crusaders. The final touch to this historical marinade was that the Viennese court and governments were dominated for sixty-eight years by the personality of Franz Joseph, a most traditional monarch who disapproved of any innovations and viewed himself as a grand enforcer of the past from the very establishment of his rule.

Before 1914 almost all European countries were monarchies, and certainly all had their royal pomp and rituals. Nevertheless, they also had other claims for political legitimacy and the most obvious of them was the national idea. In this respect Austria-Hungary was an exception—it had to emphasize feudal loyalty because of the lack of a comparably attractive national idea. Many modern historians emphasize analogies among the multiethnic empires of the Habsburgs, the Romanovs, Ottoman Turkey, and occasionally also Hohenzollern Germany, but in fact contemporaries rarely acknowledged them. Russia and Germany eagerly and noisily claimed to represent their respective national ideologies as sources of their political legitimacy. Austria-Hungary was the only large European country that could not follow this highly prized ideal, not because so many ethnic groups inhabited it—indeed, Russia had more of them—but because it was supranational by definition.

Austria attempted to impose German language and culture on its non-German subjects in the epoch of the enlightened absolutism of Joseph II and in the early nineteenth century. However, these attempts were undertaken in the name of civilization, not of the German nation. The enlightened emperors viewed much of their realm as backward territory inhabited by barbarians, and their mission as a *mission civilisatrice*. This semicolonial idea constituted the second most important pillar of Habsburg political ideology at the beginning of the twentieth century. Central Europe, it assumed, needed Austria as its protector against aggressive foreign powers and the contradicting claims of its own nationalities, and as its cultural and economic supervisor and leader. It was still appealing to such mid-nineteenth-century politicians as František Palacký, a Czech historian and national ideologist who claimed that if Austria did not exist it should have been invented. Half a century later, however, the conception of Austria as a *protectrice* of the "small," and relatively underdeveloped nationalities provoked little enthusiasm. All of them were trying to gain as much as possible from Vienna, but their expectations already went further, toward the ideal of independence, and they were frustrated with the price they were paying for being Habsburg subjects.

Another idea that accompanied the Habsburg monarchy until its breakdown was its status as a great power. The assumption that countries should be naturally and reasonably divided into the great powers and the rest, and that Austria-Hungary belonged to the former group, was omnipresent in contemporary literature. Since interwar authors commented on this issue extensively, I devote a separate section to it in the chapter on historiography. Here I would just like to stress that the great power concept was typical of the interwar perception of the monarchy, and of the contemporary historical imagination in general. Although the national idea, as well as the problem, of class struggle and social emancipation had already entered the sphere of interest of numerous professional historians, the vast majority of them still focused on questions of high politics: treaties, alliances, campaigns, and personalities of powerful statesmen. The Habsburgs, with their almost seven-hundred-years-long history as a major political factor in Europe, perfectly fit this model.

Nevertheless, seen from the post-1918 perspective, the history of Austria was also remarkably atypical. The main reason for this was quite simple; namely, this history had a clear-cut end: the death of the main protagonist. This profoundly influenced the narrative strategies of the monarchy's historians and the conceptual framework of their writings: all histories of the monarchy had to lead to its breakdown and provide an explanation for it. Consequently, the breakdown became the final stage of the process, whose causes and previous stages had to be described and explained. None of the authors giving a detailed account of Austrian history could avoid discussing them and taking a position in the debate.

In other words, histories of Austria-Hungary had to be written in the "decline and fall" paradigm. The alternative, the Romantic paradigm of rise and successful struggle, did not work. Historians who viewed Austria mainly as an obstacle on their nationalities' way toward independence paid little attention to its nature; the histories they were writing were those of their respective nations, and the monarchy appeared in them as a monolith, an unsympathetic and obscure background.[10] The decline and fall paradigm, however, offered a remarkable variety of arguments, explanations, and rhetorical figures from the repertoire of the most distinguished history writers of antiquity and modernity such as Thucydides, St. Augustine, Montesquieu, Gibbon, Niebuhr, and Mommsen. It embraced moral and political theory, as well as sentimentalism and nostalgia, bitter criticism, cynicism, and mockery. Thus, it should not be surprising that while seeking analogies for the decline and fall of Austria-Hungary, many interwar authors found the Roman Empire to be the best example. Evidently, their education in the classical *gymnasia* made this choice even more tempting.

Another classical analogy was less evident but also essential: the

Greek tragedy. Seen from the post-1918 perspective, the history of Austria-Hungary was a story of its doomed struggle for survival. Hence, its authors could only choose between presenting it as a farce or as a tragedy—a tragedy of vain attempts to avoid a fatal destiny. In both variants the narrated events and acts of characters are essentially equivocal. Successes are only partial, failures are never decisive, and decisions may seem smart but cannot really change the course of history. Actually, most historical debates about the monarchy focused on the interpretation of a relatively small number of events and developments. In interwar historical discourse about Austria-Hungary, controversies concerning factual events were quite limited. They mainly arose around the interpretation of facts and developments popularly known and acknowledged by all sides in the debate—and these very interpretations were typically used to make moral judgments.

Roughly speaking, the choice between farce and tragedy depended on whether the author sympathized with the monarchy. By "sympathizing" I do not mean being uncritical toward the Habsburgs. On the contrary, sympathy for the monarchy usually implied some serious criticism of its rulers, for it was they who actually failed, and who were to blame for the final result. In other words, the sympathetic account of the monarchy's history was a demanding intellectual and narrative challenge, since Austro-Hungarian statesmen did not know the future results of their actions, and their actual intention was to strengthen the monarchy, not to weaken it. Even if they recognized the gravity of the threats and properly diagnosed where they were coming from, they could not know that the final catastrophe was unavoidable. The challenge was yet more complicated for those who acknowledged that the monarchy's most fatal weakness was the multiethnic composition of its population, and that its mortal disease was its inability to satisfy these nationalities' expectations. Indeed, this assumption seemed quite obvious after 1918, and many authors adopted it even if they disapproved of what had happened—that is, if they found these expectations unreasonable or unfortunate. This, however, indicated that the monarchy had been struggling against history itself, against some invincible power, against the very nature of the modern age. Consequently, some authors concluded that it was not surprising that the monarchy fell, but that it had managed to last so long. Others, of course, sought some "mistake," a moment when the breakdown had still been avoidable, a moment when the monarchy became infected with the disease that killed it. In consequence, they produced numerous more or less amusing counterfactual scenarios of "what certainly would have happened if . . ." Astonishingly, none of these authors considered the simplest, and indeed the most optimistic, of such scenarios; namely, assuming that the monarchy might have proudly buried the unfortunate archduke Franz Ferdinand and given up the idea of declaring war on Serbia in the summer of 1914. Actually, some of them argued that it might have entered the war better prepared militarily, or having secured the allegiance of its multinational subjects by some internal reforms; others claimed that if only a particular battle in 1917 had been won, the monarchy could have survived. The Great War, however, seemed to be a curse, a fate of modern times, and no one dared to imagine history without it.

Finally, one should also remember that the dreadful but also ambiguous legacy of the Great War was fertile soil for theories of history. The catastrophist visions of the decline of Western civilization mesmerized the exhausted Europeans, whereas utopian visions of the imminent victory of communism were fueled by the triumph of the revolution in Russia. The war and revolution seemed to be a turning point in European history, indicating that some sort of Hegelian-like synthesis was taking place in the real world. Lenin, Spengler, and Toynbee were all foretelling that the West—labeled as the world of capitalism, Latin civilization, or democracy—was soon to expect the next stage of the crisis, or perhaps a mortal catastrophe. The quick and final breakdown of Austria-Hungary, the weakest of the old great powers, appeared a logical and consistent element of this puzzle: the rottenest link in the chain had to break first. For various reasons, the fall of the Habsburg monarchy pleased many. For the Western democrats it was too aristocratic and conservative; for Hitler and Mussolini it was too liberal and tolerant; for Lenin and Stalin it was both, which they found a sign of corruption. However, they were all too eager to forget it, so I will focus on those who remembered it well.

Postwar Discourse on Austria-Hungary

The writings on Austria-Hungary under discussion here were produced by those who could actually remember it. In order to explain why I concentrate on those authors, and to emphasize why I consider their role in shaping discourse on the monarchy as crucial, some remarks on the later developments of this discourse are necessary.

World War II had a decisive, though not immediate, impact on the image of the monarchy. First, it silenced, if not nullified, most of the moral and political claims of the European nationalists. Second, the new status quo in Europe became fully determined by the rivalry between capitalist democracy and Soviet-style communism. The entire hodgepodge of Central European political ideologies, national rivalries, and animosities became frozen in the zone dominated by the Soviets, and melted off among those who wished to oppose the communists. In other words, the ideological and political implications of interwar writings about the Habsburg monarchy lost most of their significance. Before the war, dreams about the monarchy's resurrection were rather abstract, but at least the Habsburg legacy—or, more frequently, challenges to this legacy—played an important role in legitimizing the status quo in Central Europe. After the war the only contest that mattered involved just two participants, communists and anti-communists.

The moral bankruptcy of nationalism had a different impact on the image of the monarchy. Right-wing movements were stigmatized in all countries where they had cooperated with the Nazis and the Fascists, and the most radical change, obviously, took place in Germany itself. Its importance for discourse on Austria-Hungary was tremendous for three reasons. First, the nationalist German (or pan-German, *grossdeutsch*) ideology played a crucial role in this discourse between the wars. A number of pan-German authors, whose writings will be discussed in the next chapters—such as Viktor Bibl, Heinrich von Srbik, and Edmund von Glaise-Horstenau—easily adapted their views to the ideology of national socialism when the Nazis took power in 1933. After 1945 they all remained professionally active, but the tone of their writings was, of course, different. Second, quite paradoxically, the idea of Austria's Anschluss to Germany, which united all major political parties and enjoyed undeniable popularity among the majority of Austrians between 1918 and 1938, now had to be abandoned, for it was Adolf Hitler who had accomplished it. As a sort of political sabotage, Britain had acknowledged Austria as Hitler's first victim during the war, and this disputable definition became the basis for the foundation of the Austrian Republic in 1955.[11] Consequently, a separate Austrian national identity emerged, and this meant that for the first time the country was popularly considered to be neither a part of Germany nor the "hereditary land" of the Habsburgs. Austrians could finally look back at their history swerving from political discussions considering their larger neighbor and their dynasty.

Furthermore, the decline of aggressive nationalism shed some new light on Austria-Hungary's most characteristic feature: its multinational composition. Supranational political unity as a remedy against national conflicts, even in its imperfect Austro-Hungarian version, did not seem so ridiculous and anachronistic anymore.[12] Embodied by the European Union and its predecessors, this idea has been growing more and more popular, to the point that the Union now embraces almost all of the ex-Habsburg lands except for Bosnia, the Serbian Banat, and Ukrainian Galicia. Of course the ideologists of the unification of Europe never openly pointed at the Austro-Hungarian example. The Habsburgs as ancestors of this very democratic and "modern" idea would not seem a promising or persuasive political argument. As a matter of fact, even the interwar Austrian aristocrat Count Richard Nikolaus von Coudenhove-Kalergi, whose *Paneuropa* is popularly acknowledged as one of the fundamental writings on the idea of unification of the continent, did not dare to promote the monarchy as a pattern to follow. Nevertheless, simultaneously with the federalization of Europe, a sympathetic interest in the monarchy has been growing in the postwar decades, resulting in a gradual and profound change of its popular reputation.

Most importantly, in the postwar decades Austrian studies emerged as a popular subject in the English-speaking (or indeed English-writing) world. As mentioned, many authors writing about the monarchy after World War II in America were in fact émigrés from Central Europe, and this was perhaps why their attitude toward Austria-Hungary was from the beginning a bit more sympathetic than that of British authors. The first major synthesis of Austrian history in English was *The Habsburg Monarchy, 1809–1918*, first published in 1948, by A. J. P. Taylor, who viewed the monarchy mostly as the Habsburgs' *Hausmacht*. A number of more elaborated, thicker, and also more Austria-friendly studies followed: *The Hapsburg Monarchy 1867–1914* by A. J. May (1951),

The Habsburg Empire 1790–1918 by C. A. Macartney (1969), and *The Multinational Empire* (1950) and *A History of the Habsburg Empire 1526–1918* (1974) by Robert A. Kann.

Parallel to this impressive progress in historiography was the "discovery" of Austro-Hungarian literature by the international public. Such authors as Robert Musil, Hermann Broch, and Franz Kafka all became world-famous after the war—and posthumously. Only Elias Canetti, perhaps the most international of the Austro-Hungarian writers, lived long enough to be rewarded with a Nobel Prize. Simultaneously, a number of ex-Habsburg subjects emerged as world celebrities in the arts and sciences. The generation of the 1950s and 1960s was obsessed with the writings of Sigmund Freud, dominated by the economic theories of Frederic Hayek, impressed by the argumentation of Karl Popper, and amused by the movies of Billy Wilder—to name just the few of the most famous. Turn-of-the-century Vienna, which had been viewed as a provincial and conservative cousin of Berlin by contemporaries, now appeared as the crucial intellectual and artistic milieu of twentieth-century Europe. In other words, half a century after its collapse Austria-Hungary became very popular.

Obviously, this popularity attracted scholars. The first major foreign achievements in the field of Austro-Hungarian cultural and intellectual history, basically unchallenged until today, were two studies, *The Austrian Mind: The Intellectual and Social History, 1848–1938* (first published 1972) by William Johnston, and *Il mito Absburgico nella litteratura austriaca moderna* (1963; a German edition followed in 1966) by Claudio Magris. Johnston's book enthusiastically listed all the major Austrian achievements in the arts and sciences, providing their social and political contextualization. Magris created the concept of the "Habsburg myth" as a key to understanding Austrian prose and poetry concerning the issues of the ambiguous Austrian identity. Both approaches appeared extremely fruitful.

Another major turn in the studies on the Habsburg legacy was *Fin-de-Siècle Vienna: Politics and Culture* by Carl E. Schorske (first published 1979). This extremely influential book proposed to view the declining Habsburg monarchy as "the laboratory of modernity" in arts, architecture, poetry, and mass politics. In other words, it presented the allegedly anachronistic empire as a major trendsetter, which it has indeed become, at least if we consider its posthumous popularity.

At least two of Schorske's numerous followers need to be mentioned: Péter Hanák and John Lukacs, whose *The Garden and the Workshop: Essays on the Cultural History of Vienna and Budapest* (1998) and *Budapest 1900: A Historical Portrait of a City and Its Culture* (1988) broadened and balanced Schorske's view by including the Hungarian part of the monarchy in the picture.

In Central Europe, interest in Austria-Hungary has been growing at least since the 1970s. Obviously, it has always been most vivid in Austria, because of popular sentiment there as well as the freedom to research and publish. The most impressive, perhaps, of all postwar Austrian studies on the monarchy was the multivolume *Die Habsburgermonarchie 1848–1918*, tirelessly edited by Adam Wandruszka, which aimed at covering all the available knowledge on all the Habsburg provinces. Under communism both academic and non-academic writers choosing Habsburg-related topics had to struggle with censorship, varying from country to country, protecting Marxist and also national orthodoxy. In Poland, for example, where censorship was perhaps less harsh than anywhere in communist Europe except for Hungary, a number of valuable and original studies concerning the nation-building processes in the Habsburg empire were published in the early 1980s,[13] and in 1978 an open debate took place in the popular press concerning recent novels dealing with the Habsburg Galicia. Their authors were accused of evoking nostalgia for the Austro-Hungarian epoch and idealizing anachronistic values, which were considered to be inappropriate for a society struggling to build socialism. Socialism fell, however, just eleven years later, while nostalgia continued to grow, left the realm of belles lettres, and entered the popular culture. Eventually, after the breakdown of communism, all Habsburg provinces and major cities earned a monograph, and the stream of studies regarding politics, everyday life, cultural and social history, and national and economic questions continued to spring from all major academic centers of the region, echoed by the flow of works by Western European and American authors.

During the interwar period Austria-Hungary was still not a popular subject, and if some people wrote about it, it was because they considered it rather more important than fashionable. And yet, the seeds of the future spectacular career of the politically dead monarchy were already there; the major processes, paradoxes, personalities, events, and conflicts had been identified and described. In other words, this book attempts to take a closer look at the origins of what appeared to be one of the most vibrant, internationalized, and profoundly studied problems in modern European history, because origins always matter. Austria-Hungary has its clear-cut end, and the discourse on the monarchy has a beginning, but it is actually one and the same moment: the late fall of 1918. The scenery is being changed, and people are impatiently looking toward an uncertain future—and one of the things that need to be constructed anew is their history.

CHAPTER ONE

AUSTRIA-HUNGARY IN HISTORIOGRAPHY

The following three chapters of this book discuss three genres of historical writing about Austria-Hungary: academic historiography, political essays, and literary fiction. One of my goals is to demonstrate that the interpretations expressed by these genres are complementary, and that they fuse in an image of the monarchy that would not be complete if we ignored any of them. I begin with historiography for two reasons. First, academic history may seem to many readers to be the most difficult to get through—and I cannot sincerely deny this intuition. Indeed, interwar historians of Austria-Hungary fiercely debated numerous issues that have been largely forgotten since that time, and we shall have a look at a number of them, because understanding the nature of writing history is impossible without the knowledge of certain facts and preconditions. So I have decided to serve the readers the heaviest course first, hoping that appetite grows with what it feeds upon. Second, we shall return to academic history once again at the end of the book; it will be the history written, or re-written, after World War II, when the context changed dramatically. Hence, I will argue that this history, the one we know as the last word in the discourse about Austria-Hungary, owes a lot to its interwar predecessor, and that one needs only to scratch the interpretations of some post–World War II Western scholars to find the themes and motifs introduced in this discourse in the 1920s and 1930s. This is to say that history writing develops as a dialogue with its own past as much it does as with the changing world.

Before we begin the analysis of the interwar histories of Austria-Hungary, it is necessary to realize two things. First, the main concern of these histories was the decline and fall of the monarchy. Shortly after 1918 no history of Austria-Hungary could avoid asking the question of the causes of this process. The monarchy had been one of the main European powers for the previous four hundred years, and even though its internal problems and weaknesses were well-known before 1914, scarcely anyone expected its total breakdown in such a short time. Historical writing at that time was still dominated by political issues, and historians could hardly imagine a more intriguing topic than the rise and decline of empires. The history of Austria-Hungary provided them with a fresh, clear-cut example of such a process. They had to rush before others would provide the public with their interpretations and explanations of what had just happened. Only one thing seemed certain: the monarchy fell because of the dissatisfaction of its nationalities. Hence, the national question dominated interwar debates regarding Austria-Hungary.

As noted in the introduction, I do not actually deal with historians of the successor states of the monarchy who considered its dissolution a fortunate episode in the histories of their respective countries. My motivation is not to deny the validity of such an approach. Obviously, for the authors whose main focus was the history of the nations "enslaved" by the Habsburgs, it made perfect sense: the monarchy was indeed an obstacle on their respective nations' road to independence and sovereignty, and thus it is more than natural that all they had to say about its dissolution was that it was good that it had finally happened. Therefore, I concentrate on authors for whom the history of the monarchy constituted an intellectual problem. Some of them considered it a problem because they sympathized with Austria-Hungary. They combined intellectual curiosity with emotional engagement by inquiring what had gone wrong in Austria-Hungary, and who was to blame for it. Some of them had actually been politically active before 1918, and they were personally interested in proving that they had been always right in their opinions and their choices. Obviously, their declared scholarly objectivity did not remain intact as a result of such an engagement.

Some of them were liberals, who had advocated reforms that would have changed the dual monarchy into a multinational federation. Some of them had been members of a party, or an informal group around the archduke Franz Ferdinand when he had been the heir to the throne and raised many hopes for a new opening in Austro-Hungarian politics. The most famous project for a reorganization of the monarchy along the new lines created under the umbrella of the archduke was authored by a Romanian, Aurel Popovici, who named it "The United States of Great Austria." Popovici postulated breaking up the Austro-Hungarian dualism and dividing the monarchy into a federation of cantons according to ethnic borders. The Social Democrats, the only pan-Austrian and the greatest opposition party in the monarchy, advocated a different solution. They assumed that animosities between nationalities could not be solved by drawing new frontiers, because the ethnographic map of the monarchy was a patchwork, and no such settlement would satisfy all—it would simply produce new malcontents and new oppressors. Thus, they proposed that members of the respective nations associate in communities resembling religious communities, organizing their own schools, clubs, and other institutions. Obviously, after 1918 their assumption that nations could give up their desire for their own territory and live peacefully under a supranational (but still linguistically German and politically Habsburg) administration seemed hopelessly naïve. On the other hand, they were right: the peace settlement of 1919 indeed produced new malcontents and oppressors in numbers no less than the pre-1918 order. Finally, there were conservatives, and some German nationalists, who claimed that if the main cause of the monarchy's problems was the dissatisfied nationalities, it was not because these nationalities had been oppressed but because they had been granted too many liberties and treated with too much respect and tolerance. The Habsburgs' gravest sin, they believed, was allowing their nationalist politicians to speak in parliament instead of having them properly locked in prisons.

In addition, of course, there were authors who had not been involved in Habsburg political life before 1918, among them some Westerners. Notably, however, there were few of them, and their position was special because they wrote for a public that knew little more than nothing about Austria-Hungary. In other words, the second thing we need to bear in mind before we have a look at the interwar histories of

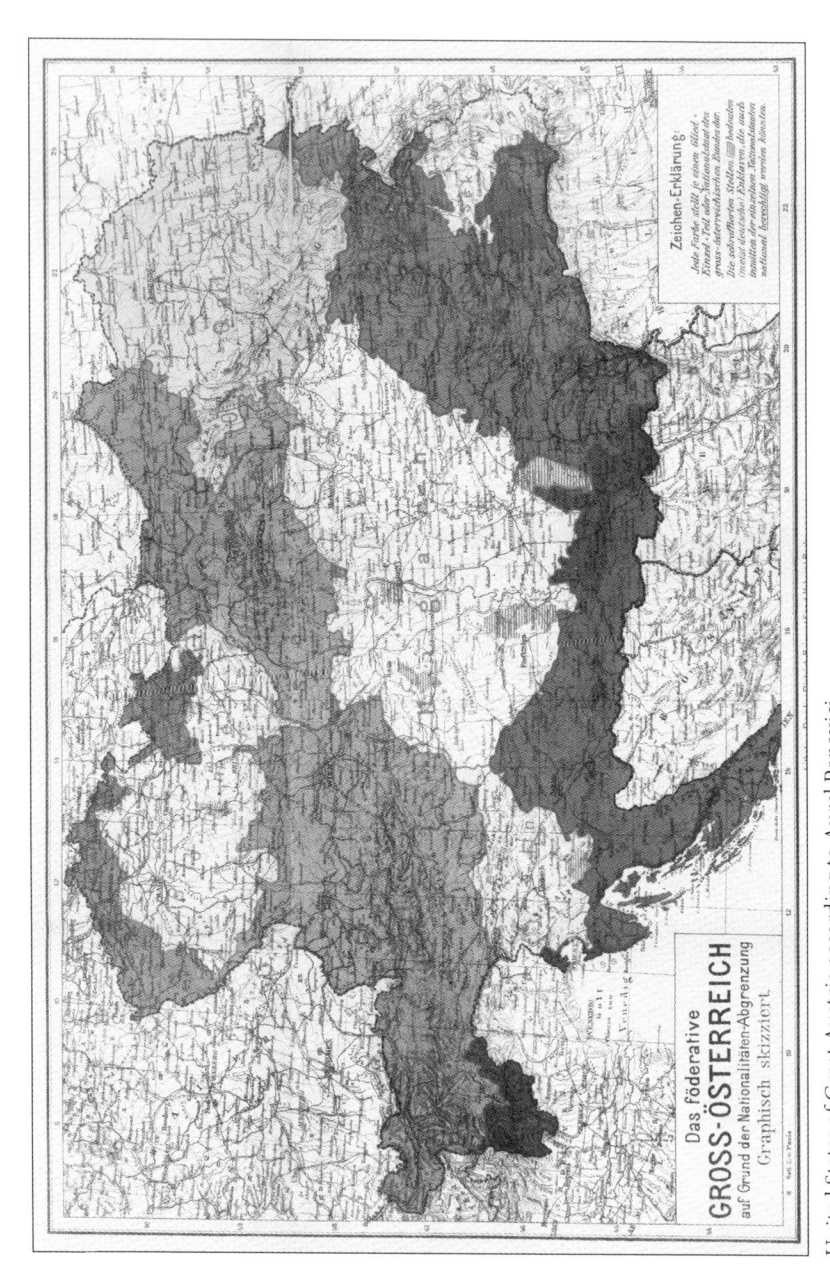

United States of Great Austria according to Aurel Popovici
(the most famous project of federalization of the monarchy according to ethnic borders)

Austria-Hungary is that by the time it fell, this country was still exotic to the majority of European readers, not to mention Americans. Works in English or French about the monarchy were few, the peculiarities of its internal politics were mysterious even for the Germans, and the ethnographic map of the monarchy was full of names that remained unknown to its citizens inhabiting the other corner of the country. As Henry W. Steed, one of the few Englishmen who wrote about Austria before World War I, informed his readers, "The Austrian problem is a problem *sui generis*, not to be solved on principle or in light of theory."[1] His compatriot C. A. Macartney, who was to become one of the best specialists in Austrian history of his generation, introduced the monarchy using sophisticated phraseology that might seem surprising if we consider that he was referring to the country against which Britain had fought its most exhausting war only a few years earlier: "The venerable dynasty [the Habsburgs] was not like others. . . . Treaties, campaigns, marriages, barters had all played their role. If the campaigns were often disastrous, the marriages were most brilliant by contrast; and perhaps the almost uniform incompetence of his generals was one of the brightest gems in the Monarch's diadem . . . Austria, the incorporated seat of the Habsburgs' will to power, changed its frontiers every decade: it was indefinable, it was almost a poetic idea."[2]

Dualism, or, the Hungarian Perfidy

Analyzing the writings of interwar historians of Austria-Hungary, one immediately finds how familiar they were with the realities they described. Armed with temporal and emotional distance, modern historians have no problem stating that the monarchy failed to satisfy the aspirations of its nationalities. They identify their demands, reconstruct their political programs, and demonstrate the nature of the national movements—and they find no reason to suppose that anyone could find it controversial, or that anyone could doubt that it led unavoidably to the fall of the monarchy. Interwar historians knew all that, but they could hardly synthesize the entire process; they saw all its elements separately, each of them in its own dynamics, and full of sub-elements: the language question, the problem of frontiers, the army, the press, the political parties with their leaders, and many others. More importantly, they did not see the process of decomposition of the monarchy as obvious or "natural"; rather, they were inclined to find who was to blame for it. This is one reason why the post–World War II image of Austria-Hungary is more serene than the post–World War I image, in spite of the Habsburg nostalgia evident in many interwar writings on the monarchy: their authors, in contrast to the historians of the next generation, were still irritated by what had gone wrong in the history of the monarchy.

Appearances notwithstanding, the majority of Austro-German authors agreed that the co-rulers of the monarchy, the Magyars, were to blame. This should not be surprising if we realize that Austro-Hungarian antagonism had troubled the monarchy for the entire period of dualism (1867–1918) and, technically, was the most problematic political issue. The Czechs, Poles, Romanians, or Ukrainians made a lot of noise about their rights and position vis-à-vis other nationalities within the monarchy from time to time; sometimes their postulates were fulfilled, sometimes they were pacified by some minor concessions, and sometimes the entire fuss was replaced by other, more urgent problems. Dualism, in contrast, was there during the entire epoch and caused similar problems year by year. Moreover, the dualist agreement of 1867 included a common budget that was supposed to be renewed every ten years. Accordingly, at the end of every decade the monarchy was paralyzed by bitter fights between Cisleithania and Transleithania (as the Austrian and the Hungarian halves of the monarchy were popularly called) about how much each was supposed to contribute.[3] In the eyes of the Austrians, the Hungarians seemed very difficult partners, and it soon became a ritual to blame them for all stagnation, unrealized plans, and failed initiatives of the government. In short, Austria-Hungary was like an arranged marriage with no love, and constantly short of money. The Hungarians, the Austrians unanimously claimed, should have been more cooperative; and some Austrians believed that all the troubles of the monarchy had their origins in Transleithania—or, in Joseph Redlich's words, in the "nationalist megalomania of the Magyars."[4] Interwar historians still knew what the next generation (looking at the monarchy from a distance and arriving at a synthetic view of its problems) would easily forget: that the Poles, Croats, Slovenes, Ukrainians, and even some Czechs—although some Czechs had been so irreconcilable—could have been compromised, or bribed, with concessions, and then they would quietly consume their little successes for a time. The Hungarians, by contrast, vetoed Austrian initiatives almost incessantly. The obvious reason for this, which Austro-German authors usually preferred not to mention, was that the Hungarians enjoyed legal and political equality with the Austro-Germans, and hence they simply could afford to oppose Vienna. Their weapon was the Compromise of 1867, which was therefore unanimously criticized by the Austrians.

The monarchy had no common constitutional bodies, but did have in common the emperor-king and his joint government, composed of three ministers—of war, foreign affairs, and common finances—whom he chose himself. Hence, Cisleithania and Transleithania could not even quarrel properly, nor could they formally discuss their mutual problems. They could, however, veto the initiatives of the other. The joint government was fully controlled by Franz Joseph, who did not allow it to mirror Austro-Hungarian antagonisms. The Austrian Empire and the Hungarian Kingdom of St. Stephen had only one common property: the province of Bosnia-Herzegovina, acquired in 1908 after thirty years of informal occupation. It was an exception in the dualist structure, born out of jealousy of both countries. Neither could agree that the other one should incorporate it, and so they decided that this semi-colony would be governed by the joint minister of finance. The last one of these before the war was Leon Biliński, a Pole from Galicia. Characteristically, he wrote in his memoirs that his office was paralyzed by "a thousand symptoms of the Hungarian constitutional phantasy," and that "a Hungarian, unwelcomed by Austrians, was always in a less uncomfortable position than a joint minister designated by the Austrians."[5] Similarly, the ex–imperial and royal ambassador to Rome, Count Heinrich von Lützow, observed in his memoir that the political mentality of the Hungarians remained "exotic" to the Austrians, and that Austro-Hungarian negotiations had usually been more difficult than negotiations with foreign partners.[6]

Indeed, the dualist order created by the Compromise of 1867 was easy to criticize. It resulted from the moment of crisis after the lost war against Prussia in 1866, when Viennese statesmen realized that the monarchy needed more popular support and decided to seek it among those who had been its most stubborn opposition, the Hungarian nobility. After continuous conflicts to do with the common budget, emblems, and symbols, some thirty years later it became obvious for many Austrians that the support of the Hungarian nobility did not suffice to make the monarchy really popular. Hungarians, however, stubbornly maintained the status quo and fiercely opposed any changes—including any parallel agreements within Cisleithania, such as the one that Vienna was considering in the early 1870s to win over the Czechs. On the other hand, at the turn of the century the majority of the Hungarian public desired changes in the compromise that would give Hungary even more independence from Austria, which caused much frustration in Vienna and met with the decisive resistance of the emperor-king. In short, as often happens with compromises, both sides believed that the other participant interpreted it egoistically. As Oszkár Jászi—a democratic liberal and a minister in the last Hungarian government before the Bolshevik Revolution in 1919—observed, the Hungarian attitude was marked by a certain legal fiction: the compromise was formally conducted between Franz Joseph as the Hungarian king, and his Hungarian subjects, and thus it did not take into consideration Austria as an involved part at all. Hence, Hungarian nationalists could maintain that their country was linked to Austria only by the fact that the Hungarian king also happened to be the Austrian emperor, and by a number of bilateral agreements, such as the ones regarding the joint army, foreign affairs, and finances. In other words, the Kingdom of St. Stephen only had accidental and temporary common interests with Austria, but no common legal nature; Hungary was married only to her king, and Austria-Hungary was just a joint venture.[7] Jászi called this attitude "constitutional dogmatism," and sadly remarked that in spite of this doctrine, which seemed to prevail in Hungarian public opinion at the turn of the century, Austria-Hungary was a real power that could call millions of its citizens to arms.[8]

    Jászi was also the only interwar historian of Austria-Hungary who critically emphasized the special element of its constitutional structure: the joint government. Hungarian nationalists, he argued, dully focused on the legal fiction of their country's independence, denying all its connections to Austria, whereas what really harmed this independence was the joint government. What was unacceptable for Jászi as a democrat was the fact that this government, located between the political structures of Austria and Hungary, was not controlled by any of the respective parliaments but solely by the monarch, and was therefore "an instrument of Habsburg absolutism."[9] It may seem astonishing that no other author of the interwar generation stressed this evident fact. Obviously, Jászi had his grounds; he was a progressive democrat and thus he disliked absolutism on principle, but he was also a Hungarian patriot, and was therefore particularly allergic to the Habsburg absolutism. Austro-Germans, even if equally democratic on principle (although there were few such authors in this generation), opposed dualism and "the Magyar megalomania." Thus, they viewed the joint government—and the monarch who controlled it, of course—as the only institution that could exercise some influence on the Hungarians, which they regarded as more than desirable. And since their custom—inherited from the epoch when the monarchy had still existed—was to incessantly complain about the notoriously strong position of Hungary within the monarchy, they omitted the problem.

German nationalists emphasized that the powers of the monarch were much more limited in Hungary than in Austria, and the absolutism they condemned was the absolute domination of the Magyars over the ethnic minorities in Transleithania. Wilhelm Schüssler, for example, who dedicated his book to "all who believe in the Great Germany," claimed that the monarchy was ruled by "Hungarian absolutism"—because in Austria the parliament was de facto impotent after 1897 and the country was ruled by the emperor, who remained under the pressure of the Hungarian parliament.[10] He was partly right: the Hungarian parliament exercised control over its government, whereas in Austria it was impossible to form any parliamentary majority after Count Kazimierz Felix Badeni's government mortally antagonized the Czechs and the Germans over the language question in Bohemia. Since that time, the country was ruled by governments appointed by the emperor on the basis of article 14 of the constitution, which gave the monarch this privilege. But Franz Joseph's position was strong in Hungary, too: he had the right to veto all bills and to approve all bills proposed by the government. What truly irritated the Austrians was that the Hungarian political system functioned more smoothly than their own. Most importantly, it did not run from crisis to crisis because of national antagonisms. This was possible because the Hungarian nobility managed to sustain an electoral census that effectively favored the Magyars (or more precisely the Magyar upper classes), and left the ethnic minorities, composing about half of the population, with just a few parliamentary seats. Facing no serious opposition, they could efficiently govern the Kingdom of St. Stephen, encompassing almost half of the monarchy's territory, and, last but not least, they pursued a consistent policy of Magyarization of Jews, Slovaks, Romanians, Ukrainians, and Serbs.

Austrian authors viewed this situation with a combination of jealousy and contempt. Most of them assumed that the monarchy could have been reformed, and therefore saved, if the Hungarians had not resisted any change to the dualist settlement so stubbornly. And they were infuriated by the Hungarian Independence Party, which did want to change this settlement so that Hungary would be even less dependent on Austria. Already during the Great War, the author of a patriotic booklet *Österreich-Ungarns Neubau unter Kaiser Franz Joseph I* (The reconstruction of Austria-Hungary under Emperor Franz Joseph) called Hungarian separatism "blinded chauvinism."[11] Other authors eventually acknowledged that dualism was a relatively good solution, but it was soon ruined by Hungarian separatism.

Hugo Hantsch was the only interwar Austrian historian who dared to praise dualism overtly. Like a true Hungarian patriot, he even claimed that "the great power status of the monarchy was saved due to the cession of part of the Hungarian sovereignty." Moreover, he argued that dualism was profitable economically for both sides, and that Hungarian parliamentary life inspired the Austrians positively.[12] However, he also believed that the Independence Party, which undermined dualism, was the most destructive political force in the monarchy because it failed to understand that, as the Czech historian and politician František Palacký had put it, "the Austrian government should be neither German, nor Hungarian, nor Romanian, but Austrian in the higher and common sense, i.e., it should treat all its subjects equally." Count Albert Apponyi, the leader of the Independence Party, Hantsch concluded ironically, could have tasted the results of his ruinous policies as the head of the Hungarian delegation to the Paris Peace Conference in 1919.[13] The modern reader may not see the bitterness of this remark, but Hantsch's generation knew very well that contemporary Hungarians regarded the settlement of 1919 as the greatest catastrophe, and the greatest humiliation, in their history—and some Hungarians today still view it in this way.

Friedrich Kleinwächter—a nationalist who converted to Nazism after the Anschluss, and then again to Austrian patriotism—also claimed bitterly that "the Magyar politicians simply failed to understand that the union of Hungary and Austria was profitable for both

István Tisza, Hungarian prime minister, 1913–1917—the "strong man" of Hungarian politics, particularly detested by Austrians and Hungarian democrats

sides, and that only this historical union could protect the racially and linguistically lonely Magyar nation."[14] Similarly, Heinrich Benedikt argued that dualism, in the Magyar interpretation, was "a purposeful system of decomposition of the state," which owed its status as a great power to the "economic cooperation of the small nations." Expressing his frustration with the unreasonable Magyars, however, he also acknowledged the purposefulness of their nationalist policy. It was, he stated, "wise and humane," for it encouraged everyone who accepted the Hungarian language and citizenship to join the Magyar national community, so "a Serb, a Romanian, and even a Jew" could have become a Magyar. Had the Magyars, he reasoned, had "a few more decades" to pursue this policy, they would have assimilated all non-Magyar Hungarian citizens.[15] Still, narrating the events of the Great War, Benedikt did not hesitate to blame the Magyars for the final catastrophe of the monarchy. When Germany and Austria-Hungary conducted their customs union on May 2, 1918, he reasoned, the Allies began to seriously fear the monarchy, and so they concocted a plan of inspiring the irredentist movements among the monarchy's nationalities. Facing this threat, Emperor Charles and the Austrian government responded with the so-called October Manifesto, promising the federalization of the monarchy. The Hungarian government, however, protested against any changes in the dualist settlement, and so, claimed Benedikt, it "fired the bullet that killed the monarchy." He concluded that "the four-hundred-year-long struggle of the Hungarians against Austria has finished with their one-day victory. Their part of the monarchy has been dismembered too," joining in unison the common opinion of Austrian historians.[16]

To sum up, the attitude of interwar Austro-German historiography toward Hungary was a continuation of the Cisleithanian public opinion's resentments from the time before the Great War. The Austrians could not forgive the Hungarians for not wanting to share responsibility for the entire monarchy, and consistently pursuing the policy of national egoism. And yet, this policy caused ambivalent reactions. On the one hand, Austrians emphasized how disastrous Magyarization was for the monarchy's image as a supranational power and a common home for its many nationalities; on the other hand, its efficiency also caused some respect, not to say jealousy, of those who regarded the Slavs, Romanians, and Italians as problem-makers rather than real partners. Old animosities became grudges inspired by the painful memory of the downfall of the monarchy; the rhetoric of bitter accusations was fueled by the trauma of their common failure. Basically, however, the main theses of the Austrian authors—apart from the claim that only Hungarians were to blame for this failure—have survived till our times, petrified by post–World War II Western historians; in short, Hungarians profited from dualism more than they contributed. Already in 1937 C. A. Macartney wrote: "In appearance the position of the Crown was one of neutrality: in reality it proved a strong support for the Magyars. The whole conservative power of one of Europe's most conservative states stood behind Hungary's own system, which itself depended so largely for its efficiency on its oligarchic character. More important still, through her partnership in the Dual Monarchy, Hungary belonged to one of the Great Powers of Europe, whose might constantly overawed the little Romanian and Serb states which were now to constitute the real threat to Hungarian integrity."[17] Macartney also stressed that Magyarization, although occasionally forceful and generally animated by chauvinism, was in part a natural consequence of rapid industrialization and urbanization—and that it was parallel to the processes that had been taking place in the West, for example in France, a few decades earlier. As a matter of fact, Macartney's opinions cannot be contrasted with those of other contemporary Anglo-American experts, except Robert William Seton-Watson. The latter, however, had been an implacable enemy of the Magyars even at the beginning of the century, when he also became friends with Tomáš Garrigue Masaryk, the future leader of the Czech national movement and the first president of Czechoslovakia. Seton-Watson expressed his relentless contempt for the Magyar policies in his *Racial Problems in Hungary* (1908), and later actively supported the Slavic irredentist movements within the monarchy. Other Western scholars simply relied on secondhand information, usually derived from publications in German. Only during the next generation, when refugees from Hitler- and Stalin-dominated Central Europe found shelter at Western universities, did politically neutral studies on the monarchy flourish in America, Britain, and France.

It would also be difficult to compare interwar Austro-German discourse on the monarchy with contemporary Hungarian discourse. Only their dynamics were similar, in that Hungarian historians also remained preoccupied with debates that had their origins long before the Great War. More importantly, they were busy reacting to the traumatic experience of the Peace Treaty of Trianon of 1920, which deprived Hungary of two-thirds of its prewar territory and half of its population (including all minorities except the well-assimilated Jews). In consequence they had even less interest in the problems that rankled in the minds of their Austrian ex-partners than before. "In the Hungary of the 1920s and 1930s, the focus of the explanatory endeavors was not the dissolution of the Dual Monarchy, but of the historical country," claims Gergely Romsics in his recent study on the memoirs of the Austro-Hungarian elite. He also points out that interwar Hungarian authors "consecrate to it [the dual monarchy] one chapter and, at times, only a page or two, while whole volumes are devoted to the breaking up of St. Stephen's Hungary."[18] Péter Hanák adds that the interwar Hungarian historians basically remained divided into two camps that had already formed during dualism: the pro-Western and pro-Habsburg *labanc*, and the nationalist *kuruc*, which saw the Compromise of 1867 as a "moral capitulation." The most radical representative of the latter was probably László Németh, who regarded the Hungarian elites of the dualist era simply as Habsburg (and Jewish) agents—in short, traitors of the nation. The most significant authors of the former, liberally-conservative trend, who were also ardent critics of Hungarian nationalism, were Gusztáv Gratz, Gyula Szekfű, and Szandor Pethő.[19] Moreover, there was a small group of Hungarians whose personal careers predestined them to identify with the entire monarchy and who, therefore, were extremely critical toward the separatism of their compatriots. For example, ex-Austro-Hungarian diplomat Count Julius von Szilassy claimed that "because of this folly the one-thousand-year-old Kingdom of St. Stephen collapsed, and also everything that was humane and cultural, and that build up the Austrian spirit."[20] Still, the majority of the Hungarian public, united in their outrage against Trianon, remained faithful to the concept of the indivisibility of the "lands of St. Stephen's Crown," which had fueled Magyar resistance against all reforms of dualism before 1918. This legalist dogma was so widely praised that when a professor of constitutional history at the University of Budapest questioned it, its scandalized adherents brought the issue under the discussions of the national parliament in 1931.[21] One of the most vehemently protested points he made was to compare the history of Hungarian constitution with that of the Polish or the Czech, rather than with the English constitution—which the Hungarian tradition regarded as the sole appropriate analogy in the entire world history.

Nationalists and Bureaucrats

Friends of Austria-Hungary unanimously claimed that the supranational state was a better solution to the problems of Central Europe than the patchwork of nation-states that replaced it. As a great supranational power, the old Austria had, they reasoned, guaranteed security, promoted culture, and provided necessary resources for economic growth. It may therefore seem that their sympathy for Austria-Hungary was founded upon a negative assessment of nationalism as such. Of course, things were not that simple. What the majority of Austro-German historians liked about the monarchy was not only the fact that it was supranational but also that it privileged Germans over other nationalities and kept the barbaric Slavs under the influence of German culture.

The most sincerely and consistently anti-nationalist of all interwar accounts of Austro-Hungarian history was perhaps *Nationalgeist und Politik* (National spirit and politics), by Friedrich Hertz. This multivolume book covers the development of nationalism in all major European countries in the nineteenth century, involving typical (and stereotypical) analyses of their "national characters." Hertz overtly expressed his negative opinion about nationalism as a predominantly destructive force, which he characterized with Thucydides' words that adherents of nationalism care more about causing damage to their enemies than about avoiding it themselves.[22] Austria-Hungary occupies an eminent position in the book—and enjoys some evident sympathy from its author. He emphasized that the monarchy always protected its nationalities against domination by their mighty and aggressive neighbors; first the Turks, later the Germans, and eventually the Russians. He argued that "no other government has ever worked so hard on achieving reasonable compromises" in its attempts to realize the contradictory claims of its nationalities, and denied the popular opinion that Vienna, and particularly Franz Joseph, consistently pursued the *divide et impera* policy, supporting weaker nations against stronger ones in order to play the role of an arbiter and rule them more efficiently. This he called "a democratic prejudice"; nationalism, he reasoned, is not inspired by "Machiavellian politicians," nor is it a camouflaged intrigue of capitalists. It is a popular ideology of the immature masses, animated by irresponsible demagogues.[23]

Thus, Hertz's account of the history of national movements in Austria-Hungary is extremely critical. Like other German historians of his time, he was not indulgent toward the Magyars. There is, however, more logic in his reasoning, for he argued that their nationalist policy contributed to the escalation of nationalist feelings of the Hungarian minorities oppressed by the Magyars. Furthermore, he spared no Austro-Hungarian nationality in his criticism. He seems to have been particularly disgusted by the pettiness and absurdities of the German-Czech conflict, and mocked the Czech tendency to focus on (as he estimated) purely formal issues and questions of prestige. Still, he claimed that German nationalism was ideologically deeper and eventually took the form of racism, and that Germans were mostly responsible for spreading anti-Semitism throughout the monarchy. This ideology, he emphasized, was inseparable from the nationalism of the

Austro-Germans, whereas among other nationalities of the monarchy anti-Semitism was simply "a primitive reaction of the non-educated classes against the German-Jewish businessmen." Astonishingly, in contrast to the Czechs and the Germans he praised the Poles; they were constantly ready to compromise in internal Cisleithanian conflicts, and such was also the attitude of the Polish politicians who influenced Austrian diplomacy, such as Prime Minister Badeni or Minister for Foreign Affairs Agenor Maria Gołuchowski, who both advocated compromises with Russia.[24]

Hertz's uncompromisingly negative approach to nationalism was, however, rather atypical for his time. Other Austro-German authors were more openly biased; they criticized all nationalities of the monarchy except Germans, whom they presented as victims of their own tolerance. This approach was perhaps most overtly and consistently presented by Harold Steinecker in the opening chapters of *Das Nationalitätenrecht des alten Österreich* (The law of nations in old Austria). The book was edited by Karl Gottfried Hugelmann, who cannot be accused of hiding this bias—in the preface he proudly informed his readers that only German authors had been asked to contribute to it. In the opening chapter Steinecker reminded readers not to underestimate the power of nationalism, as his contemporary Polish and Czech scholars did (he mentioned Franciszek Smolka, Oskar Halecki, and Emanuel Radl). First, as the 1919 peace negotiations in Paris proved, Steinecker observed, national antagonisms reach as far back as the medieval epoch; second, nations, and races—the difference between the two is not clear—are biologically predestined to compete for territory. Characterizing the situation in Austria-Hungary, he generally claimed that its nations got what they deserved, and their share in the "common cake" was determined historically. He divided the Austro-Hungarian nationalities into "historical" ones and the "nations without history." The former—the Poles, the Hungarians, and the Germans—had political and cultural traditions and institutions of their own; the latter were only acquiring their national consciousness in the course of the nineteenth century. Interestingly, this popular theory is usually ascribed to Friedrich Engels, Karl Marx's friend and editor (and will therefore be discussed again in the next chapter). Finally, explaining the relatively privileged position of the Germans in the monarchy, Steinecker presented at length their merits for the region. In accordance with the contemporary German dogma he claimed that all culture and civilization enjoyed by Central Europe had been brought there by German colonists. Paradoxically, he maintained that German colonization had never had political claims, and that the Habsburg policy of centralization, which Vienna had several times attempted before the Compromise of 1867, had nothing to do with Germanization.[25]

Contradictions of the attitude of conservative Austro-Germans to the national question in Austria-Hungary can be best observed in the concluding chapter of the volume, written by its editor Karl Gottfried Hugelmann. Hugelmann declared that he wanted "to render justice to the great monarchy for the sake of historical truth" although "it is well known" that he did not support the idea of its reconstruction in any form. On the one hand, he argued that the monarchy guaranteed its nationalities an almost perfect equality, suggesting that, at least legally speaking, the notorious national problem of the monarchy was much ado about nothing. Even if the excellent Austrian law did not work perfectly everywhere, he added, the situation of any of the Austro-Hungarian nationalities was incomparably better than the situation of any of the ethnic minorities in the successor states after the Great War. On the other hand, he emphasized the German primacy in the monarchy. The German nation not only contributed the most to the common state but it also gave example to the other nations and inspired the rise of their respective national movements. Most importantly, the Germans sacrificed for Austria-Hungary their most precious national ideal: the unification within "the great power of their own nation" that was the German Reich.[26]

As far as the alleged notoriety of the national question in the monarchy is concerned, Heinrich Benedikt proved basically the same, employing a reversed argumentation. Discussing constitutional matters, he claimed, tells us little about the actual conduct of politics, for as Alexander Pope had already pointed out, "For forms of government let fools contest / Whate'er is best, administrated is best." His choice of an eighteenth-century English poet was not accidental; like most enthusiasts of Austria-Hungary he chose Britain as the best analogy to analyze the political order of the monarchy. This rhetorical manipulation had two advantages: First, considering Britain's international prestige in the first half of the twentieth century, it was obviously flattering for Austria-Hungary. Second, Britain enjoyed the reputation of the motherland of parliamentary democracy, and yet its political system was also undeniably conservative and founded upon traditions rather than abstract principles. And this was exactly what the admirers of the Habsburgs wanted to prove about Austria-Hungary; that despite its conservatism, it actually guaranteed its citizens more liberties than did formal democracies. Eventually, Benedikt went even further and proved that the old Austria was in fact governed better than Britain itself. In Austria-Hungary, he reasoned, all citizens enjoyed perfect legal equality, whereas in Britain the electoral census and tradition reserved the positions of power in the parliament and the government for the privileged classes exclusively. Quite illogically, but with much vigor, he continued by saying that the genius of Austria rested upon the truly aristocratic spirit of its bureaucracy, with its politeness and good manners. Furthermore, he stressed that one should not overestimate the notorious obstruction of the Austrian parliament, because this institution, controlled by modern political parties and divided along national lines, was not truly Austrian, and therefore "no one took it seriously." The truly Austrian spirit was supranational, monarchical, and Catholic, even though in the last decades of the monarchy's existence some nationalistic, atheist, and Protestant elements managed to disturb its harmonic functioning.[27]

This image of idyllic harmony, tolerance, and liberty under the umbrella of the flawless Habsburg bureaucracy, which eventually deteriorates into an unmanageable chaos of war of all against all, is typical for Austro-German historians. Joseph Redlich, for example, himself an ex-Austrian parliamentary member and minister, believed that the monarchy, at least since the establishment of the Supreme Administrative Court in 1876, embodied the idea of a *Rechtsstaat* "in the most perfect fashion." His enthusiastic eulogy of the Habsburg bureaucracy is worth quoting at length:

> This bureaucracy . . . deserved in many respects to hold the first place among the administrative services of the great European states. It was absolutely incorruptible. The scale of salaries was by no means great, but in the exercise of its functions it was animated by a very lofty sense of social and juridical right. As part of its old Austrian inheritance it possessed a humane outlook which honorably distinguished it from the bureaucracies of other nations and

states. . . . . As the prestige of the *Reichsrat* [the Viennese parliament] and the Diets fell, that of bureaucracy, the silent, faithful, and efficient crew of the ship of state, rose."[28]

Of course, other Austro-German historians did not praise the Habsburg bureaucracy in such a naïve, or perhaps even sentimental way; still, the assumption that it was free of national prejudices and that it epitomized the most precious Austro-Hungarian virtues, was certainly a dogma. Characteristically for such patriotic assumptions, it is in fact impossible to determine its origins. Austro-German historians might simply have been motivated by their memories, but they might also have arrived at this opinion driven by logic: since bureaucracy, alongside the army and the person of the monarch himself, was considered one of the few institutions uniting the monarchy and surpassing ethnic divisions, an admirer of the monarchy had no choice but to praise it. This is easily seen even in the writings of the sober critics of the monarchy such as C. A. Macartney. The British historian, not surprisingly, also decided to compare the Austro-Hungarian institutions with those of his homeland. Obviously, his evaluation was opposite that of Heinrich Benedikt's; in other respects, however, they were strikingly similar, like images of one object in two mirrors. According to Macartney, "Franz Joseph's absolutism was the most thoroughgoing that Austria ever experienced," despite all constitutional liberties, precisely because of the growth of the bureaucracy that, freed from the feudal limitations of earlier times, actually ruled the monarchy. And the Austrian bureaucracy, in contrast to the English one, served not the needs of society but the autocratic will of its sovereign. And yet, in an apparently Habsburg style, the British historian added that "the bureaucracy felt itself Austrian, and did truly, if thinly, incorporate that elusive idea," and that it was permeated with aristocratic spirit, partly due to the personal policy of Franz Joseph, who always made a point to nominate nobles to important posts. Finally, Macartney, in contrast to his Austro-German colleagues, listed two more social groups that were also faithful supporters of the monarchy: "the Jews, the most, and the Gypsies, the least influential of all races."[29]

However, as mentioned, Austro-German historians also acknowledged some clouds on the bright firmament of the Austro-Hungarian political scene. According to Viktor Bibl, the primordial sin of dispatching from the appropriate course of Austro-German politics was committed by Prime Minister Eduard Taaffe, who first decided to seek support for his government among the Slavs and against the German liberals, who were omnipotent in the 1870s and early 1880s, and hence "governed the monarchy up to death." By doing so, Bibl suggested, Taaffe encouraged the rebellious nationalities to fight for a more and more powerful position within the monarchy, and finally to destroy it. It was by no means an unavoidable process, he argued, quoting the most famous nineteenth-century Austrian poet Franz Grillparzer, who wrote, "If only we had a Bismarck for five years—he would be done with them."[30] What came after Taaffe was an "agony" of "political morphinism." Other Austrian authors were not so openly chauvinistic; nevertheless, their image of the last decades of the monarchy is equally pessimistic: driven by the national antagonisms, it ran from crisis to crisis. Redlich argued that "the Habsburg realm was doomed from the moment when the constitutional principle was smashed, in parliament, by Germans" in November 1897, when Badeni's government fell after the prime minister tried to solve the Czech-German conflict in Bohemia with his language ordinances.[31] Since that moment Austria-Hungary had been dominated by a permanent conflict of the nationalities. As he bitterly remarked, "If Germans had brought three governments down on the language ordinances, the Czechs must do the like to one."[32]

Actually, admiration for the alleged Habsburg virtues could not protect the monarchy in its confrontation with nationalism. This can perhaps be best observed in the essay "Erzherzog Albrecht, Benedek und die altösterreichische Soldatengeist" (The Archduke Albrecht, Benedek, and the old Austrian military spirit), by Heinrich von Srbik. Srbik was one of the most distinguished Austrian historians of his generation, and a conservative nationalist who oscillated between nostalgia for the Habsburgs and fascination with the Nazis in the late 1930s. In "Erzherzog Albrecht," he reconsidered the mentality of the Habsburg military—another supranational institution regarded as one of the pillars of the monarchy—using the examples of the archduke Albrecht and the general Ludwig August Ritter von Benedek, as those who embodied the Habsburg virtues most perfectly. Archduke Albrecht was an evident example; Benedek was a controversial one. The general won questionable fame for his mistreatment by the emperor during the fatal 1866 campaign against Prussia. The court blamed him for the defeat, although he had been nominated as commander of the northern army against his will shortly before, and then forbade him to comment on the issue in public. Humiliated by his emperor, Benedek remained loyal—and Srbik praised him for this loyalty, emphasizing that the general saw the future of the monarchy in dark colors. "*Vorwärts ist ungrisch und böhmisch*" (Our prospects are Czechish-Hungarish), he was supposed to have said in his last years. Srbik shared this pessimistic view; in his opinion the Habsburg army—brave, loyal, and admirable—lacked an "animating idea" in 1866. The only such idea available at this time was the national one.[33]

Eventually, Austrian historians had no choice but to admit that the monarchy had been in trouble already at the end of the nineteenth century, and that during the next two decades it was declining politically. They sought consolation in somewhat desperate arguments. Wilhelm Schüssler argued that the monarchy "fulfilled its basic functions," that it protected its citizens against external and internal enemies, and "promoted culture" until the last days of its existence and during the four years of its glorious combat in the Great War. This implies that the monarchy's condition was not as lamentable as it was popularly assumed, he concluded, and crowned his argumentation with an astonishing analogy: "It still possessed a will to life, and a strong one, not like the old Poland of the eighteenth century!"[34] Furthermore, Austrian historians found relief, or perhaps satisfaction, in comparing the monarchy with its successor states. Germans and Hungarians were not the only victims of the peace settlement of 1919, observed Max Hildebrandt Brehm in *Das Nationalitätenrecht des alten Österreich;* the situation of the Slovaks, the Ukrainians, the Croats, and the Slovenes, who exchanged Austro-Hungarian domination within the monarchy for domination by the Czechs, Serbians, and Poles in Czechoslovakia, Yugoslavia, and Poland, had not changed for better. "The destructive policies of their leaders carried their old problems into contemporary Europe," Brehm argued. In contrast to its successor states, the monarchy did its best to guarantee the equality of its nationalities; if it did not succeed in practice, it at least left "an impressive theoretical literature on the subject," he desperately concluded.[35] A similar reasoning made Edmund von Glaise-Horstenau, an Austrian officer who, like Srbik, in the 1930s exchanged his nostalgia for the Habsburgs for admiration of the Nazis, forget his anti-Hungarian sentiments! It would be unfair, he argued in the book *Die Katastrophe* (The catastrophe), to discuss the policy of Magyarization before the Great War without mentioning that with respect to national assimilation the successor states pursue similar policies much more ruthlessly today—that is to say in the 1920s.[36]

Untimely Meditations, or, Historical Alternatives

Professional historians usually deny that the question "what would happen if . . . ?" can be answered within the framework of their discipline. They know that the world of historical alternatives is an unmanageable chaos, a Pandora's box of potential, or the so-called counterfactual developments that were more or less likely to happen. Nevertheless, in practice they employ this sort of reasoning constantly in their narratives. Alternative historical scenarios have been a part of historiography since Livy, who meditated on what the potential consequences for the history of Rome would have been if Alexander the Great had decided to invade Italy instead of Asia. There are several reasons for this. Today, when alternative history has become a separate genre, it seems obvious that one of them is simply the fact that it is amusing and attracts a large number of readers, who prefer to exercise their imagination rather than feed their minds with facts and interpretations that have been established a long time ago, and digested a number of times since that moment. Another reason is the logical premise immanent for all evaluations, particularly for all moral judgments: it is impossible to say that some past agent was good or wrong in his or her decisions and choices without imagining an alternative. Hence, alternative scenarios are generally more frequent in histories written by authors who are frustrated or dissatisfied with the outcome of their story; the winners do not need to bother with this problem that much. Obviously, historians of Austria-Hungary often referred to the problem of alternatives. All authors who had some sympathy for the monarchy more or less openly inquired what could have been done to save it.

This feature of the discourse about Austria-Hungary is extraordinary for one more reason: authors almost unanimously agreed on the causes of the monarchy's decline and fall. It is enough to look at any reasonable analogy to realize how special it was. In the case of the Roman Empire—and this example was dear to interwar historians, educated at classical *gymnasia*—dozens of volumes had already been written before World War I on the causes of its decline. The debate involved some of the most prominent names in historical studies all over Europe, such as Montesquieu, Gibbon, Ferguson, Niebuhr, and Mommsen; and the problems discussed included geography, agriculture, religion, manners, political institutions, military affairs, and, last but not least, the laws of history—or Providence. In the case of Austria-Hungary, the entire debate evolved around the national problem. Of course, this problem is itself complicated and multifaceted, and has never ceased provoking controversies of historians and theoreticians. In the interwar epoch it seemed to be *le dérnier cri* of history, an indisputably modern trend that was just arriving at the peak of its might and significance. Austria-Hungary, in contrast, was overtly anachronistic; it epitomized the feudal principle of dynastic power, typical of the Middle and Early Modern Ages. As Max Hildebrandt Brehm put it, sarcastically but straightforwardly, the monarchy fell in consequence of the principle of the self-determination of nations, which had its origins in the French Revolution, and which allowed Tomáš Garrigue Masaryk, leader of the Czech opposition before 1914 and the first president of Czechoslovakia, to justify his high treason as duties toward his nation. "Monarchical charisma" was all that Austria could oppose against "enlightened prejudices," and that indicated that it was "alienated from the modern spirituality."[37] To be sure, this opinion had been highly popular already before the Great War, when the monarchy was still one of the great powers. Austrians might have been accustomed to their national complications and hoped that the constant animosities could be appeased, as they had been in the past. Still, if we take a look at the contemporary opinion on the monarchy abroad, we will hardly find anyone who did not suppose that the Austro-Hungarian ethnic bomb would one day explode. For example, the author of a statistical-legal compendium of information on the monarchy, published in Warsaw in 1907, concluded, "The national struggle is constantly rising, involving all strata of the society. It covers the entire territory of the state, disturbing its political development, and at the moment no solution for this lamentable condition seems available. The future of Austria appears to be dubious, and it is possible that the changes that we now observe taking place in the entire East of Europe will destroy this artificial construction that has become a cage for so many peoples."[38] Seven years later, and a few months before the outbreak of the Great War, Francis Gribble in the first biography of Franz Joseph in English painted an even darker image of the monarchy's prospects:

> The real rivalry of the Europe of today and tomorrow is the rivalry between Teuton and Slav; and that is a rivalry which has its origin not merely in conflicting material interests, but in fundamental antipathies of character. As long as Teutons are anywhere ruling over Slavs, no policy of "live and let live" is feasible; as the Slavs increase in numbers and in racial self-consciousness, the clash is bound to come. When it does come—when the unredeemed Slavs, assisted by the unredeemed Romanians, insist upon their redemption—Austria will have played her part in the stage of European history, and the curtain may be rung down.[39]

Thus, providing that nationalism was Austria-Hungary's main enemy, it might seem that the monarchy had been unquestionably doomed, and all scenarios considering its chances for survival were pointless. Still, interwar historians of the monarchy, and particularly the Austro-German ones, tried to speculate on them. To modern readers these speculations may make little sense, but they were writing for their contemporaries who were hungry for such counterfactual scenarios, as readers of history are always considering recent developments, especially if they find them unfortunate and frustrating.

Generally speaking, Austro-German authors suggested to their readers two kinds of alternative scenarios regarding the national question. They may be called the liberal and the conservative, provided that we understand both terms relatively, in the context of the actual Austro-Hungarian policies, rather than their standard interpretations in political philosophy. Thus, the liberal alternative implied some sort of compromise with the rising national movements, and the conservative one opted for a more decisive and vigorous centralization of power. However, as I shall demonstrate, the latter also acknowledged the need for some concessions, such as the replacement of dualism with a federation of more than two ethnocultural territorial units, assuming that such a structure would be more efficiently governable for Vienna.

The conception that I call liberal was, as a matter of fact, highly critical toward the German and Magyar liberals who ruled Austria-

Hungary for about three decades following the Compromise of 1867. Its most representative adherent, next to Oszkár Jászi, was perhaps Joseph Redlich. In contrast to the majority of his Austrian colleagues, he found the Compromise of 1867 unsatisfactory not simply because it privileged the Hungarians vis-à-vis the Austrians but because it left the other nations underprivileged. Hence, he believed that the monarchy should have been further federalized, so more nations would get their fair share in power. Characteristically, he never specified which nations actually deserved to be put on equal footing with Germans and Magyars. Still, he supposed that the monarchy could have been transformed into "a union of national democracies" as a result of a general democratization of the country, and thus he argued that the best moment for that was the introduction of the popular franchise in 1907.[40] Analogically, Heinrich Rosenfeld pointed out the Kremsier Constitution of 1848—introduced in immediate response to the revolution and soon revoked by Franz Joseph—as the moment when the nations of the monarchy "were closest to each other," and therefore the constitution, if only it had lasted, could have been a basis for a more fortunate development of the monarchy.[41] Rosenfeld's argument had the advantage that in 1848 nationalism was still an innocent baby, so his scenario assumes that it would never become Austria's mortal enemy; Redlich's scenario had the advantage that by 1907 everyone knew that nationalism was Austria's problem. Viktor Bibl, who himself claimed that Austria's existence had been "problematic" since its union with Hungary and Bohemia in 1526/1527, listed a dozen books published between 1902 and 1910 that advocated federalization of the monarchy according to the national lines—without, however, specifying which particular solution he found the best.[42]

The conservative conception, on the other hand, advocated that nationalism should have been put down rather than tamed by concessions, assuming that no concessions would be radical enough to satisfy the nationalists' appetite—or simply that German domination was the best solution for the monarchy. Heinrich Benedikt, for example, was disgusted by the German riots in Vienna following Badeni's language ordinances of 1897; however, he fully accepted their premises—the refusal of the German officials in Bohemia to learn Czech. Why should a German learn Czech? Benedikt found no justification for such a peculiar idea, since, as he stated, no literature of any value existed in this language, except for a number of translations from Balzac and Maupassant.[43] A. F. Pribram, a Viennese professor, also pointed to 1848 as the turning point in the history of Austria; it was then, he argues, that the nationalities of the monarchy became irrevocably hostile toward their German masters. The Habsburg emperors of the previous two and a half centuries "left nothing undone in using the power of the dynastic absolute state which was at their disposal to transform the various nationalities of their Empire into a German Greater Austria." If they failed nonetheless, it was because they had other obligations too, such as fighting other great powers, and could not concentrate fully on this task. "Ever since the idea of nationality began to pervade the whole public life of Europe," he concludes melancholically, "the time for the Germanization of the Monarchy was past."[44]

What irritated the conservatives the most was that the Austro-Hungarian authorities watched the growing potential of their enemies passively and avoided "decisive measures." Such a measure was war—because wars, provided they are victorious, improve the morale and prestige. They did not bother noting that this was exactly what Austria-Hungary did in the summer of 1914: it attacked the small but notorious Serbia, hoping to teach it a lesson and discourage all other irredentists, but in fact provoked the outbreak of a world war and its own downfall. The conservatives simply assumed that this war came too late, and blamed the indecisiveness of the authorities for the fatal delay. As Pribram put it, "With advancing age [Franz Joseph] preferred advisors who knew how to untie a knot instead of cutting it." And he précised, "Time passed by and nothing was done. The South Slav sore, allowed to fester on the body of the Empire, spread over it until it brought about its death."[45] Similarly, Bibl claimed that after the annexation of Bosnia-Herzegovina in 1908, the Balkan policy of the monarchy was "progressively paralyzed," and that it played the role of "a kind uncle who surrenders to everyone's wishes and watches them having fun at his cost."[46] Thus, they argued that the war against Serbia could have been a success that would have reversed the unfortunate rise of irredentism and nationalist ambitions, if only the timing had been better. Bibl suggested that the perfect moment was 1909, shortly after the annexation of Bosnia. Josef Schneider pointed to several moments: the 1903 inner crisis in Serbia after the assassination of its royal

Young Franz Ferdinand

couple, or the years 1904–1906 when Russia, Serbia's main protector and ally, was engaged in the conflict against Japan and weakened by the revolution. Unfortunately, he concluded in unison with Pribram, all these opportunities were lost because of Franz Joseph's unwillingness for decisive action and risk.[47]

Of course, this reasoning, counterfactual as it was, was also shortsighted. A victory over Serbia could have improved the monarchy's prestige for a time, but in the longer run it would not influence its internal tensions. Redlich was aware of this, and in order to support his argument he quoted Adolf Fischhof, author of the first project of the federalization of the monarchy from the 1870s, who commented on the crisis of 1878, when Austria faced the danger of war against Russia: "A victorious war against Russia might delay, but could not prevent the downfall of Austria so long as our constitution, instead of being the wax which welds our territories into a whole, is the wedge to drive them apart. Thence and thence only can salvation come!"[48]

Still, the majority of Austro-German historians agreed that salvation could have come from a man who had indeed embodied many hopes for a reform of the monarchy before his premature death: the archduke Franz Ferdinand. It was a public secret that the archduke, who had been the heir to the throne for almost four decades, was not a friend of Franz Joseph's policies. As the old emperor was aging, more and more malcontents looked up to the archduke as the symbol of future changes—as they imagined them. At the beginning of the century Franz Ferdinand was already a powerful man with numerous protégés in crucial institutions in Vienna, and many others hurried to present to him their projects for reforms.[49] Since it was well known that he was not an enthusiast of dualism either, he was particularly admired by all who were upset with the Magyars, and therefore, for example, a Romanian-Slovak delegation presented him with a memorandum postulating the reform of the monarchy into a federation. But Franz Joseph never allowed the archduke, whom he openly resented, to exercise too much influence—and so no one knew what direction the monarchy would take, had he lived long enough to rule it. Thus, his legend suited many: the pigeons who advocated a federation that would compromise the nationalities, and the hawks who missed a strong man.

Therefore, Edmund von Glaise-Horstenau, a German nationalist, and Richard Suchenwirth, a pro-Nazi, reminded us that all Austro-German patriots (except for the Social Democrats!) united around the archduke before 1914, and that he was "the last hope for Austria" and the only strong man who could still save it. This, suggested Glaise-Horstenau, was exactly why Franz Ferdinand was assassinated.[50] On the other hand, Christian Socialist Wilhelm Schüssler argued that Franz Ferdinand was the only man who could replace dualism with trialism, adding to Austria and Hungary a third component of the federation embracing ten million Croats, Serbs, and Bosnians, which would have solved "the Balkan question."[51] The Catholic activist Alfred Missong named Franz Ferdinand the first martyr of the future federation of Central European nations that, he hoped, should one day succeed Austria-Hungary.[52]

However, there were also skeptical voices. Viktor Bibl, for example, agreed that Franz Ferdinand was initially an enthusiast of a radical reform of the monarchy. The archduke first favored the supranational federation, and then opted for a trialism that would be the next compromise, which would create a Southern Slav state within the monar-

General Conrad von Hotzendorff. Chief of the General Staff, protégé of Franz Ferdinand and leader of the war party

chy, enjoying equal rights with Austria and Hungary. Finally, however, Bibl claimed, the stubborn Hungarian resistance and the constant conflict of the nationalities of Cisleithania made him disappointed and disillusioned about these plans. He realized that the contradictory claims of the monarchy's nations were unsolvable.[53] Moreover, other authors observed that although Franz Ferdinand indeed raised many hopes for reforms, as a matter of fact he could only be considered the leader of the war party in the monarchy, since his most important protégé was General Conrad von Hotzendorff, chief of the General Staff and the most ardent advocate of war among the Austrian decision-makers.[54]

Obviously, historical alternatives could not compete with the history of the monarchy as it actually was. The consolation they brought was ambivalent—if Austria-Hungary eventually had some chances for survival, why had they remained unrealized? At this point, the old animosities could speak again, and the old political opponents could be blamed. Nonetheless, it seems that the grounds for employing alternative scenarios in the historical narratives were also technical. The monarchy indeed was passive in its struggle against the rising centrifugal powers and nationalism. History does not tolerate a vacuum, and thus the story of the struggle for emancipation of the nationalities of Austria-Hungary had to be balanced with some reaction by the other side. The alternative scenarios were only shadows of the real developments, but at least they slightly dramatized the story of the colorless, bureaucratic routine of the monarchy vis-à-vis energetic initiatives of its enemies.

Austria and Prussia: The Big Sister and Great Power Problem

Eugene Bagger, a critical biographer of Franz Joseph, summarized the entire national problem of the monarchy in a bon mot: "The tragedy of Austria-Hungary was that it resembled a social-economic pedagogical institute for the nationalities, whose students burnt the building after having successfully passed the exams."[55] Of course, this elegant formula represented the Austro-German point of view, rather than that of the other nations of the monarchy, whose historians preferred to compare it to a cage or "a prison of nations." And yet, the comparison of Austria-Hungary to an educational institution in a way captured the essence of the controversy. The teachers saw it as a blessing for the students; the students felt oppressed and abused; both sides reciprocally resented the other's stubbornness, insensitivity, and stupidity.

Following this rhetoric, one could say that the Austro-Germans viewed the monarchy as a mother who had been betrayed and abandoned by her ungrateful children, and their bitterness was strengthened by their awareness of the fact that the children insisted that she was a nasty and abusive stepmother. Similarly, their anti-Magyar sentiments could be compared to an outburst of complaints after the divorce of a couple who never had love for each other, only a common budget. However, there was one more important member of this family: Austria's mighty sister, the Germany united by Prussia. In this hate-love relationship the resentments were the deepest and most complex for, let me repeat, at that time the difference between Austrians and Germans was indefinable. The border between the two countries was regarded as an artificial remnant of the past, preserved by the victorious Allies; the border between the two identities and loyalties ran across the personal biographies of a number of interwar historians.

Austria and Prussia had had no love for each other since the eighteenth century, when the younger Prussia questioned Austrian domination in Germany, and humiliated the Habsburgs in a number of wars; the last of them came in 1866 when Bismarck pushed Austria out of Germany, and then offered Franz Joseph an alliance. Austrian patriots never forgave the new German Reich this blow. German nationalists never pardoned the Habsburgs for the fact that because of them more than ten million Germans were left outside of their newly united fatherland. Finally, the two empires were united by the catastrophe of the Great War, the memory of which, however, also alienated them, as the Austrians felt that the monarchy had pointlessly fought, and perished, for the German cause. Many non-Germans shared this feeling. For example, let us have a look at one more colorful, metaphorical epitaph for the monarchy, this time by Polish aristocrat Leon Sapieha: "Austria, who sacrificed everything for the Prussian, her calmness and the relative sympathy of the world, was blinded by her ridiculous faithfulness. And so, approaching her doom, she watched with her fading eyes the Teuton flirting with the great, red Russia, who stimulated his desires, weaning with the faithful Austria, for Russia could murder better than he could, even at her own home. The Teuton still needed to learn that. Your idiotic sentiment caused your destruction; Austria, such stupidity must have been punished!"[56] Austrian authors would never employ Sapieha's erotic metaphors, and yet a number of them agreed with his diagnosis, that Austria perished because it fought in the war that served Prussian interests, and the reasons for getting involved in the combat were indeed difficult to explain. In other words, the German problem provided another key to the question of the monarchy's breakdown. In contrast to the national problem, it allowed for reasonable alternative solutions. All Austria needed to do in order to survive was not to enter the war. Hence, its solution was technically simpler than that of the rise of nationalism, which in fact constituted an unsolvable dilemma for admirers of the monarchy. It also suited the contemporary historical imagination better, for it concerned "high politics"; that is, treaties and alliances, whereas the national problem was about mass consciousness and ephemeral projects of reforms whose alleged consequences remained enigmatic. Still, the German problem was also more ambivalent because of the noted ambiguous identity of Austro-Germans. Some of them indeed resented the German Reich and deplored its policies, but they nevertheless sympathized with the German nation. Furthermore, it involved the issue of the monarchy's participation in the Great War, which could hardly be reduced to an "idiotic sentiment" for Germany. Moreover, scarcely any Austrian author could imagine that the monarchy, which actually started the war by attacking Serbia, could have simply avoided it. Apparently, the Great War was such an overwhelming and emotionally engaging experience that it did not allow for such speculations. All interwar historians could do was to criticize, and to regret, several decisions of the Austro-Hungarian men in power.

Obviously, it was not an easy task for pro-Habsburg historians to prove that the monarchy had to start the war that turned out to be suicidal. Nevertheless, they found some arguments for this thesis. One of them was A. F. Pribram—who, however, marked his reasoning with a typical restriction: "It is not at all my purpose to justify the decision of the Viennese statesmen. They were certainly too hasty." Moreover, his argument is remarkable for its confusing the capitals and their newspapers for the alleged Austrian nation, "It must be considered that in all quarters of the realm the opinion prevailed that a Great Power could no longer tolerate the attitude of the Serbian Power. Have not nations their sense of honor the same as individuals? Is it therefore so very strange that the Austro-Hungarian statesmen should have thought it impossible to bear any longer the insolence of the Serbs?"[57]

The logic of national psychology and national honor, which allowed abandoning, at least for the moment, political logic, was frequently employed by Austro-German authors when describing the Great War. Equipped with this flexible explanatory tool, they were able to explain to their readers the meaning of this devastating experience. Indeed, they were able to present it as a kind of Austro-German triumph, neither in the political nor in the military sense of the term, of course, but as a moral and psychological victory. As Hermann Gsteu acknowledged in his textbook for Austrian history from 1937, this was the interpretation actually expected by his compatriots, and his role was simply to confirm it in a skillful way. Teaching about the war, he confessed, was a special challenge in interwar Austria. When the lecture began, an intense silence ruled in the classroom, while pupils removed all unnecessary objects from their desks so as not to be disturbed while listening to this painful topic.[58] Glaise-Horstenau, an Austrian officer (who was to become a Wehrmacht general in the next war), also emphasized that entering the war was foremost a question of prestige. "A great state [Reich] and a great army should not surrender without fighting," he claimed, adding that escalation of the conflict was against the strong German will for peace.[59] There were, of course, other variants of speaking about honor and glory while discussing the war, and especially its beginning. Richard Suchenwirth, for example, who tried to combine his pro-Habsburg sympathy with a *grossdeutsch* nationalism in the Nazi era, acknowledged that the decision by Franz Joseph to start the war "reanimated the greatness of his ancient house."[60] In this version, the glory of the Habsburg family was seen as a gem in the diadem of German honor, shining particularly brightly during the war. Seen from this perspective, the fact that most citizens of the monarchy were not Germans, and therefore could scarcely share German patriotic feelings, was simply unnoticeable. One could suppose that it was the result of the intensification of nationalist emotions caused by the war, but this was not the case. To be sure, the war inspired chauvinists and admirers of "national honor" who normally did not have a high opinion of the monarchy. Yet ignoring the non-German nationalities was unique neither for descriptions of the war nor for the chauvinists. It was rather typical for the German, and particularly for the Viennese, bourgeoisie.

However, not all authors who claimed that the war was a question of honor for Austria assumed that it was precisely German honor at stake. The argument was flexible and used by authors of various political and emotional affiliations. Apparently, the above-mentioned Pribram, who wrote for English readers, also did not mean German honor when describing the bellicose mood prevailing in the summer of 1914, although he presumably knew it from Vienna. The Austria he personified as an individual possessing a sense of honor was the supranational Austria. A remarkable characterization of the passage from German Austria to Austria the good mother (or a good-spirited but inept stepmother) of her nationalities is to be found in a book by a Christian Socialist, Friedrich Funder, who said, "States are organisms too. They cannot exist without respect for their legal rights and their honor. This state did not belong to a particular dynasty or governing clique. It was a space [Lebensraum] of a community of nations, which protected their national identity and liberty. It also protected the European balance of power."[61] It is not clear what kind of organism Austria was, according to Funder, and what kind of honor it did possess—if it was simply the Lebensraum inhabited by the nationalities. Karl Werkmann, a young collaborator of the last emperor Charles, expressed this opinion a little more consistently: "Austria-Hungary entered the war to defend its existence," he claimed, and explained that "Emperor Franz Joseph reached for the sword for no other reason but to save the multinational state. The war was fought by Austria-Hungary to preserve its boundaries, sovereignty, and its European character."[62] Abandoning the opinion that Austria was a nation—an organism, having just one voice and one sense of honor—Werkmann arrived at the paternalistic concept of Austria as the protector of Central European nationalities. Hugo Hantsch argued that "in order to understand the tragedy of Austria-Hungary" one needed to realize that its war aims were purely local, in contrast to those of Germany, and that they in fact did not contradict the aims of France and Britain. Finally, he also emphasized that "everyone knew" that Franz Joseph strongly opposed the war party in the monarchy, and that he gave up involuntarily.[63]

The question of prestige that appears in the quoted opinions of Austrian historians is closely connected to Austria-Hungary's status as a great power, and the balance of power concept. Interwar historians liked these notions, which they inherited from nineteenth-century diplomats, and notoriously overused them. A skeptical British scholar observed already in 1923 that they were so frequently used in so many contexts that it was impossible to define them or ascribe any precise meaning.[64] Nevertheless, the great power status was obviously precious and desirable, and Austrian historians were proud that their motherland had been one. When they spoke about the honor of Austria they meant national German honor, the dynastic honor of the Habsburgs, and the prestige of a great power; and this prestige was defined by the ability to conduct wars. It is actually impossible to separate these concepts in Austro-German historians' argumentation. When the decision to attack Serbia was discussed, the problem of the great power status prevailed, because a great power could not tolerate an offense by a minor power like Serbia without risking its reputation—and its claims to this status. Great powers could negotiate controversial issues among each other, but in a case of a conflict with countries that did not enjoy this amiable status, they had to dictate their will. This scheme, or principle if you like, was not openly discussed, but silently accepted by interwar historians, more or less like the principle that gentlemen had to duel against each other but could refuse a challenge by a person of minor status. Moreover, a number of Austro-German historians regarded preserving the great power status as a raison d'être of the monarchy, as did Austro-Hungarian diplomats. Hantsch based his positive evaluation of dualism on the argument that the Compromise of 1867 "allowed for the preservation of the great power status."[65] Schüssler argued that either a federalization or a successful war could have saved the monarchy.[66] Richard Suchenwirth claimed that the dynasty prepared its own downfall, for it allied itself with the Czechs and the Poles, ignoring the Germans, who were "historical carriers of the great power position" of Austria (historischen Trägern der Grossmachtstellung).[67] Also, critics of the monarchy emphasized its decision-makers' suicidal obsession with prestige and their fear of losing the reputation of a great power. Heinrich Kanner pointed out that the mobilization against Serbia in 1914 could have been recalled, as had actually happened twice before, but the Austro-Hungarian government desired war in the panic of a humiliation.[68] Eugene Bagger agreed with the opinion of admirers of Franz Joseph, that the emperor wanted to avoid war, but stressed that he was aware of the preparations and consequences of the war memorandum presented to Serbia, and still agreed on it because of his sense of dynastic honor.[69] Viktor Bibl who, as mentioned, suggested that it would have been desirable if the monarchy had crushed Serbia before 1914 and so avoided the Great War, approvingly quoted the Serbian foreign minister Stojan Protić, who stated, "Peace and good relations between Austria-Hungary and the Balkan states will only be possible if the monarchy decides to play the role of an eastern Switzerland. As long as it plays the role of a great power, it will also desire new conquests on the Balkan Peninsula."[70]

Finally, there was also a Catholic-legitimist point of view, strikingly combining religious idealism, unyielding Habsburg loyalty, and prejudices against all things modern. Its authors believed that Austria-Hungary was a peaceful empire that was unfortunately manipulated by the Prussians and their allies, the cunning race of Hungarians. They were legitimist because they emphasized Austria's connections to Germany; nevertheless, the Germany they meant was not a modern nation but the country that had been ruled by the Habsburg emperors before it was dominated by Protestant Prussia. It was the innocent Germany of the feudal idyll, whose soul was not yet polluted by riotous modern political ideology. They also respected the balance of power theory, and thus they claimed that Prussian domination of Germany destroyed this balance. They pointed out that Germany had been a peaceful country under the Habsburgs, and it became an aggressive power only when the Hohenzollern took control over it.

Arthur Polzer-Hoditz, for example, a biographer and collaborator of the last emperor Charles, was an adherent of this tendency. Nature, he argued, wanted Germans to cohabitate Europe in harmony with other nations within the Holy Roman Empire of the German Nation, which, however, failed because of the Reformation, Napoleon, and the Austro-Prussian War of 1866. Prussians ruined this noble idea by making Germany a nation-state, although it was predestined to remain a supranational Reich. Germans also played a destructive role within Austria-Hungary, he claimed, for they maintained their disastrous deal with the Hungarians, inspiring frustration and nationalism among other nationalities. "Austria was asleep," he concluded, "whereas Germans and Hungarians controlled it, and its enemies united to work against it." Finally, Germans and Hungarians made Austria fight in the Great War to realize their imperialist dreams. These dreams, he stated, were just silly, because Germans are idealistic by nature, and therefore they should not participate in global capitalist and political competition, which, moreover, produces such destructive ideas as communism, socialism, and anarchism.[71] Polzer-Hoditz was evidently biased because of his involvement in the unfortunate policies of Charles, who had a reputation of being naïve and virtually incapable of governing the monarchy in the time of its harshest crisis. The only independent political initiative Charles made was his awkward attempt to negotiate a separate peace with the Entente, which resulted in his humiliation and total subjugation to the German Reich. Hence, the adherents of Charles had no reason to love Germany and the pro-German clique in the Austrian government. This sentiment is also easily seen in another biography of the last emperor, by Karl Werkmann. Both Polzer-Hoditz

Wilhelm II and Franz Joseph, a World War I propaganda postcard

and Werkmann had little sympathy for Franz Joseph, who yielded to German-Hungarian influences and left his monarchy on the edge of destruction. Moreover, Werkmann openly argued that Charles had a moral right to abandon his German ally during the war, for loyalty toward children (that is, the nationalities of the monarchy) goes before loyalty toward friends. The monarchy lost the war and collapsed because of the German-Hungarian resistance to Charles's plans.[72]

To sum up, the logic of the anti-German argumentation was based on a disappointment perhaps more painful than that caused by disloyalty of the monarchy's nationalities. Like all other admirers of the monarchy, they too intended to answer the question: who was to blame for its decline and fall? Like all other interwar historians, they did not have too many new facts to present to their readers; rather, their task was to organize them in a whole that would imply a convincing answer to this question. The fact that Austria-Hungary had problems with its multinational composition was no secret to any potential Central European interwar reader. The idea that maintaining the dualist settlement did not allow for necessary political reforms was only a bit less evident for all who remembered constant Austro-Hungarian animosities before 1914. The idea that Germany, too, contributed to the monarchy's troubles was, politically speaking, the simplest, for Germany was naturally considered responsible for the escalation of the 1914 war into a global conflict that exhausted Austria-Hungary until its death. Emotionally, however, it was the most difficult, because in the interwar time Austria and Germany were more than sisters; they were still considered one nation. Moreover, the Great War might have served German imperialist ideology but, after all, Austrians and Germans fought arm in arm for four years, they were fed the same war propaganda, and they suffered similar doses of humiliation and disappointment as a result of the common defeat. These things were not easy to forget.

Nevertheless, interwar Austro-German historians also remembered what a blow it had been for Austria when Bismarck had pushed it out of Germany. A number of them also emphasized that Germans were actually the champions of nationalism in Central Europe, and that other nations of the region developed their nationalist ideologies while enchanted with German Romanticism, and then fascinated with the successes of the German "blood and iron" ideology. Furthermore, the unification of Germany was obviously not only an inspiring stimulus for nationalists but also the first step to the destruction of the European balance of power that guaranteed Austria-Hungary's international position and prestige. Heinrich von Srbik, a German nationalist but also an intelligent historian sentimental about the Habsburgs, ambiguously argued that Austria-Hungary tamed "German imperialism and Eastern barbarism," and that the monarchy was "a harmonious combination of the German and the European interests."[73] He evidently realized that these interests were in fact difficult to combine, or that they were indeed contradictory; however, in order to save the fragile harmony of his own mind he avoided stating it openly. The concept of Austria as a more peaceful, tolerant, and politically reliable version of Germany, popular among interwar Austrian conservatives, will be discussed in detail in the next chapter.

Finally, let us have a look at a double outsider who saw the entire problem differently. His name was Albert Fuchs and he was a communist—and Austria, this happy subalpine country of waltz and creamed coffee, had very few communists. Hence, he wrote his *Geistige Strömungen in Österreich* (Spiritual currents in Austria) as a refugee from his Nazi-occupied motherland. As a devoted partisan of his ideology he despised nationalists, conservatives, and social democrats equally, and considered them agents of imperialist capitalism, and quoted Stalin's *Marxism and the National Question* as the supreme source of authority in these matters. However, Fuchs was also an Austrian patriot, and therefore he argued that the gravest sin of the Social Democrats was exactly their inability to recognize the importance of the national problem, their "blindness," which, as he put it, was forgivable in the case of bourgeois liberals but not in the case of people who called themselves socialists. Most importantly, the socialist leaders and theoreticians Karl Renner and Otto Bauer, he pointed out, failed to understand that all nations deserve their own territory.[74] In other words, Fuchs, despite his communism, also attempted to answer the question, "Who was to blame for the dissolution of Austria-Hungary?" The responsibility for "the miseries of Austria," in his opinion, rested mainly with the German nationalists, who, on the one hand, made the monarchy ally itself with the German Reich, and on the other hand did not allow the Austrian national consciousness to rise properly. This fact did not imply that Austrians were not a nation; to the contrary, Fuchs was probably the only author who argued that "everyone who takes the concept of nationality seriously has to agree that the nation-building process in Austria had been accomplished in 1871."[75] He was almost right; only by the next generation it became obvious that the nation-building process in Austria started in 1871.

What Remained Untold

As demonstrated, in the interwar epoch the breakdown of Austria-Hungary was still a highly controversial issue. The majority of the authors whose writings were analyzed above had personal reasons to be emotional about it. Austro-German historians regarded it as a "catastrophe" that should have never occurred. Pan-German authors had little sympathy for the monarchy, but they viewed it as a tool of German domination in Central Europe; moreover, the immediate cause for its breakup, the Great War, was evidently a catastrophe for the German nation, and so they also viewed the entire process that led to it as a historical tragedy. Since internal problems of the monarchy had been no secret to any watchful observer of the political scene before 1914, the main challenge that interwar historians faced was to explain who was responsible for them, and why nothing was done to solve them. In short, interwar historical debate on Austria-Hungary resembled a public trial in front of an audience hungry to identify the guilty of a national tragedy. A number of its participants were themselves suspects or had been partisans of the political groups that had been active in the decision-making processes before 1918, which they therefore treated like a hot potato and desperately tried to ascribe to someone else. It was the Magyars who blocked all reforms or the liberals who neglected them; it was the nationalists who resisted all compromises, or the Germans who manipulated our government; it was Franz Joseph who started the Great War, or Charles who was unable to conduct it, they argued angrily or regretfully. Needless to say, the situation left little space for a rational and impartial analysis of the historical process in question.

There is nothing like an impartial analysis in history, as the postmodernist experience teaches us. Still, some interwar historians at least tried to hide their bias behind the analytical apparatus. Let us regard two such attempts, by David Strong and Oszkár Jászi. They are worth our attention because, on the one hand, they skillfully organized the main arguments used by interwar historians, and, on the other hand, they constitute an evident link to post–World War II historiography on Austria-Hungary.

In *Austria: Transition from Empire to Republic,* David Strong listed the "important weaknesses" of the monarchy. First is the fact that in consequence of the Compromise of 1867 "Germans and Magyars were given disproportionate advantages" vis-à-vis other nationalities in the monarchy. Second is the perpetual antagonism between Cisleithania and Transleithania created by the compromise, which he found "a vague and inadequate provision for the solution of mutual problems." He argued that "although in 1867 a temporary modus vivendi had been obtained, the conflicting ideologies of the two parties to the Compromise were not brought into line, and the period from 1867 to 1918 witnessed the recurring conflict of their opposing principles." Furthermore, Strong observed that the Austrian constitution of 1867 had serious deficiencies. For example, "qualification for voting was such as to favor the Germans, Italians, and Poles," and the two-thirds majority necessary to pass any bill in the lower chamber of the parliament prevented any constitutional changes and thus "protected Dualism from Trialism." Finally, Strong claimed that the Austria created by the settlement of 1867—that is, Cisleithania—"was not a geographical unit."[76]

All this, except the last point, could be repeated by a modern historian, although after World War II scarcely any of them still believed that trialism would have saved the monarchy. Notably, Strong's last point, which seems astonishing today, was characteristic for the historical imaginary of his time. "Geographical unity" was an argument often employed by interwar historians and, as most other arguments used in the debates on Austria-Hungary, it was easily reversible: the same territories were identified as "unity" or "disunity" according to the authors' political preferences. Eventually, partisans of the reconstruction of Austria-Hungary, or some Central European federation that would replace it, almost unanimously argued that such a federation was a necessity exactly because geography indicated that the post-Habsburg territories were united and indivisible.[77]

Oszkár Jászi formulated two groups of factors contributing to the fall of the monarchy, the first group "undermining its unity" and the second "causing its disintegration and final dissolution." They were the following: (1) contradictory goals and principles of dualism and the growth of the national consciousness of the nationalities, (2) economic exploitation of the provinces by "feudal land owners" and the "semicolonial" character of the German capitalism, (3) "lack of serious civic education" that could promote state patriotism and prevent the rise of nationalism. And in the second group, of immediate causes of the monarchy's fall: (1) disappointment of nationalities with the status quo and their unfulfilled hopes for territorial-national autonomy, (2) irredentist propaganda of the neighboring countries (Italy, Romania, Serbia, and Russia), (3) the political impact of the Great War, which made it possible for nationalist politicians to organize national committees and profit from the support of the Entente.

The list seems almost complete; modern historiography has added little to it. What it has done is analyze more carefully motivations of particular social and political groups involved in the process called "the decline and fall of Austria-Hungary." In the interwar time hardly any historian, except for Jászi, stressed the social inequalities in Austria-Hungary, correlated them with national divisions, or analyzed their political potential. Their critiques of nationalism were monotonously one-sided, invariably focused on conflicts between nations regarded as political entities, and paid little attention to the processes that were taking place "below" this level, such as social mobility, political engagement, urbanization, or mass communication. Their narratives were dominated by political ideas such as nationalism, socialism, or the highly politicized concept of culture; ephemeral projects such as trialism or various plans for federalizing the monarchy; and decisions of political leaders and men in power. Moreover, they generally preferred to interpret these decisions in light of principles rather than interests of the historical agents. Joseph Redlich's remark, for example, that Franz Joseph had no interest in a Czech-German compromise, for such a compromise would limit his personal power, was unusual for interwar historians. The majority of them dismissed such suppositions as, in Friedrich Hertz's words, "a naïve prejudice of democrats who always regard the nations as reasonable and the authorities as unreasonable."[78] In doing so the interwar historians of Austria-Hungary were not at all behind the standards of academic history of their time. Nonetheless, the fact that they concentrated on political ideas, programs, and leaders did not allow them to answer the question why, after all, Austria-Hungary lost the confidence, loyalty and support of its citizens, whose majority watched its dissolution indifferently.

Finally, let me comment once again on the problem of ideological bias of the authors whose writings have been analyzed in this chapter. As noted, my choice is not representative for the interwar time; it leaves aside all those who regarded the decline and fall of Austria-Hungary as a natural process that liberated their nations from the domination of foreigners. The authors analyzed in this chapter did not view the monarchy simply as "a prison of nations." Even German nationalists, who indeed thought that some twelve million of their compatriots had been imprisoned in the monarchy after the unification of Germany in 1871, appreciated the privileged position that Germans enjoyed in Austria-Hungary. Moreover, they appreciated the role Austria-Hungary played as Germany's ally during the Great War. The Austro-Germans simply considered the monarchy their motherland and viewed its dissolution as a historical tragedy, even though some of them believed it was unavoidable. In short, the authors whose writings have been analyzed in this chapter sympathized with Austria-Hungary—and there is nothing wrong with that, for all historians have their sympathies and antipathies. All we need to do is to realize their motivations and remember them while reading their interpretations of past developments. Thus, we need to realize that the interwar historians, all their criticism toward Austria-Hungary notwithstanding, idealized the monarchy in certain aspects. One of them was the image of Franz Joseph, the monarch who became a symbol of his country during his lengthy rule—this problem will be analyzed in detail in chapter four. Another such problem was Austria-Hungary's responsibility for starting the Great War. The majority of authors discussed in this chapter desperately tried to free the monarchy's authorities from this responsibility, claiming that they had been, in a way, forced to declare war against Serbia in 1914. Only a few of them, mostly outsiders (Jászi, Kanner, Fuchs, Strong), sought an explanation that involved the mechanisms of decision-making and the mentality of the political elite and its long-distance goals. As I shall demonstrate in the conclusion of the book, this tendency was to be continued by future generations of historians. Particularly in comparison with the tens of volumes written on the Wilhelmine German Reich and the Great War, Austria-Hungary's role in it seems underestimated.

CHAPTER TWO

AUSTRIA-HUNGARY IN ESSAYISM AND POLITICAL THEORY

The frontiers of historiography as a genre have always been leaky. Interwar historians wrote multivolume books, just as their novelist contemporaries did, but their language had not yet been as professionalized as it is today, and they addressed a broad public of nonspecialists as well. They used standard vocabulary and phraseology and rarely tortured their readers with methodological problems and sophisticated terminology. They did not hesitate to include extensive quotations in Latin and French, but knowledge of these languages was still mandatory for alumni of the classical *gymnasia*. Familiarity with a number of literary classics, particularly Goethe and Schiller in the post-Habsburg space, was also expected, and historians eagerly supported their arguments with citations from their national poets. Delimiting academic history from other forms of historical writings may therefore seem an artificial operation. It is, however, purposeful because it will help us to see the difference between these authors whose aim was to write about the Habsburg monarchy as it was—and may thus be rightfully called historians of the monarchy—and those who involved certain images of it in their narratives as arguments in some more general debates. One of these debates concerned the nature of history as such, the mechanism that governs it and its aims, for in the interwar period it was still popularly believed that history has an aim, and that one can penetrate its mechanisms.

For an academic historian it was natural to declare, as A. F. Pribram did in his *Austrian Foreign Policy*, that he would "avoid any higher standpoint" than "the purely historical one," and conclude his narrative stating that "regrets, however, are of no avail. History has pronounced its verdict. Austria-Hungary is no more."[1] To be sure, a mistrustful, and certainly a postmodern reader would challenge this declaration, observing that no "purely historical" standpoints exist, and that the historian included a lot of ideology, emotions, and Austrian patriotism in his narrative. Still, I am going to credit interwar scholarship with some straightforward confidence and differentiate their writings from those whose main interest was not the history of the monarchy but the present and the future of ideas it represented. Academic historians have to emphasize this difference, even though it may sometimes seem that they do so naïvely or perfidiously, in order to remain within the framework of their domain and to protect it against those who do not respect its rules. As the first chapter of this book indicates, they scarcely avoided "higher standpoints"; their writings are full of ideology and sentiments that have little to do with scholarly standards, but a lot with their political and national sympathies. And yet academic accuracy, source-based data, and the necessity to acknowledge various opinions and interpretations (including those that did not please them), seriously limited their inclinations to express their sentiments. In other words, academic standards worked imperfectly, but they had their undeniable impact on historians' narratives.

In this chapter I am going to deal with another kind of historical writing, which acknowledges "higher standpoints" overtly and freely. The past is a rich, dark soil that can feed various kinds of writers, including these who do not really cultivate it but exploit it for their "higher" purposes. Authors discussed in this chapter did not really care about Austria-Hungary as a monarchy with its peculiarities and paradoxes, institutions and monarchs, and its history that ended in the fall of 1918. What mattered for them were the timeless ideas that for a moment anchored in the Habsburg monarchy. In other words, they did not care whether democracy, socialism, or nationalism had strengthened or weakened the monarchy but whether the monarchy had hastened or slowed down their "march through history."

More precisely, there were three main problems discussed by interwar authors inspired by the fate of the Habsburg monarchy. First was the shaping of an Austrian identity, one that could rival the ethnic nationalisms that were popularly believed to have been the deadliest enemies of the monarchy. One should remember that before 1918 nothing like that actually existed in Austria. There were two reasons for that. First, all Austrians who cared about such things as the still relatively fresh national identification considered themselves members of the German nation—except those, of course, who considered themselves members of some other nationalities, and whom we may nevertheless retrospectively call Austrians because they were good Habsburg patriots. This refers to many Slavs, Hungarians, or Romanians who settled in Vienna or who made careers in the state administration or the imperial and royal army; to the supranational aristocracy; and, perhaps most importantly, to the numerous Austrian Jews, who might have had the same Austrian identity regardless of whether they lived in Vienna or in eastern Galicia. These people, dispersed throughout all corners of the realm and combining their ethnocultural self-identification with Austrian patriotism, were the true pillars of the monarchy. Needless to say, before the Great War, when the monarchy had still been powerful, stable, and prosperous, it seemed that their number was huge and that they built up the social elite of Austria proper and all its crownlands. When the monarchy fell, however, and was replaced by new successor states, their number also fell drastically, and most of them quickly forgot their old loyalty. Second, Austria did not need any national identity. The monarchy had enough problems taming the all-too-vigorous nationalisms it eventually had to face, which undermined its dynastic-patriarchal order, so it never made any serious or coherent attempts to promote anything like Austrian nationalism. Austria, in contrast to Hungary, was supranational by definition and political necessity. However, after 1919, when the German Republic of Austria was created, and its unification with Germany was forbidden by the victorious Allies, it immediately became a problematic issue. How should Austria have functioned without the empire and without Austrians? Of course, the majority of Austrians were busy with other, more pragmatic problems, and they rightly assumed that the article of the Saint-Germain treaty that forbade the Anschluss to Germany was a political trick, and that one day the Anschluss would nevertheless take place and the problem would be over. However, there were still intellectuals who were upset that at the time Austria was neither a nation nor a part of Germany, and they considered it their duty to try to change the consciousness of their compatriots. Some believed that Austrians should finally become a nation, instead of remaining Germans; others insisted that Austrians had always been Germans and should immediately get rid of their artificial Austrian identity, which they had erroneously caught from the Habsburgs; and some argued that history made Austrians a distinguished, superior part of the German nation. Appearances notwithstanding, it is important to remember that the Austria they meant did not equal the Austria from historical writings we came across in the previous chapter. It was no longer the empire stretching from the Carpathians to the Alps and from the Adriatic to the Dniester, but the German-speaking republic that still bore the name inherited from the so-called hereditary lands of the House of Austria, embracing some six and a half million people. The imperial episode in her career was over, and Austria was back home, which she had left four hundred years earlier to conquer, annex, and dominate her neighbors and their relatives. She had to adapt to the embarrassing new situation, and it was not at all clear if her spectacular memories were an advantage or a burden.

The second issue that permeated interwar historical essays on Austria-Hungary was the character of Central Europe. Deprived of the empires that had ruled over it—Habsburg, Ottoman, Hohenzollern, and Romanov—Central Europe needed an identity, too. It was after the Great War that Central Europe ceased to be the borderland of these powerful states and became a region. The political implications of this idea were, however, quite different than they seem today, when Central Europe is, presumably, ceasing to be a region and gradually becoming the eastern borderland of the European Union. The new nation-states that emerged from the post–1918 settlement had no wish to be seen in such categories; their ambition was to be perceived as nations of their own, as younger and poorer, but technically equal, members of the European family including Spain, Holland, or Sweden, and, fantastic as it was, their powerful *protectrice* herself, *la grande nation* of France. This was exactly the idea that had penetrated the minds of Hungarian and Romanian statesmen a few decades earlier, when they started constructing such buildings as the Westminster-like parliament in Budapest. Now the concept of belonging to a special region also seemed politically undesirable and psychologically humiliating for Poland, Czechoslovakia, and Yugoslavia. The elites of these countries all hopefully looked toward Paris and London; they did not know the languages of their neighbors, but all spoke French volubly and learned English diligently, carefully avoiding using their perfect German. They competed for the sympathy of the Western Allies, and approached each other with mistrust and animosity founded upon their border conflicts from 1918–1919 and their common desire to forget as quickly as possible that they had been the underprivileged pariahs of the multinational empires just a few years before. The origins of the idea of Central Europe were indeed imperialistic: if it stressed the originality and specifics of the region, it did so in a truly patronizing manner and suggested that this patchwork of nations and ethnic groups needed a powerful protector. In other words, it was a perfectly Austro-Hungarian idea, although the monarchy itself never officially promoted it under this label. It was first formulated by Friedrich Naumann in his *Mitteleuropa* in 1915, which argued that the region was a natural goal of German territorial expansion, which would be profitable both for the German Empire and for poor and backward Central European nations unable to govern themselves. After the Great War, Austrian patriots, looking back nervously at the history of their country, adopted and developed this concept. The raison d'être of the Habsburg empire, they argued, was not to serve the interests of the Habsburg dynasty, but those of Central Europeans. This was, they believed, the Austrian idea.

The third issue that post-Austro-Hungarian essayists intensively debated was closely related to the problem of the political organization of Central Europe and the legacy of the Habsburgs. Liberated from their loyalty to the dynasty, Austrian intellectuals could rethink the history of their country in a new context. The old dynastic privileges, rights, and connections, and the numerous royal and imperial titles did not seem to explain much. Nor did the European balance of power theory, since both the balance and the monarchy as its irreplaceable element disappeared. Nevertheless, in the age of triumphant nationalism, Austrian patriots turned to Austria-Hungary as an example of a country that had successfully resisted this powerful force for many decades. Nationalism caused the Great War and still inspired animosity among Europeans, particularly the East Europeans, they claimed, and it should be counterbalanced. They advocated a supranational state or a federation of states, which unavoidably resembled the Habsburg monarchy and was supposed to learn from its mistakes. Conservative, sentimental, and unrealistic as it was in the interwar years, the idea was also prophetic. After all, it was the Austrian count Richard Nikolaus von Coudenhove-Kalergi who, in his *Paneuropa*, first formulated a vision of the federation that finally came into being in the form of the European Union.

The Historical Necessity and the Mission of Austria

Generally, there were three standpoints from which post-Habsburg political writers and ideologues assessed Austria-Hungary: the progressive-democratic, the Austro-German nationalist, and the Catholic-conservative. Of course, none of them had a monopoly on a certain type of argument and interpretation, and they shared a number of them. If we begin with the first group, to the left of the political scene, we immediately arrive at one such paradox. Leftist authors were by definition also internationalists, and hence, in spite of their progressive-democratic inclinations, they had to appreciate the anti-nationalist character of Austria-Hungary. Despite being highly critical of this backward, monarchical state, they could not deny that it fought against the enemy that was also theirs. This ambiguity makes the leftist authors' opinions about the monarchy a complex and instructive example of the marriage of ideology with historical realism. However, the Austrian Social Democrats—like their socialist colleagues from all over Europe—also did not lack patriotism, and this included some healthy national pride and some prejudices toward the poorer, underdeveloped Easterners.

This fascinating mixture of democratic, national, and cultural ideas is to be found, for example, in *Die österreichische Revolution* (The Austrian revolution), by Otto Bauer, one of the leaders of the Social Democratic movement during the last decades of Austria-Hungary and the short life of the Austro-German Republic. On the one hand, Bauer did not hesitate to contradict the taboo of the post-Habsburg Austrian patriots, and he openly claimed that the monarchy's decision to start the war against Russia had been suicidal, for it antagonized the majority of its own Slavic population. Furthermore, he emphasized his and his party's hostile attitude to the Habsburgs. He had good reasons to do so: the Social Democratic Party had been one of the few allies of the throne after the imperial governments irrevocably lost the parliamentary majority in the mid-1890s, so many of his readers might have had some doubts whether the party and the monarchy had really been enemies. Indeed, at one point it becomes evident that in Bauer's eyes the monarchy served some valuable purposes: it was the historical mission of Austria as a *Kulturträger*—a force civilizing East-Central Europe. "When its supremacy over other nations broke down, the German bourgeoisie saw the end of its historical mission, for which it tolerated the separation from its fatherland," he claimed.[2] His reasoning is evidently ambiguous. On the one hand, he advocated the Anschluss of Austria to Germany, and he retrospectively suggested that this goal was also true before 1914, when the monarchy still existed and the Anschluss seemed utopian for all but the minority of German nationalists. Furthermore, he justified his own and his party's policy from that time, claiming that when the monarchy still existed, its existence was purposeful, for it served a cultural mission that, on the other hand, explained the German supremacy in the monarchy. Hence, the ambiguity is solved by dialectics. Evidently, some people have difficulties understanding dialectics, and so Bauer complained that after the war "the Viennese grand and petit bourgeoisie could not believe that the old, great Austria was gone forever. They still hoped it would come back, perhaps in some other shape."[3] He had no doubts of this kind: once the monarchy was over, its mission was over too, although it is not at all clear whether the mission was accomplished.

Another author who elaborated on the Austrian *mission civilisatrice*, distancing himself from the Habsburgs politically because of his democratic ideals, is Walter Kolarz. His *Myths and Realities in Eastern Europe*, published just after World War II, is more eloquent and detailed than Bauer's *Die österreichische Revolution*. He was writing for British readers, for whom the splendors and miseries of the Habsburg rule were not as obvious as they had been for Austrian readers thirteen years earlier. He was remarkably indulgent toward the monarchy: "The Austrian Monarchy died of infirmity of old age, and indeed, in the form in which it existed in 1918, it had no right to survive in a modern world. But this is no reason for refusing to recognize the international cultural values of the old Austria, its position as a bridge between East and West and the possibilities latent in it for the development of a supranational solidarity."[4]

Kolarz was an enemy of nationalism and a friend of civilization. Hence, he found the supranational states, including not only Austria but also Russia, attractive, and claimed that the "advantages of living in contact with other nationalities to a certain extent even outweighed the evils of police terrorism in Austria." Of course, the nationalities he had in mind were the "young nations without history" who had no civilization or culture of their own, and for whom contacts with culturally superior peoples was by definition beneficial, even though it involved some oppression and exploitation. Austria, Kolarz emphasized, occasionally supported such nations against their neighbors; for example, it protected the Ukrainians against Polish domination in Galicia, or the Romanians against the Hungarians in Transylvania. He had no illusions that the monarchy did so for some higher purposes; facing the more powerful national movements of better-organized and -developed peoples, the government simply balanced them by supporting the poorer nationalities according to the old *divide et impera* principle. Most importantly, however, they all profited from the blessings of the imperial status of Vienna, "from which enlightenment and culture radiated into the area of peoples without history and where the representatives of all the various small and young peoples could come into contact with world civilization."[5] Again, the modern reader may be astonished to find a truly democratic author writing in such an openly imperialistic style. And yet British readers of Kolarz in the late 1940s, who were just saying goodbye to their Indian empire and probably could still not imagine they would soon have to accept the independence of their colonies in Africa, presumably found it reasonable and convincing. Furthermore, Kolarz was certainly not the first leftist to distinguish between nations "without history" and "historical nations." He was, rather, one of the last representatives of a tradition going back to Friedrich Engels, who is popularly believed to have introduced this simple but appealing distinction in the 1880s, when such nationalities as the Ukrainians, the Slovaks, or the Slovenians might indeed have seemed "young" peoples who had just emerged from the anonymous masses of the illiterate East European peasantry.

Engels and his mentor and friend Karl Marx were among the first to believe that Austria-Hungary was a sort of "lesser evil." In the writings of their pupils, such as Bauer, this idea was still present, but in a diluted, unclear form. Authors like Bauer still hoped for the socialist revolution, and yet they believed it should take place within a unified, strong national German state. They were friends with foreign socialists, and they had a lot of sympathy for their parties; nevertheless, these socialists were working for revolutions in their respective countries and, as a matter of fact, they all favored national loyalties over party loyalties, as the Social Democrats' support for Hitler's Anschluss best demonstrated. Marx and Engels might have had their cultural-German prejudices—for example, they believed that such nations as the Czechs had no right or indeed any chances for an independent existence—but they were true internationalists. They did not value Germans higher than all other nations because they were themselves Germans; they supported the socialist cause also in countries that were not friends with Germany at all. They looked coldly at contemporary Europe and assessed particular nations according to their advancement on the way toward the revolution. Of course, Austria-Hungary was not their pet; they found its aristocratic-bourgeois political order rather disgusting. The monarchy was far behind other countries on its road to socialism according to the Marxist paradigm, and Marx himself called it "the European China" to emphasize its backwardness, for in the eyes of nineteenth-century Europeans China was the symbol of stagnation and anachronism in politics and economy. And yet, Marx and Engels also appreciated Austria-Hungary for one reason: it was an enemy of Russia, and Russia seemed to be the most powerful defender of political reaction, and the most powerful enemy of revolution in Europe. In contrast to the "Asiatic" Romanov despotism, Austrian "paternal despotism" appeared relatively harmless. Thus, as long as Austria counterbalanced the tsars, it served the cause of socialism.[6] Essentially anachronistic, it was functionally progressive, and therefore its existence was purposeful.

Marx and Engels are famous as masters of historical dialectics, a method of reasoning first introduced by Hegel. However, in discourse on Austria-Hungary the leftist thinkers had no monopoly on it; as a matter of fact, they used it rather sparingly in comparison with German nationalists. Paradoxically, the latter referred to it most intensively because of the same argument that Marx and Engels had introduced: Austria was an enemy of Russia. Hence, the monarchy protected Central Europe against the preponderant influence of its mighty neighbor. Of course, the nature of this task in the eyes of German nationalists was not to protect the region against Russian reactionary despotism but against Russian "barbarism" and, in the end, against its own population, which was predominantly Slavic and therefore could easily have been won over by Russians, the mighty enemies of the German culture. We have already come across these ideas in the previous chapter, especially in the context of the Great War, when keeping the Austro-Hungarian Slavs immune to Slavophilic propaganda seemed a crucial element of the Habsburg military effort. On the one hand, there was nothing particularly unusual in this reasoning, except for the special combination of German chauvinism and paternalism toward Central European nationalities—enemies of our enemies are our friends not only in German eyes. On the other hand, however, the reasoning became interesting in context of the breakdown of Austria. It was then that dialectics was applied, and when the Austro-Russian antagonism became the Austrian mission.

This retrospective assumption is omnipresent in interwar Austrian literature. Apparently, it seemed so obvious for Austrian authors that most of them did not bother to comment on it extensively. A textbook on national history published in 1937, for example, informs us that after 1848 the goal of Austria was resisting the Russian impact on Central Europe. Therefore, the author argued, the Austro-Prussian War of 1866 was a success for Prussia but a defeat for Germany, for since that time the Slavic influences in the monarchy had grown. Still, the monarchy achieved its historical goal, having forced millions of Slavs to fight against Russia during the Great War. When the war was over, he concluded, the monarchy broke down because its mission was fulfilled.[7] Oskar von Mitis, author of a biography of the unfortunate crown prince Rudolf, presented his hero as yet another potential savior of the monarchy. Rudolf, Franz Joseph's only son, achieved even less than Franz Ferdinand before becoming addicted to drugs and committing a double suicide with his teenage lover (a colorful life that resulted in his being made into a Hollywood character portrayed by Omar Sharif). Still, Rudolf was supposed to have published anonymously in the press, expressing remarkably liberal-progressive opinions, and thus he won posthumous fame as an advocate of profound reforms. Enumerating virtues of the prince, Mitis also briefly mentioned that Rudolf under-

Archduke Rudolf

stood that the historical mission of Austria was to resist Russia—and to spread German culture in the East.[8] Echoes of this idea are also present in *The Economic Policy of Austria-Hungary during the War in Its External Relations,* a book by two distinguished Austro-Hungarian émigré economists, Gusztáv Gratz and Richard Schüller. Again, the authors did not really elaborate on it; it appears as a truism that needs no serious explanation. Still, they located it in the historical context much deeper than the Austro-Russian antagonism preceding the Great War. Commenting on the breakdown of the monarchy, they wrote, "We may regret its fall; for it is possible still to hold, with Palmerston, that if an 'Austria' did not exist, it would be necessary to create one; and the menace of the Slav, against which the East Mark was erected as a barrier in the days of Charlemagne and Otto the Great, is certainly not less than it was in Palmerston's day. Yet the Monarchy, whatever its uses, it was an anachronism."[9] This shows that the theory that Austria had its "uses"—another name for its mission—was so popular that hardly anyone actually explored it. Gratz and Schüller felt obliged to acknowledge it, although it did not really go with their own conclusions, which had little to do with the enigmatic idea of the eternal German-Slavic rivalry.

Appearances notwithstanding, this idea was certainly a part of the Habsburg legacy. Of course, the Habsburgs did not promote it openly—it would have been suicidal for them to antagonize the majority of the population of the monarchy, as the Great War actually proved. Their German subjects, however, adopted and developed it in order to remain within the paradigm of German national history and explain the sense of their own position within the monarchy. The multinational, liberal monarchy, they retrospectively reasoned, was the only way to control the underdeveloped, semi-barbarian Slavs and impose German culture on them. Other nationalities preferred to view it as Western Civilization, and under this label Habsburg propaganda was, more or less efficiently, selling this idea, especially during the Great War. For example, Ludwik Kulczycki, an Austrian Pole, in his book *Austrya a Polska* (Austria and Poland) in 1916, encouraged Poles who might have their doubts about whom to support in the conflict to compare the conditions that Austria offered them with those they might expect from Russia. Moreover, he argued that Austria-Hungary and the old Polish-Lithuanian Commonwealth, which Austria, Prussia, and Russia had dismembered in the late eighteenth century, were actually very similar. They both fulfilled the great historical mission of promoting Western Civilization in Eastern Europe; furthermore, they both expanded territorially by dynastic marriages rather than conquests, and they both had comparable dual constitutional structures. Finally, Kulczycki reminded his Polish readers, Austria-Hungary was more successful in pursuing its great historical task—indeed, the Polish-Lithuanian Commonwealth had been dead for more than a hundred years in 1916, whereas the Habsburg monarchy was at the peak of its military achievements during the Great War.[10]

Furthermore, the idea of the lesser evil was strikingly abstract in a particularly Habsburg way. It did not imply that Austria was a nation, nor that it was a real motherland—it was, rather, a better solution than an open German-Slavic confrontation. It produced a technical patriotism rather than the "normal" one. This idea was silently omnipresent in the writings of post-Habsburg writers; again it was so obvious that there was scarcely any need to express it. For Stefan Zweig, one such rare occasion was the funeral of Joseph Roth, who was best known for his writings full of nostalgia for the monarchy. Remembering his colleague, Zweig said, "astonishingly, in our unusual Austria one could hardly find its true admirers and connoisseurs in its German-speaking capital Vienna, but there were plenty of them in the remote peripheries, where one could compare the tolerant and lenient Habsburg rule every day with the harsher and less humane conditions abroad."[11] Roth was surely an admirer of the Habsburgs, having been born and raised close to the Austrian-Russian border and having spent several years in Russia and Poland. And yet the words of Zweig represent his own opinion of a rich Viennese who only traveled westwards, and he was nonetheless convinced that the poor inhabitants of the eastern borderlands should have been very happy to be Habsburg subjects, and that the Viennese whom he really knew did not appreciate this enough. He did not mention another crucial fact that certainly influenced Roth's Habsburg patriotism: he was a Jew brought up in German culture who left his native Polish-Ukrainian Galicia to make his career in Vienna because he considered Vienna a center of this culture. Zweig's argument nevertheless perfectly matched the Viennese point of view of the monarchy as a lesser evil for its numerous nationalities. Exactly the same logic made Austrian historians claim that Austria-Hungary was a lesser evil not only in comparison with its neighbors but also in comparison with the successor states that followed it. Their favorite point to stress was that the protection of national rights, which Austria was supposed to have oppressed, actually declined after the monarchy fell. Some authors went further: Hugelmann, for example, claimed that the legal protection of national minorities as guaranteed by the Austrian constitution of 1867 was the best in the world, and if some of their rights were violated in practice it was still undeniable that the monarchy did everything that was possible to protect them.[12] Similarly, Count Heinrich Clam-Martinic, the Austrian prime minister in 1917–1918, rhetorically questioned whether the equality of all nationalities, guaranteed by the constitution, could ever be achieved. According to him, the monarchy did more to realize this ideal than any other country, particularly the successor states.[13]

The necessity of the existence of Austria as the bulwark against Eastern barbarism remained in a dialectical relation with yet another necessity, the national unification of Germany. Apparently, those two principles excluded each other: either Austria was to rule over the Slavs or it was to be included in the unified German nation state. Hence, some authors viewed the entire history of Austria as one great heroic deed of the German nation, which sacrificed its unity at the altar of Western Civilization. Wilhelm Schüssler, for example, claimed: "Now, having accomplished their incomparably difficult historical task, the Austrians may come back to their Native Home."[14] This was Otto Bauer's idea, a little more pompously formulated: Anschluss is now necessary, because the Austrian mission has been accomplished. In other words, the necessity of Austria's existence has been replaced, or followed, by the necessity of its being incorporated into Germany.

To be sure, there were also authors who simply found Austrian history to be an error that should have been avoided. "The Austrian Germans have been pushed off their fatherland without their will, and indeed against it. They became victims of rivalry between the Habsburgs and the Hohenzollerns," claimed F. G. Kleinwächter, adding that Austrians missed the Reich (that is the unification with Germany), although not all were aware of it.[15] Alfred Rapp, who published under the Nazis, was less sentimental about this. According to him, the Habsburgs were a tragedy in German history, and the result of their degenerate rule was the delay of four hundred years in the formation of a German nation-state. Moreover, he argued, a consequence of this delay was that when Germany was finally united, more than one-third of Germans were left outside of it: the Austrians, the Swiss, and the Dutch.[16] The degeneration of the dynasty, he emphasized in the true Nazi style, was both moral and physical—as numerous diseases and the notorious "Habsburg nose" proved.

Austrian patriots, however, had their doubts about the Anschluss. These rose from the assumption that the Austrian mission had not finished and should be continued. The dissolution of the monarchy made this assumption questionable, but Western Civilization still needed Austria. A. R. C. Jaschke, for example, believed that Austria perfectly fit the general paradigm of history that, as Herodotus had first observed, was all about the perpetual conflict between Europe and Asia. Europe, he argued, has always been protected by two powers: England

and Germany. The English took care of the seas, and controlled the Japanese menace, and Germany guarded the eastern frontier against the Russians. Austria fulfilled the crucial role in this national mission of the Germans—*Schutzherrentum*—as the most eastern bulwark of Europe—the Eastern Mark. Jaschke, who published his book in 1934, a year after the Nazis took power, did not support the Anschluss, though. He rightly assumed that Germany, striving for the next European war, was the greatest threat to the continent. Austria, by contrast, with its traditions of peaceful leadership over the Slavic nations, was predestined to begin the process of unification of the continent. The small nations, such as Czechs or Hungarians, he claimed, would never agree to an integration with a unified German state of 72 million people instead of the mere seven million Germans of Austria.[17] This claim resembled the argument by Heinrich von Srbik, discussed in the previous chapter, that the sense of Austrian history was to protect Europe against the barbarism of the East and against German imperialism.[18]

Other Austrian authors also looked optimistically to the future in spite of the fall of the monarchy—because Austrians still had their mission or task (Aufgabe) to accomplish. Bruno Brehm, author of numerous lengthy historical reportages, pointed out that Germans were unable to understand that the goal of this task was not imperialistic; indeed, they were scarcely capable of differentiating between Central European nationalities such as Slovenes and Slovaks. It was to "make possible peaceful coexistence of the small nations in the Danube region."[19] Of course he failed to notice that if Austrians were not a part of the German nation, they were themselves "a small nation in the Danube region." Friedrich von Wieser argued in his book published just a year after the fall of the monarchy that Austrians were predestined for "cultural work" more than any other European nation. He hoped that the military defeat had strengthened Austrians like it had strengthened the French after 1815 and 1870, and that they would soon prove their "silent heroism" and give "a peaceful response" to the unjust peace imposed on them. All they needed, he believed, was a truly great leader—*ein Führer*.[20]

The Austrian Idea

All attempts to present the history of the Habsburg monarchy as a part of a purposeful process were undertaken in the name of a certain philosophy of history. According to the authors discussed above, history as such was a purposeful process leading to an ultimate goal: for the socialists it was the revolution, for the German nationalists it was the unification of all Germans in one Reich, for other authors it was the triumph of Western Civilization in its eternal struggle against the barbarians. Regardless of their sympathy or antipathy for the monarchy, they did not view it as anything more than an element of a larger scheme; its history did not have a meaning on its own, only as a stage of the general scenario. Hence, regrets that the monarchy had fallen were of no avail.

There were, however, Austrians who did not agree to view the history of their country in such terms. This history, after all, was the only basis for the creation, or indeed the definition, of an Austrian identity—which, as noted, was still a shaky and labile concept. Therefore, they attempted to make sense of this history, to discover "the Austrian idea" hidden in their country's past. It was a unique attempt to create an identity of a country that had ceased to exist. It was supposed to fill the ideological vacuum left by the monarchy abandoned by its citizens.

As mentioned, while the monarchy still existed it did not lack loyal subjects. When it fell, however, it left few orphans. It was not a real motherland like the nation-states, but a lesser evil or a technical solution of the political problems of the region, guaranteeing a decent level of civil rights, culture, and economic development. People appreciated it as long as it worked, even though many of them truly respected Franz Joseph for, in the end, love for the monarch was the essence of Habsburg patriotism. To be sure, many observers had been aware of this weakness of the monarchy when the old emperor was still alive. Henry W. Steed, for example, one of the few authors from the West who extensively published on Austria-Hungary before the Great War, argued,

> True, Austrians and Hungarians alike employ the term "fatherland," but they usually limit its application to their own half of the Monarchy; *Gesamtpatriotismus* or patriotism embracing the whole Monarchy is the principle of the few. Such "soul" as "Austria" possesses is mainly dynastic; and the principal bond between the Habsburg peoples is devotion to the person of the Monarch, who, ruling by the right Divine in various constitutional guises, is the chief factor in each state separately and in both states jointly. The

> Dual Monarchy depends on the Crown more fully and more truly than any other European realm.[21]

The monarchy lacked more than its own nationalism. It was an ancien régime par excellence: it lacked any popular modern ideology. All it could offer was splendor of tradition, rituals, and monarchical pomp. Still, loyalty to the dynasty meant little to the people at the beginning of the twentieth century, and the personal popularity of Franz Joseph could not change that; apparently, it was rather misleading, for the more popular he was, the more evident it was that no one could replace him. Moreover, his reputation could not change the fact that more and more of his subjects viewed the dynastic right as an obsolete principle that did not match the standards of modern political life. Even those who believed in the historical mission of Austria as a civilizing force were often disappointed that this mission was actually notoriously obscured by dynastic interests. As a Polish journalist from Galicia remarked in 1913,

> And so it has been established, almost paradoxically, that the Austrian state that was mainly built upon the remnants of the Ottoman Empire . . . has not managed to create the resources, neither the plan, nor any ideology suiting its eastern mission that would justify it at least in the eyes of its own population. . . . The Austrian state-idea has not been able to rise above promoting the most primitive dynastic interests, neither in this respect nor in many others. The stubborn emphasis on these interests caused the state to lose numerous opportunities to widen and strengthen itself.[22]

Franz Joseph was indeed a stubborn man. Apparently, the ideological vacuum that everyone in the monarchy sensed, and which many intellectuals feared, did not trouble him. He viewed the monarchy as a *Hausmacht*—a dominion of his dynasty whose possession was guaranteed by divine right, and although he cared for his personal popularity, he considered all democratic reforms that could turn his subjects into citizens undesirable compromises. He understood that some concessions were necessary because the absolute power that he had inherited had been criticized as tyrannical by 1848, when he ascended to the throne. Still, neither he nor any of his governments sought any source of legitimacy for the political order of the monarchy other than tradition and divine right. The old emperor regarded the Compromise

Ferenc Deák, father of the Compromise of 1867

of 1867 with Hungarians as his final concession. As the conservative Hungarian politician Albert Apponyi recollected, when the emperor's collaborators asked him to consider some changes in the Dualist settlement created by the 1867 agreement, he refused and replied: "There were three of us who made the agreement: Deák, Andrassy and myself. I'm the only one who is still alive, so you have to trust me about what we had in mind."[23]

The most painful blow suffered by the ideological foundations of the monarchy was the unification of Germany in 1871. This triumph of national principle, preceded by the unification of Italy, shook the minds of many of the most loyal Habsburg subjects—and the monarchy had no good response to this question. Nevertheless, as long as the economy went well, the administrative apparatus of the monarchy functioned smoothly, and the trains were punctual, the majority of the population did not bother itself with such problems too much. It was the Great War that made the question burning, antagonizing the population according to national divisions and demanding sanguinary proofs of loyalty. Fighting and dying for the monarchy called for more determination than paying taxes and celebrating the imperial-royal family members' birthdays. Immediately after the outbreak of the war, millions of Serbs and Ukrainians were stigmatized as potential enemies; in the following months Italians and Romanians joined them, and Czech loyalty was also publicly questioned. It soon became evident that the war would bring enormous sacrifices, and this made the legitimacy of bloodthirsty authorities a problem. Other belligerents were supposed to fight and die for their nations; their governments were doing their best to make citizens feel proud of their countries and hate the enemy. The ambiguous Austro-Hungarian identity, composed of a number of loyalties and identifications, was hardly a solid basis for mortal combat. It was perhaps already too late to ask about the meaning of being Austrian and to attempt to construct an Austrian patriotism; nevertheless some intellectuals, and to an extent even the imperial and royal authorities, who had been neglecting this problem so lightheartedly, believed it was exactly the right moment to finally rethink this issue.

In such circumstances the Austrian idea was born: when the ancient walls of the monarchy were crumbling and its people were beginning to look around for new motherlands and, most importantly, for themselves. It was the child of blind determination and war hysteria, which grew with increasing chauvinism, war censorship, and spy mania. It sought to fill the ideological vacuum of the old monarchy with some essence that could feed the Austrian soul. Presumably, it never had many true enthusiasts, even though it might seem that the crowds marching on the streets of Vienna and Budapest in the summer of 1914, shouting "Down with the Serbs!" were doing so in the name of imperial and royal patriotism. Actually, its military and propagandist entourage earned it powerful enemies from the beginning. Karl Kraus, publisher of *Die Fackel* (The torch) and the most famous Austrian pacifist, claimed that the cheerful fat hangman from the fabricated picture of a public execution of an Italian deputy to the parliament who was accused of treason was the true face of an Austrian. When the so-called literary group of Austrian writers formed for purposes of war propaganda, he called it "supplementary service for [those] unfit for literature."[24] Astonishingly, the group included some of the most well-known Austrian authors: Rudolf H. Bartsch, Franz Karol Ginzkey, Alfred Poglar, Franz Theodor Csokor, and, for a short time, Rainer Maria Rilke and Stefan Zweig. They edited an official journal called

Franz Joseph and Elisabeth—one of the last common photos

Donauland, wrote for the press of the neutral countries, and organized public lectures. Some of them—Zweig, for example—were to be regretfully ashamed of this activity in the future.

Hugo von Hofmannsthal, a poet, playwright, and the rising star of prewar Austrian literature, was the one who coined the term "the Austrian idea," and first formulated its basic characteristics. Still in 1913, in his letter to Leopold von Andrian, the poet complained that Austrians did not have a fatherland, but only a *Heimat*—a regional or local identity within Germandom.[25] During the war he served the monarchy giving public readings in neutral countries, in which he argued the Habsburgs' case. His essay entitled "Die österreichische Idee" (The Austrian idea) was based on the speeches he delivered in Scandinavia in 1917, when the majority of his colleagues, and indeed the majority of Austrians, were already disillusioned with the war. Nevertheless Hofmannsthal argued with much optimism that the war, which "laid bare all values," also uncovered unexpected vital forces of the Habsburg monarchy. Obviously, the Austro-Hungarian vigor he referred to was actually epitomized by the ability to conduct military operations. Still, the poet emphasized not only the fact that the monarchy was able to resist its enemies during the preceding three years of the war but its long historical duration in general, which he viewed as the true source of its power and the proof of its superiority over its enemies. Duration, Hofmannsthal claimed, recalling Machiavelli, is the real aim of all governments, surpassing all other qualities. It was not of secondary importance, he stressed, that the history of Austria as a Mark of the Holy Roman Empire had lasted a thousand years, and as a Roman colony claiming the legacy of Charlemagne it had lasted two thousand years. More importantly, for all that time Austria preserved its "idea" that held it together, determined its identity and its uniqueness. He argued,

> The essence of this idea, which through centuries enabled Austria to survive chaos and cataclysms with her face ever younger, is constituted by its inner polarization. It is an antithesis: a borderland between the European empire and the chaotic conglomerate of the half-European and half-Asian peoples, and a moving frontier, open for colonization and cultural expansion eastwards, but also ready to receive the waves moving westwards. . . . Realistic up to perfection, and hence super-real in its consequences[,] . . . this idea in its spiritual amplitude surpasses everything that the national and economic ideologies of our days can produce.[26]

Evidently, Hofmannsthal's patriotic fervor and his attempt to embrace the entire history of the monarchy made his vision an overtly maximalist hodgepodge of concepts, motifs, and desires. Enigmatic as it was, however, it was not essentially new. It mainly consisted of concepts popularly associated with the monarchy in his time: the historical claims for legitimacy dating back to Charlemagne and ancient

Rome, "inner polarization," and the frontier character of the monarchy located between the West and the East. What was new and unique in this was its uncritical enthusiasm about issues that normally worried supporters of the monarchy, such as its anachronism and complicated cultural and ethnic composition. The greatness and splendor of Austria, according to Hofmannsthal, was actually its weakness *à rebours:* it was an essentially polemical construct intended to challenge all the critics of the monarchy. Technically, the same characteristics led to sad conclusions about the future of the monarchy when regarded by authors who employed cold calculation and who were not immune to influences of modern ideology; the mystic imagination and patriotism of the poet resulted in hopeful enthusiasm. Despite all the terror and fears caused by the war, he trusted that it was the time of fulfillment of the Austrian mission. The decades preceding the war, which critical observers considered a constant political crisis of the monarchy, were for him the time of "silent work" and preparations for "the only task of Austria"; namely, "the reconciliation of the old Latin-German world with the new European world of the Slavs." Appearances notwithstanding, the war seemed to have been the next, but not the last stage of this process; it was the climax in the formation of a new Europe and the triumph of Austria. His bombastic prophecy went as follows: "The language of Austria was too great for the epoch that followed Napoleon. We have had to wait for this war in order to be able to speak freely again. We are more carefully prepared for the things to come than anyone else in Europe.... The ideas of reconciliation, synthesis, and overcoming the divisions have their own power and spontaneity, they rise from situations instead of arguments, from true experiences instead of slogans: socialist, nationalist or parliamentary.... The Europe that intends to form itself anew means Austria."[27]

To be sure, Hofmannsthal's rhetoric contains elements typical for war propaganda of the Central Powers. Particularly the ideas of a "synthesis" and a "new opening" were ubiquitous in the German discourse of the first years of the conflict—they belonged to the so-called ideas of 1914, when numerous German authors were enthusiastically greeting the outbreak of war as an opportunity for national reconciliation and a challenge that would finally unite the divided nation. In that time Germans were also obsessed with the alleged differences between their national culture and that of their Anglo-French opponents, which they called civilization and accused of superficiality and artificiality in contrast to the alleged depth and spontaneity of the German *Kultur*—which the "true experience" of war was supposed to demonstrate. Again, the Austrian poet borrowed some of their vocabulary and gave it his own meaning. At the first glance, his interpretation seems more logical indeed: it was Austria rather than the new German empire that stood against all modern political doctrines and seemed predestined for the "synthesis" of its nationalities. Still, in the context of the world war his prophecies of reconciliation and overcoming antagonisms appear totally irrational.

Nevertheless, the Austrian idea outlived the monarchy. In the interwar years Austrian intellectuals cultivated and developed it, dreaming about the resurrection of the monarchy, or simply about invigorating their feeble republic and providing it with some distinctive identity. Most of them claimed that this identity was not national in the ordinary sense of the term. It was, rather, a consequence of the particularly Austrian historical experience. In a way, this claim mirrored the paradox that troubled the monarchy itself, which on the one hand had attempted to discourage its citizens against all nationalist feelings, and on the other hand had desired to be a motherland like any other.

Seemingly, the Austrian idea did not need the monarchy. As we shall see, it was an abstract and mystic concept—an idea in eternal search for its application rather than an idea derived from reality. In a word, it was a fantasy. It was created, to be sure, in the epoch when patriotism was considered the noblest of all political ideas, and nationalists in many countries feverishly praised their nations beyond any reasonable limits. Apparently, the Austrian idea was a response to this concept of people who had no nation to attach their emotions to; therefore, it was enigmatic, mystic, and complex. It constantly had to struggle against the paradoxes it was itself generating.

Austrian intellectuals themselves acknowledged that it was a difficult and demanding task to realize what the monarchy was and what it meant to be Austrian. In 1917 Anton Wildgans, Hofmannsthal's colleague, still had his doubts about it. "What is Austria-Hungary? What justifies its existence?" he asked rhetorically, and replied, "History? There is no justification by history."[28] In 1930, in his "Austrian speech," broadcasted on radio, he was already positive about the nature of the Austrian historical experience. He claimed that being Austrian was "a particular capacity to serve a certain idea, because the Austrian state of the past was more conceptual than any other state. It was the condensed idea of the power of its dynasty, and the conglomerate of fatherlands, fusing into one country as a result of the most complicated legally-political intellectual process."[29] Consequently, being Austrian was not like being a member of a nation; it was the mental state of someone who understood the meaning of the political credo of the old monarchy and acknowledged its meaning. Authors of the Austrian idea realized—indeed, they insisted—that being Austrian was as complicated, complex, and incomprehensible as being human. Like many religious ideas the Austrian idea was presented as originating from pure experience. Its authors denied its conceptual character and claimed it was self-evident; it was therefore supposed that only those who possessed the necessary experience, its bearers, could understand it. However, since experience as such can scarcely be considered the soil of any particular idea, conceptualizing was nevertheless needed in the process. In other words, it was a mystery waiting to be revealed. Accordingly, in 1918 Richard von Schaukal argued that Austria-Hungary itself should be regarded as the human condition (*Dasein*). He explained it in the following way:

> An Austrian, in the sense given to him by the old Austria, historically seems to be an idea consisting of the nationalities. What unites him is not the people's dynasty, neither the state with its not the most fortunate upbringing, but his fate, the fate of his legacy, that pulsates in him with a thousand of suppositions and feelings, silently and forcefully, not in any particular direction, but constantly toward itself. Austria-Hungary . . . is a living expression of an organic unity, whose components are capable of the common, purposeful activity. Its meaning is here; one only needs to discover it.[30]

Similarly, in 1936 Oskar Benda warned his readers not to confuse the Austrian idea with a "national myth," an "ideological superstructure," or a "political claim." The definition he provided was, however, not much clearer than those produced by Wildgans or Schaukal. Namely, he argued that the Austrian idea was "the true experience embodied in an idea; the historically formed, spiritually-material substance of the Austrian humanity; the deeply grounded reality of a higher rank, rising outside and above the entire European reality."[31]

To sum up, the grandiose expressions of the Austrian idea contain a number of common points. First, they desperately emphasize the difference between Austria and a nation. This is clearly a part of the Habsburg legacy, even though monarchism was not necessarily the ideology of the enthusiasts of the Austrian idea. Second, their vocabulary invariably resembles that of contemporary mystic nationalism: it stresses experience with its uniqueness and ineffability, and history perceived as shared fate and heritage; it speaks about soul rather than reason, and rejects all "modern political theories" feverishly. It is full of pompous but hazy and occasionally vague claims. And third, the Austrian idea proudly ignores reality: it denies all critiques of the monarchy and refuses to acknowledge the humble status of the German Republic of Austria in interwar Europe. It confuses the past with its glories with the miserable present, as it often confuses Austro-Germans with all inhabitants of the monarchy, refusing to acknowledge their distinctive national identities, simply because of their impressive numbers.

Nevertheless, with time the Austrian idea evolved, and sheer expressions of patriotism were accompanied by more concrete considerations regarding history and contemporary politics. The mysterious Austrian historical experience was reinterpreted, and Austrian identity more precisely discussed. Naturally, the problem of the Austro-German relationship seemed crucial.

How did Austrians differ from Germans and what were the political consequences of their distinctive historical experience? It is important to remember that interwar authors had no easy answer for this question. Modern readers may be astonished or confused by the arguments employed in this debate, because they usually did not answer the question of whether Austrians did belong to the German nation or not. It may seem that the adherents of interwar Austrian ideology had no choice but to acknowledge that Austrians were culturally German, and yet they insisted that this fact did not make them German politically. Still, things were more complicated: Austrian intellectuals refused to regard Germany as a nation in the way the German nationalists did. They believed that Germany was more than that, and Austrianness was a particular form of Germandom, and hence being Austrian did not exclude being German. On the other hand, they wished to distance Austria from Germany in the form given to it by Bismarck and the Hohenzollerns, and they believed that their country was politically and spiritually superior to Germany, because politics was for them—the powerless, isolated, and few in number—basically a spiritual phenomenon. Full of contradictions as it was, this thinking was not as inconsistent and irrational as it may appear. The main obstacle to apprehending it today is that it was fruitless: the Austrian nation formed after World War II had little to do with this ideology, because its main political objective was to forget about the Austro-German kinship. Adherents of the Austrian idea could not know the future; all they knew was the past, and this past had the form of the Habsburg empire. They all hoped that this empire would one day be reconstructed in the form of some Danubian federation with Vienna as its capital. Obviously, they were naïve and their hopes were soon proved wrong; the reconstructed Austria-Hungary they imagined was a conservative utopia. However, today, when most of Europe, including most of the ex-Habsburg lands, is a federation, they do not seem to have been as fundamentally wrong as they seemed to be during the Cold War.

Analyzing the attitudes of partisans of the Austrian idea toward Germany one also has to remember that they faced strong opposition from German nationalists, or pan-Germans, who insisted that Austrians had always been Germans. The pan-German argumentation was actually no less rooted in history than the Austrian idea. It rightfully pointed out that Germany was not a united country during most of its history, and that strong regional differences between various German lands did not exclude the national, or pan-German identity. As a matter of fact, in the eyes of pan-Germans, Austrians had even more national consciousness than their compatriots from the Reich, because they had to reaffirm it in constant contacts with foreigners—contacts that, according to the nationalist philosophy, invariably meant a struggle of two nationalisms. The author of the essay "Das Deutschtum der Deutschösterreichischer" (The Germandom of the Austrian Germans), published in 1927, claimed that "a Bavarian or a Wurtemberger, an Oldenburger or a Thuringer, needed not to confirm his Germandom. He was surrounded by it and considered it self-evident. . . . It was otherwise with an Austrian. He guarded the south-eastern border. It might easily have happened that he would have lost his nationality; however, what actually happened was that he reaffirmed his natural mandate for leadership over other nations."[32] In other words, insisting that Austrians were true and indeed distinguished members of the pan-German family, he nevertheless acknowledged their exceptionality within it. Adherents of the Austrian idea did almost the same, but they put the emphasis on the exceptionality. As it often happens in national ideologies, this exceptionality was presented as a result of the unique historical experience of the Austrians, and simultaneously as one of its causes—because Austrians, as many others, were predestined for their experience.

One of the most powerful and characteristic expressions of this ideology is Leopold von Andrian's book *Österreich im Prisma der Idee* (Austria through the prism of the idea). Andrian claimed that the belief in the Austro-German community (*Doppeldasein Ideologie*, ideology of the dual nature of Austria) was one of the greatest misfortunes for his country. Among other things, it caused the Prusso-Austrian War of 1866 and contributed to Austria's participation in the Great War. Naturally, he considered the dissolution of the monarchy as another, perhaps the greatest of Austrian catastrophes. And yet he remained relatively optimistic: Austria, he believed, could still be reconstructed—reborn. He supported his hope with the example of Poland, which reemerged as an independent state after more than a century of foreign occupation, because of the power of their national idea and their Catholicism. After the dissolution of the monarchy, Andrian argued, God remained the only guarantee of Austrian independence, which he blessed with the Austrian idea. According to him, the idea emanated on the country, and the Austrian provided it with shelter, like the Monstrance protects the Holy Sacrament. He trusted in the religiosity of his compatriots, and in their immunity against the attractiveness of foreign modernity, embodied in such novelties as "Berlin radio."[33]

Andrian's book is uncritically pro-Habsburg and epitomizes the spirit of "old Austria" in its profound hostility toward modernity. However, written in the mid-1930s, it did not advocate the restoration of the dynasty openly. The monarchy was Andrian's ideal and his inspiration; his practical goal was rather to support the conservative regime of Chancellor Kurt Schuschnigg, desperately struggling against

Otto von Habsburg, the eldest son of Emperor Charles, in a propaganda picture from the 1930s

both the Social Democrats and the Nazis. Schuschnigg occasionally played with the idea of the restoration of the Habsburgs, which won him popularity among conservatives, but he was aware that it would be suicidal for his government and for the Austro-German Republic. Instead, he promoted a bizarrely archaic social ideology that partly imitated Mussolini's concept of corporations, which should have replaced social classes. Andrian's book perfectly mirrors this ideology. It has the form of a conversation of representatives of four social groups or "estates." The author claimed that these groups, inspired and animated by the "historical nobility" should form "the united Austrian nation" (*Gesamtnation*).[34] However, half of his book is devoted to discussions of the moral and spiritual deterioration of his epoch, which he viewed as resembling the early medieval era: a time of the triumph of barbarism over the higher civilization that had fallen, a landscape full of ruins and ghosts of past glory. Paradoxically, the only positive element of this landscape was the prospect of the construction of an Austrian nation—a very modern concept. This prospect, however, was constantly being shaken by German (and other foreign) influences, welcomed by the cosmopolitan Austrian bourgeoisie, which eagerly denied its "Austrian soul" and preferred the standard German language instead of the musical Austrian folk dialect.

The Austrian idea was most radically formulated in the edited volume entitled *Die österreichische Aktion* (The Austrian action), published in 1927. Its contributors were probably the most pro-Habsburg, Catholic, idealistic, traditionalist, and anti-German intellectuals that Austria had between the wars. Their radicalism is easy to prove: *Die österreichische Aktion* is presumably the only interwar Austrian publication in which an approval of the Treaty of Saint-Germain, which delineated the frontiers of the Austro-German Republic, was formulated. Its author Alfred Missong claimed that, against all appearances, the treaty was a just punishment for the country for repudiating its emperor, and its great advantage was that it forbade the Anschluss to Germany.[35] Apparently, *Die österreichische Aktion* is the best source to reconstruct the ephemeral Austrian idea: it contains all its ingredients and discusses them more openly and affirmatively than any other contemporary text. Other authors focused on a particular aspect of it, or omitted some elements because they found them self-evident; the contributors to *Die österreichische Aktion* included all of them and insisted that they formed a coherent entity. The volume covers the necessity of the creation of a Danubian federation, the cultural-religious mission of Austria, the historical legacy of Rome, the superiority of Austrians over Germans and the tragic consequences of Prussian domination in Germany, and the demonic character of nationalism, liberalism, and atheism. It is a manifesto of interwar Austrian patriotism, and its apogee before the rise of Nazism reopened the question of the Anschluss.

According to the authors of *Die österreichische Aktion,* Austria embodied all virtues of a Catholic state: it was peaceful, aristocratic, tolerant, and ethical. Austria-Hungary had not fully realized this ideal, and therefore it was understandable that it fell. As Alfred Missong claimed, Austria-Hungary broke down because it became a modern "a-Catholic" state, penetrated by the spirit of Joseph II, who imitated Frederic the Great of Prussia. The final clash of Prussia and Austria in 1866, was, as he put it, the conflict of "an aristocrat and a parvenu, Saint Clemens

Maria Hofbauer and Luther, a cathedral and a dungeon." In consequence, he continued, Prussia triumphed in Germany, and the Prussian influences penetrated Austria, inflicting it with parliamentarism, interconfessionalism, and nationalism, which caused its decline and fall. The Prussian victory and the decline of the Catholic art of government (*Staatskunst*) brought Arianism, Votanism, and Protestantism (and Protestantism is the revolution in the mask of liberalism) that undermined the German tradition. The only analogy to this process in the history of the Christian civilization, he bombastically concluded, was the repudiation of Jesus by the Jews.[36]

Despite all criticism toward Austria-Hungary, authors of the essays included in *Die österreichische Aktion* purposefully confused the ideal Austria with the real one. Their relations were not reciprocal: the ideal, embodied in the Austrian idea, influenced the reality but not vice versa. The ideal remained pure even though its applications may have seemed disappointing. As a consequence, the image of Austria that emerges from the volume is rather enigmatic; it has little to do with the realities of Austria-Hungary and of the interwar Austro-German Republic. Two introductory essays, *Der europäische und der österreichische Raum* (The European and the Austrian space) and *Die österreichische idee in der Geschichte* (The Austrian idea in history), by Ernst Karl Winter, are symptomatic of this approach. Winter put much effort into demonstrating the geographical and cultural unity of the lands of the old monarchy, and emphasizing their location at the border of civilizations and races (the Latin, the Germanic and the Slavic). He attempted to make his rather unoriginal remarks seem as scientific as possible; however, he crowned them with conclusions that are as general as they are vague. He claimed, for example, that "thinking Austrian means thinking European," and that the true mission of Austria, which undertook the true mission of Germany, was "to be everything and remain oneself." Finally, he explained that this meant "responsibility for the Central European fate," and that it would only be possible after the restoration of the monarchy. The so-called successor states could not reunite with Austria before it returned to its true legacy. If Austria failed to take leadership in the region "in the European spirit," either Prussia would do it "against Europe," or the demonic "united borussianism-bolshevism" (by which, apparently, he meant a communist revolution in Germany that would easily dominate Central Europe).[37] In other words, Winter again argued, Austrians were better Germans, and his country's destiny was returning to its glorious past.

The subsequent essays, by Alfred Missong and H. K. Zessner-Spitzenberg, focus on the problem of the supranational Christian state. Austria, the authors claimed, was the only peaceful modus vivendi of Germans with other European nations. Since Austria-Hungary broke down, the opinion prevailed that supranational states were anachronistic. This was a mistake, observed Missong, for Austria-Hungary, in its shape created by the Agreement of 1867 and the Austrian constitution of that year, was only a dual monarchy and not a true federation, and all attempts to form such a federation were prevented by the German and Hungarian nationalists. The unification of the region, Zessner-Spitzenberg added, had nothing to do with imperialism; it only implied "the paternal care of the House of Austria" over "the international unifying force." It was not anti-national, moreover; it overcame national egoism in the name of solidarity and justice. The modern idea of the protection of national minorities, he concluded, could not be compared to the "old Austrian principle of equality" without going into the history of the practical implementation of this noble principle.[38]

Authors of *Die österreichische Aktion,* patriotic as they were, were also highly critical toward the old monarchy. Missong observed that serious attempts to federalize the monarchy in the years 1860–1861 were abandoned when German liberals came to power after 1867 and poisoned Austrian politics with "teutomania" and an obsessive fear of the Czechs. In addition, the Hungary formed by the Compromise of 1867 was sick, he argued, but for reasons quite different from those given by most of his Austro-German colleagues—namely, because it was not built upon the example given by St. Stephen, the patron of Hungary, but upon the principles of Luther and Hegel, and therefore permeated with Protestant, Jewish, and liberal influences. "Franz Joseph was tragically mistaken," the essay concludes, "to believe that he could neutralize the liberals by allying himself with them."[39] Similarly, Zessner-Spitzenberg wrote about "the tragic fault" of the Habsburgs, who neglected to seek support for their rule among all their nationalities, favoring only the Germans and the Hungarians. Furthermore, he claimed that the foreign policies of the monarchy also mirrored liberal nationalist influences in the Austrian government. He called the alliance with Germany an ersatz of the Anschluss for the pan-Germans, and characterized it as an unfortunate error, which made Austria fight against her Catholic sisters France and Italy counter to her true interests. In order to demonstrate the erroneousness of Austrian policy before the Great War, he compared the Triple Alliance of Germany, Austria, and Italy, inspired by Otto von Bismarck, to Prince Klemens Wenzel von Metternich's system, formed after the Congress of Vienna in 1815, which "made the devil carry bricks for the construction of the church."[40]

Of course, authors of *Die österreichische Aktion* advocated the reunification of the lands of Austria-Hungary. However, this did not simply imply a return to the status quo of 1914; rather, it was to be the first stage of a larger process that would involve all of Europe, although its details remained unclear. Hence, their attitude to the monarchy was exceptional: they did not view it as an anachronism, nor as a closed chapter in the European history. Austria-Hungary, according to them, was rather a model of the European federation of the future. Still, they postulated patience and, driven by their ideological premises, expressed friendly remarks about the League of Nations. Judged by appearances, Missong observed, the League had only deficiencies: it supported the status quo created in 1919, it did not recognize the authority of the pope, and it was permeated with Jewish-Masonic influences. The same, however, refers to all parliamentary democracies that "from the sociological point of view are surrogates of the socially healthy, patriarchal monarchy," and the League was a surrogate of the Empire.[41]

Obviously, the authors of *Die österreichische Aktion* had no monopoly on the Austrian idea. It became a symbol of Austrian patriotism and Austrian uniqueness, and hence many authors competing for Austrian readers ornamented their arguments with it, promoting various concepts and ideas. Again, we should not be misled by their claims for exceptionality; the majority of patriotic symbols share this fate. Still, the Austrian idea remained an undeniably conservative concept. It symbolized a conservative community that was not bound by ethnicity, but was nonetheless supposed to be "natural" and therefore "true." Thus, its main enemy was the "artificial" modernity of such institutions as parliament, political parties, and modern urban culture—as Hofmannsthal emphasized in his university speech in Munich of 1927. It was supposed to be rooted in the natural order, blessed by God and protected by tradition.[42] Austria-Hungary, with its contradictions, divisions, and flawed political life, did not represent the Austrian idea— only a few of its citizens carried it. According to Friedrich Funder, a Christian-Socialist journalist and activist, Franz Ferdinand embodied it most perfectly, as the symbol of the Austro-German hopes for the unfulfilled reform of the monarchy and the creation of Popovici's Great Austria. If Franz Ferdinand had been saved from assassination in Sarajevo, the Austrian idea would have evolved into the *Grossösterreichische Idee:* "the unwritten Magna Carta of the small Danubian nations, rising above the law and the frontiers."[43] Oskar Benda argued that it was the *Dienstaristokrat* (an aristocrat in the public service) who epitomized "the old Austrian state idea."[44] Naturally, others pointed to the imperial and royal officer corps, since officers are ubiquitously supposed to be the best patriots. Provided that the Austrian idea was a concept so vague that no one fully understood it, the supposition seems reasonable.

Finally, the Austrian idea, enigmatic as it was, also had a moment when it was for a time adopted by politicians in power, namely the regime of Chancellor Schuschnigg. This authoritarian regime is frequently described as "fascist" or "Austro-fascist" since, trapped between Nazi Germany, Fascist Italy, and the oppressed but still strong Social Democratic opposition at home, Schuschnigg and his Christian conservatives chose Mussolini as their only available ally and eagerly expressed their admiration for his policies. Their love for Mussolini was nonetheless superficial, and it resulted from desperate political calculations; what truly inspired them was their love for the imperial past of Austria. Propagandists of the small Austro-German Republic, acting under the constant threat of Anschluss to the Third Reich, argued that Austria was a spiritual empire, that it was the future leader of the region and the entire Europe, and that it possessed the key to the salvation of the limping Western Civilization. "Austria," claimed a journal sponsored by the government, "is not founded upon temporary circumstances . . . but upon values on the global scale. Austria is more than a modern continent (see America); its format is greater than of any other European country." The Chancellor himself declared that Austria "surpasses all other countries in the capacities and universalism of its culture, resting upon the cultural traditions of incomparable fame."[45] Authors of the volume *Österreich und die Reichsidee*, published in 1937, claimed that "our Austria" guarded the "supranational, federalist state idea," which originated in the Ancient Rome and flourished under Charlemagne.[46]

To sum up, the Austrian idea had been close to implementation in the past, and was supposed to rise again in the future; its only problem was the present. Politically, Austria was weak, small, and cut off from its Danubian hinterland. Ideologically, the Austrian idea suffered from the upheaval of nationalism, liberalism, and "modern culture." Socially, Protestants, liberals, capitalists, Freemasons, and Jews were seen as its enemies, even though most of them never heard of it. It appealed to "true Austrians" who were disappointed by the current political status quo, frustrated with the depression, and unhappy about the dissolution of the empire: the peasantry, the petite bourgeoisie, the patriotic middle class, and the aristocracy. It was supposed to be a response to their patriotic pride, economic fear, and prejudices against aliens such as Jews and capitalists, since these notions, as Franz Borkenau claims, "fused in the consciousness of the Austrian people."[47]

In other words, the Austrian idea resembled contemporary nationalism both ideologically and functionally and yet it was an ardent enemy of nationalism. Austria, as Oskar Benda put it, meant "national relativism," and a tendency to "melt in the universal," and being Austrian meant being a citizen of the world.[48] Partisans of the Austrian idea carefully avoided calling Austrians a nation, even though their characteristics of the Austrian identity resemble nationalistic discourse of the time. Occasionally, they used some other parallel terms. Missong, for example, wrote about "the Austrian man" (*der österreichische Mensch*) who "differs from the German no less than the Swiss. Racially he is a synthesis of the Germans and the Slavs, spiritually of the Romans and the Byzantines, and his format is Latin."[49] In contrast to other conservatives of the interwar period, who typically viewed communists as their main enemies, authors of the Austrian idea focused on nationalism as the most destructive and erroneous ideology of the modern era.

Certainly, some anti-nationalist tirades of the adherents of the Austrian idea seem too bombastic on the one hand and too vague on the other to be taken literally. Such, however, was the phraseology of the time. Nationalists of all sorts, not to mention the Nazis, eagerly referred to mysticism comparable to the one of the Austrian idea in their propaganda. There is, therefore, no reason to mistrust the authors of the Austrian idea. If they chose nationalism rather than communism as their main opponent, they had their reasons to do so. One could suppose that the Austrian idea was shaped in competition with the Nazis for the souls of the Austrians, since Hitler finally appeared as the main rival of Schuschnigg and the sexton of hopes for the reconstruction of the Great Austria. Still, the Austrian idea was already formed in the 1920s, when Nazis were still a marginal group on the German political scene. Therefore, if we want to search for the origins of the Austrian idea, we have to go back to Austria-Hungary and the shock caused by its breakdown. Imperfect as it was, it remained the source of inspiration for the Austrian idea and hopes for the future Austria as the regional leader or a mother of the future European federation. And its enemies—nationalists and the vaguely defined forces of "modernity"—remained the enemies of the Austrian idea. The fact that this idea on the one hand promoted and praised cosmopolitanism and "national relativism" and on the other hand was mistrustful or hostile toward liberals, capitalists, and Jews (the groups that had been most loyal to the old monarchy) was a paradox that none of the adherents of the Austrian idea attempted to solve.

Finally, the Austrian idea never managed to overcome its marginality; even though for a short time it became a semiofficial ideology of the government, its enthusiastic but enigmatic formulations of Austrian patriotism remained attractive exclusively for a tiny group of intellectuals. Neither the restoration of the Habsburgs nor any Central European federation with Vienna as its capital has ever been a realistic political option after 1918. The idea of the nation-state, to the contrast, triumphed all around Austria, and apparently in Austria itself. In the end, Richard Nikolaus von Coudenhove-Kalergi, the most famous Austrian interwar enthusiast of a European federation and popularly considered one of the fathers of the European Union, himself hoped that his compatriots would finally form a nation of their own. In his *Paneuropa* of 1935 he argued that "the nationalization of Austria is one of the most important events in contemporary European history. It brings an astonishing solution to the Austrian problem. Since Austria has finally acquired a national consciousness, it has ceased to cause difficulties for Europe. The Austrian question does not matter more than the Swiss one. Austria is not a problem anymore, it is a fact."[50] Of course, the reality was more complicated. Austria remained a political rather than a national entity even after World War II, when Anschluss was finally out of the question. Still, in 1955, when the Republic of Austria was finally proclaimed from the four Allied occupation zones, an Austrian journalist ironized, "We may hope that Austria, having its National Theater since 1776, the National Bank since 1816, and the National Council since 1921, will soon also have a nation of its own."[51] By that time the Austrian idea had already seemed dead and forgotten for seventeen years. And yet some of its partisans were still alive, and they were not necessarily unhappy about it. As the novelist Felix Braun put it: "Austria is an idea. All ideas remain unfulfilled in reality, also the idea of the Church. Why should Austria be excluded from this worldly law of the non-actualization of ideas?"[52]

Austria as Apocalyptic Trumpery

Identity does not imply affirmation alone. Apparently, the Austro-Hungarian identity, so shaky and questionable in other aspects, firmly rested upon a particularly developed art of complaining. Criticism, irony, and disillusionment were as important for it as pride and trust in authorities, and love for the aged monarch; they were crucial for the Austro-Hungarian auto-stereotype, especially for the Austrian Germans, who viewed Germans from the Reich as lacking a sense of humor and self-criticism. Some Austrian patriots perversely argued that the deficiencies of the monarchy actually made it a more tolerable place to live than other countries. Such was the sense of the bon mot by Viktor Adler, one of the leaders of the Social Democrats, who pointed out that the political order of the monarchy was "Ein durch Schlamperei gemildeter Absolutismus" (absolutism mediated by disarray). Indeed, many Austrians were in a way proud of the legendary higgledy-piggledy in their public life; it was their *felix culpa*.

However, when politics is concerned, it is often difficult to differentiate muddle from incompetence, and hence in comments about the Austrian *Schlamperei,* joyous irony neighbors bitter mockery. Even authors who sympathized with Austria-Hungary employed it with refined cruelty and a particularly Austrian love for paradoxes. One

Charles I (IV), a postcard on the occasion of his beatification in 2004

of the close collaborators of the emperor, for example, wrote, of the war policies of the monarchy, "Everything was top secret in Austria, and therefore nothing was kept confidential. Hence, no wonder that the famous cabaret singer Melke Mars could foretell the beginning of the first offensive against Italians with mathematic precision."[53] Obviously, the most critical toward the authorities were those who had already practiced criticism before 1914. Ignacy Daszyński, the leader of the Polish socialists in the Viennese parliament, recollected with comparable wit,

> The old emperor was succeeded by Charles, a weak man of an immature mind. Sometimes he made the impression of being simply harmlessly stupid. The two years of his rule were the time of the total decline of the entire state and resulted in its breakdown ... The government of Clam-Martinic fell because of the typically aristocratic incapability of the prime minister and his colleagues. He was replaced by a certain Dr. Seidler, an ex-teacher of the em-

peror Charles. He was the funniest prime minister I have ever seen (and I have seen a couple of dozen of them!). He was petty, sincere, relatively stupid, and so naïve, that once in my speech, causing laughter in the Chamber, I asked: "Have you ever seen, Gentlemen, a child of this age?" And such a man could have served as the prime minister of the declining Austria for an entire year![54]

Joseph Bloch, the Social Democratic Jewish deputy from Vienna, wrote in the same spirit that "in the seventh and eighth decades of the last century the Jews invariably supported the so-called liberal constitutionalists, trusting them so stubbornly that any contrarious opinion was considered as a heresy or treason. . . . Despite this fact, this party could not have been described but as 'the most stupid and unable in the entire world.'"[55] As a matter of fact, however, the Social Democrats were not the most ardent opposition in the last decades of the monarchy. Actually, after national tensions rose in the mid-1890s the socialists were often the largest party with which the government could at least negotiate, and occasionally also cooperate. Their declarative internationalism made them the only pan-Austrian party, and their willingness to support the government in reforming the monarchy—for example when the popular franchise was introduced in 1907—earned them the label of *Burgsozialisten,* from the name of the emperor's residence in Vienna. In short, they were a part of the political system, and as such were also heavily criticized. For their more radical colleagues they were simply fake revolutionaries.

Leon Trotsky, a leader of the Bolsheviks and the future rival of Stalin, spent seven years in exile in Vienna, met all the most prominent Austrian socialists, and left a characteristic testimony: "They were well-educated people whose knowledge of various subjects was superior to mine. I listened with intense and, one might almost say, respectful interest to their conversation in the 'Central' café. But very soon I grew puzzled. These people were not revolutionaries. Moreover, they represented the type which was farthest from that of the revolutionary. This expressed itself in everything—in their approach to subjects, in their political remarks and psychological appreciations, in their self-satisfaction—not self-assurance, but self-satisfaction. I even thought I sensed philistinism in the quality of their voices."[56]

Trotsky was right: Austrian socialists were much less radical than their Russian counterparts. Austrian society, moreover, was permeated with conservative values, and with respect for the splendors of nobility, ranks, and titles. Obviously, the same could be said about half of interwar Europe. In Austria, however, "philistinism" and the love for social hierarchy found relatively few critics, perhaps because the Habsburg monarchy fell in consequence of the lost war and revolutions (or revolts) in Prague, Cracow, and Budapest rather than in Vienna. Nothing like the spectacular success of the passionate social novel *Der Untertan* (*The Loyal Subject*), by Heinrich Mann, in Germany—written in 1914 and published in 1918—occurred in Austrian literature. Social critique in Austria was practically embodied by one powerful and original individual: Karl Kraus. Kraus and the journal he edited, *die Fackel,* had been active for two decades before the fall of the monarchy; during the war Kraus made himself known as the most passionate and consistent pacifist of Austria. By the time of the Republic he was already an institution. He was a talented and productive writer, and a speaker who continued to mesmerize his audience during public lectures in Vienna until his death in 1936.

Kraus, however, was not a revolutionary either. He was an aesthete and a polemical genius, but had no program, nor a social philosophy of his own. He furiously attacked the authorities, the social and intellectual establishment, taboos, and double morality—in the name of "truth" and vaguely defined humanism. He was obsessed with the purity and "sincerity" of the German language, and therefore his beloved satirical trick, which he practiced in *Die Fackel* for decades, was to quote at length public personalities of his time or, as he himself put it, "the great masters governing Austria in the absolute manner, limited exclusively by the capacity of their minds."[57]

Among other things, Kraus hated the mysticism and conservatism of the Austrian patriotism à la Hofmannsthal and other partisans of the Austrian idea. He mocked them mercilessly in his antiwar drama *The Last Days of Mankind*. In the drama, Leopold von Andrian, who was a diplomat by profession, is portrayed as an official in the Austrian consulate in Warsaw during the Great War, waiting for the imperial and royal invasion in order to grant a valid Austrian visa to the triumphant troops. "The Austrian ideology," he claimed, "is the greatest swindle that has ever taken place."[58] Radicalized by the war, Kraus had little sentiment for Austria-Hungary, which he called "a muddy brown coffee topped with a double helping of whipped cream—and displayed in the closet of the civilized world as a tourist attraction."[59] In his view, the decision to start the war was no coincidence but a consequence of the Austro-Hungarian political system and the mentality of its elite. Unable to realize and admit its own incompetence and helplessness in the modern world, the Austrian government, he argued, preoccupied with prestige more than anything else, chose to perish in a world-scale war drama rather than sink in domestic chaos. For him, the entire glory and greatness of Austria-Hungary was a mystification and a patriotic lie—and he considered it his personal mission to unmask public lies.[60]

However, Kraus was as revolutionary in his disrespect for the authorities and the patriotic taboos as he was conservative in his attachment to the cultural values and ideals of humanism. As time passed by, he became no less disappointed with the Republic as he had been with the monarchy. Its dissolution, he had to admit, did not purge the public life in Austria. In 1927 he wrote, quite in the spirit of the post–imperial and royal nostalgia:

> I am almost afraid that it might be interpreted as a confession of a monarchist, if I remind the reader that the old era had personalities at its disposal who—long before the decision of influential zombies to usher into the dawn of death—had too much red blood in their veins to taste that of their subjects, and too much human dignity to offend that of their charges as evidence of their power. . . . Even socialist quarters cannot deny that under the Monarchy the very desire for popularity and mania for saluting on the part of the head of state offered a certain amount of protection against bureaucratic excesses.[61]

Kraus, with his phobia of all duplicity and an inclination toward the grotesque, revealed in *The Last Days of Mankind,* was, nevertheless, a harbinger of a fascinating trend in the discourse on Austria-Hungary: that this country was a mystification, that it lived a shadow-life of a mass illusion. It will be discussed in length in the next chapter, for it became one of the major themes of post-Austro-Hungarian literature. It may seem natural that, retrospectively, the public life of the monarchy appeared a bit theatrical: such is the fate of most emotions and disputes of the past, and in case of Austria-Hungary there was nothing left that could carry them on into the future, because all the institutions and all the troubles of the monarchy were gone with it. However, this feeling had already been present in the writings of some of the most prominent Austrian authors before 1914, when the monarchy still lay firm on the maps of Europe. Robert Musil wrote in 1913,

> There are few countries in which politics is pursued so passionately as here, and none in which politics, accompanied by a comparable passion, remain such an indifferent affair: passion as pretext . . . Somewhere in this country a secret must be hidden, an idea, but no one knows where. It is not the idea of the state, not the dynastic principle, not the idea of a cultural symbiosis of different peoples (Austria could be a world experiment): apparently the whole thing is really only motion in the absence of a driving idea, like the weaving of the bicyclist who isn't going forward.[62]

The most comprehensive and influential diagnosis of public life in Austria-Hungary was formulated a quarter-century later by Hermann Broch, in his *Hofmannsthal und seine Zeit* (Hofmannsthal and his time). Broch also arrived at the conclusion that the Habsburg monarchy was a great producer of illusions; however, his analysis originated in his critique of the Austrian artistic production. The decline of the monarchy had begun, he argued, from the decline of its art. He believed that at the end of the nineteenth century Vienna became the global capital city of kitsch—a concept that he considered crucial to understanding the mentality of the modern era, and which he obviously despised. Kitsch in his view is an imitation of art; it is not a kind of art of low quality, but its deceitful negation.[63]

Austria, according to Broch, lived an illusory life after 1848: it was a "museum" of the baroque in which no more "baroque politics" was practiced. Viennese culture, with its theaters, operas, and the feuilleton, which he considered the essence of this culture, was pure decoration that masked the lack of any true values. All that served pure entertainment, and was therefore kitschy, but it still made Vienna, as he noted, the only great European city that was considered joyous and cheerful. He coined this process "the merry apocalypse"—and this term was to have a big career and soon lose its original sense. Austrian politics, Broch argued, was equally artificial and decorative: democracy was a pure façade, and Austro-Hungarian dualism was an abstract theory "in which no one really believed." The masses uncritically copied the hedonist style of the elites, and showed no real interest in the decision-making processes. Hence, the depoliticization of the masses, which Metternich had failed to accomplish through absolutism, turned out to be a by-product of liberalism and a particularly Austrian aestheticism. The literature, symbolized by Hofmannsthal (whom Broch never pardoned for his inclination for the word *schön*), successfully cooperated in locking Austrians in a golden cage of overaestheticized, pacifying illusions.[64]

Broch concluded his essay with an apology of Kraus and his "absolute satire," which he viewed as the only means of revealing "the devilish ridiculousness of evil," and therefore called "the central art of the twentieth century."[65] This only indicates the scale of Kraus's influence upon his contemporaries—he had only enemies and worshippers. Still, many of Broch's observations proved inspiring for future discourse about Austria-Hungary. First of all, it was his intuition that the monarchy, anachronistic and obsolete by appearances, was also a home for a number of strikingly modern phenomena in the sphere of mass politics and mass imaginary. Second, he was a pioneer of the critique of politics in aesthetic terms. Although the only form of art he valued was high art in its traditional meaning, he nevertheless viewed it as a mirror of society and its popular values. Indeed, historians and sociologists had already analyzed societies of the past this way. Broch applied this idea to his own society, and what he found was a "vacuum" instead of "values." In this, he was one of the first great pessimist thinkers of the twentieth century, disappointed and mistrustful toward their own cultures.

CHAPTER THREE

AUSTRIA-HUNGARY IN LITERARY FICTION

Many literary theorists emphasize that the most characteristic feature of literary fiction is that it constantly deceives us and questions our capacity to understand the world around us—or, more precisely, that the world of fiction is not like ours. In this chapter I propose a more naïve reading of literature dealing with the Austro-Hungarian past, arguing that it can tell us a lot about past realities, and that its authors were making real claims about them. The monarchy, after all, passed away before the postmodern era, and this was the way in which most readers interpreted the texts I am going to discuss in this chapter. Moreover, the subject of this analysis is not the monarchy as it actually was, but its posthumous image, so the theoretical question of the nature of relations between the world of fiction and our world need not trouble us too much here. We can simply assume that the majority of interwar readers believed that the world of fiction resembled and reflected their world and enjoyed this fact. The Vienna they saw described in novels was for them the city they inhabited, visited, or dreamt of visiting; the emperor Franz Joseph talking to fictional protagonists was for them the monarch they knew from newspapers; and the Great War in which these protagonists perished was the war they luckily survived. Thus, literature was a powerful tool for shaping their image of Austria-Hungary; it performed this task alongside their own memory, occasionally reshaping and reconstructing it. In that time writers were indeed supposed to make comments on contemporary political and social developments, and readers sought historical and political interpretations in novels and poetry. Interwar Central European writers met these expectations successfully.

Certainly, the higher the artistic quality a particular piece of literature represents, the more sophisticated and ambiguous is the way it reflects historical reality. And Providence was generous to the generation of authors who witnessed the agony of the monarchy, blessing many of them with a remarkable artistic talent. Still, I will argue that we can see traces of certain Austro-Hungarian realities and motifs even in the novels of Franz Kafka—and other authors whose prose seems to be set both anywhere and in no specific historical moment. Another problem we will have to face analyzing the writings of the post-Austro-Hungarian authors is that some of them had a splendid sense of humor as well. Of course, I am not going to bore readers with a scholarly analysis proving that some of my sources are actually very funny. On the contrary, I will argue that some pieces of literature that enjoy the reputation of being remarkably humorous in fact involve a lot of particularly bitter sarcasm, reflecting deep frustrations troubling their authors.

Another reason to include literary fiction in this analysis is that its role in shaping the image of the monarchy was indeed exceptional, and so is its position still today in academic discourse about the Habsburgs. Scarcely any other historical discourse is inspired by fiction to a comparable extent. Historians of the monarchy regularly quote from Robert Musil, Stefan Zweig, or Hermann Broch—because they find them informative and witty or because they simply cannot challenge the clarity and conclusiveness of the novelists who also happened to witness a turning point in European history. Perhaps the monarchy was just lucky to die at the proper moment, when a number of talented authors were entering their most creative years. Apparently, however, this moment was unusual enough to attract their attention: with the Great War and the dissolution of Austria-Hungary the entire world changed. Even those who welcomed these changes or who did not care for the monarchy, but had grown up before 1914, must have felt uneasy about them. New forms in politics and everyday life, new fortunes, new technologies, new fashions, new entertainments, the miseries of the war and the postwar crisis, the insecurity of the interwar period—all that attracted talented writers, who in some other, more peaceful and stable time, might have considered politics and history boring themes unworthy of their attention and their pens.

There are, generally speaking, three major spheres of the Austro-Hungarian experience that the belles lettres explored more profoundly than they did any other genre of historical discourse. The first of them was exactly this sense of change, the passing of the old, and the emerging of the new. Academic history in that time was hardly capable of recording the depth of such changes: focused on high politics, it was overwhelmed with facts, treaties, intrigues, and campaigns, which followed each other chronologically; some grand processes it noted were too abstract to be easily translated into the language of the individual experience. Moreover, it lacked distance in time, which historians always need, even when they do not realize it. Literature has always been capable of grasping this distance or indeed creating it, and so were Austro-Hungarian writers in the interwar period. In his famous study *Der habsburgische Mythos in der österreichischen Literatur* (The Habsburg myth in modern Austrian literature), Claudio Magris claimed that this capacity of creating a sense of the remote, the archaic past, was characteristic for Austrian literature, and constituted the basis for a phenomenon that he called "the Habsburg myth." Myth stands beyond history, and so did the Habsburg monarchy in a number of narratives devoted to it. It stood still, unchangeable since time immemorial, almost fantastic in its costume of legendary names and titles, until history—or, if you wish, modernity—intervened and destroyed it.

Literature has also always, at least since the time of Homer, been occupied with the problem of the passing away of people, families, epochs, customs, and civilizations. It sometimes has been the main or perhaps the sole tool capable of saving their memories, of immortalizing their remains. Some Austro-Hungarian writers attempted to do this because of nostalgia, because they mourned the past that was irrevocably gone. This was a powerful stimulus for Dante, who summarized it in his famous formula, "Nessun maggior dolore che ricordarsi del tempo felice nella miseria." No other medium was better capable of expressing nostalgia for "the good old days of peace" than literary fiction, nor could any of them compete with the literary images and ambiance of decadence and imminent catastrophe. Some authors, however, merely observed and recorded the process of the decline and fall of the old world, and of the emergence of the new. The change intrigued them: its unexpectedness, its paradoxes, its occasional rapidity or belatedness. Literature alone was capable of grasping (or of making such an impression) of its entirety, because the only way to do that was by referring to metaphors.

It makes little sense to distinguish between these two approaches, for many literary accounts of the decline and fall of the monarchy embraced them both. Obviously, their political implications also often remain ambiguous. Perhaps no other author expressed nostalgia for the Habsburgs better than Stefan Zweig did in his *The World of Yesterday*, full of declarations like, "Can one still imagine an Austria so lax and loose in its joviality, so piously confiding in its Imperial master and in the God who made life so comfortable for them?"[1] And yet, Zweig and many other authors filled with a sense of loss were also highly critical toward the old monarchy and, more importantly, they were aware that there was no return to the status quo from 1914. Indeed, the idea of the restoration of the Habsburgs did not materialize even in the land of fiction. Another author highly sentimental about the monarchy, Franz Werfel, introduced it into his unfinished novel *Cella oder die Überwindung*—as a farce in which twelve desperate monarchists make a ridiculous attempt at a clumsy coup d'état.[2] And that was all: the monarchy might have been attractive in the land of the past, also an object of mockery; in the present it was not capable of producing a single story.

In her study on Polish literature of the ex-Austrian province of Galicia, Ewa Wiegandt argues that the Habsburg myth embraced two main motifs: la belle époque and fin de siècle, the Arcadian and the catastrophic, and that "the unity of the two, notwithstanding their apparent opposition, defines the entire theme."[3] There was, actually, one more: the satiric, mercilessly mocking the anachronisms of the old monarchy, its pompous sense of pride and ridiculous traditions. This was the third aspect of the Austro-Hungarian experience that literary fiction alone was capable of rendering—or did perhaps literature create it? There were, certainly, no such absurd initiatives in the old monarchy as "the Parallel Action" in Robert Musil's Kakania, no policies so ridiculous as those in Fritz von Herzmanovsky-Orlando's

Tarokania, and presumably no Austrian soldier so cunning, adventurous and philosophical as Jaroslav Hašek's good soldier Švejk. But they all represented the realities of the Austro-Hungarian monarchy in a way that was understandable for the contemporary readers. In a word, this monarchy was fertile soil for fantasies.

The Empire of Peace and Quiet

Let us begin with the Arcadian motif. Interestingly, all we know about the social realities of the old Austria from historical inquiry is deceptive rather than informative for the analysis of its Arcadian literary images. The monarchy created by writers was not an ancien régime: it was not a paradise for the aristocrats and clergy, nor for the Germans and Magyars, nor for the Viennese. It was, foremost, a middle-class Arcadia. Moreover, its authors suffered from a malady typical for intellectuals and artists of all epochs: they were inclined to believe that they knew what the so-called simple people really thought, what they wanted and what they felt. Consequently, they did not praise the monarchy for the privileges it had guaranteed for the higher classes; there was no nostalgia as there had been in post-revolutionary France or Russia, for the elegant balls, the intellectual salons, or the artistic appreciation. They did not amuse their readers with the flavor of the true decadence, the taste of the last glass of champagne with caviar. The monarchy was supposed to have eaten and drunk properly, danced decently, and slept well. It was presented as a state that best suited the bourgeois, because it did not interfere in their lives. Its genius was that it was easy to ignore, to negotiate, and to tame. It did not promise equal rights for everyone, nor did it guarantee social justice, but it was stable, and reliable, and tolerant: it did not demand its citizens to be perfect. Most importantly, its power was limited.

These limits were symbolized by its legendary old age, emphasized by both the apologists of the monarchy and the ironists. Its old age was valued not because, as Hofmannsthal argued along with Machiavelli, duration is the proper goal of power and proves its efficiency; on the contrary, the old age of Austria in literary images symbolized the weakness of the monarchy, and the lack of ambition of its authorities—a virtue so dear to the generation that suffered from the growing powers of the state and its ambitions to transform society. Seen from this perspective, it seemed to be a blessing that the Austrian government lacked efficiency, that it often acted clumsily and reacted belatedly to changing realities. Instead, it acted with caution. This virtue was brilliantly characterized by the ironic Robert Musil:

> And the administration of this country was carried out in an enlightened, hardly perceptible manner, with a cautious clipping of all sharp points, by the best bureaucracy in Europe, which could be accused of only one defect: it could not help regarding genius and enterprise of genius in private persons, unless privileged by high birth or state appointment, as ostentation, indeed presumption. But who would want unqualified persons putting their oar in, anyway? And besides, in Kakania it was only that a genius was always regarded as a lout, but never, as sometimes happened elsewhere, that a mere lout was regarded as a genius.[4]

Obviously, this was a caricature, written by an author who considered himself a genius, and hence he was sensitive to all mediocrity around him. This genius, however, was also an ex-Habsburg citizen, who appreciated hierarchy, and order, and caution. People who appreciated stability and security generally missed the time before the Great War; however, in East Central Europe, when the interwar years were so turbulent and insecure, the Habsburg monarchy became the epitome of these values. Of course, bourgeois values are not easy to idealize in literature; ambitious writers, considering themselves artists, have since Romanticism been generally supposed to be highly critical toward the bourgeois mentality. Stability, security, and caution as virtues or life goals of an individual have been ridiculed by innumerable talented authors; an attempt to praise them must have been risky for an author of high self-esteem, or one simply aware of the European literary tradition. A writer should have rebelliously hated bourgeois society, splendidly ignored it, or at least ironically distanced himself from it, in the way Thomas Mann did in his *Buddenbrooks*. If interwar Austrian authors dared to idealize the coziness of the prewar, middle-class Habsburg paradise, it was because of despair. It was the imminent apocalypse of this mediocre, reasonable world that made it worth describing and remembering. The straightest, sincerest, and most appealing image of it is perhaps to be found in Stefan Zweig's *The World of Yesterday*. Zweig was also capable of insightful social analysis. For example, he wrote:

> In this vast empire everything stood firmly and immovably in its appointed place, and at its head was the aged emperor; and were he to die, one knew (or believed) another would come to take his place, and nothing would change in the well-regulated order. No one thought of wars, of revolutions, or revolts. All that was radical, all violence, seemed impossible in an age of reason. This feeling of security was the most eagerly sought after possession of millions, the common ideal of life. Only the possession of this security made life seem worthwhile, and constantly widening circles desired their share of this costly treasure. At first it was only the prosperous who enjoyed this advantage, but gradually the great masses forced their way toward it.[5]

Interestingly, in this paragraph Zweig did not simply remind us that life in Austria-Hungary was secure; he informed us that in Austria-Hungary "the feeling of security" was highly valued, as if such an attitude were something special, or as if security itself were something unusual. Zweig constructed his report from the past like a historicist author, as if the past were a different country. He did not compare it to the present explicitly, arguing that it was better or worse. He pointed out the mechanism that governed it, discreetly suggesting that it functioned smoothly, and smartly letting his readers draw the conclusion whether or not the old Austria was a good place to live.

Moreover, Zweig's eulogy for the monarchy is in fact ambivalent. The security he praised as the most precious aspect of the happy existence under the Habsburg rule did not originate in the belief in the stability of "well-regulated order" only. It was, apparently, founded not only upon ignoring all those who thought of "revolutions and revolts" but also included an unlimited trust in progress—a conviction Zweig himself evidently shared. Surely, the entire pre–World War generation shared this belief; however, it must have been confusing for someone who looked retrospectively at Austria-Hungary with nostalgia. After all, progress and tradition do not go together perfectly well. Zweig certainly understood that, but he desperately refused to draw consequences from this fact. "In those years," he claimed, "each one of us derived strength from the common upswing of the time and increased his individual confidence out of the collective confidence . . . whoever experienced this epoch of world confidence knows that all since has been retrogression and gloom."[6] Not all Austro-Hungarian writers shared such idealism, typical for the prewar middle class, nor Zweig's pessimism, which mirrored his earlier optimism and finally led him to commit suicide in 1942 in Brazil. In Robert Musil's *The Man without Qualities,* we come across a character whose simultaneous belief in progress and order guaranteed by Austria-Hungary evidently resembles that of the young Zweig—or perhaps that of his parents, who belonged to the successful Jewish industrialists of late nineteenth-century prosperity. The character is Leo Fischel, a Jewish bank director. Musil summarized his character's Weltanschauung with his characteristic lack of mercy for illusions:

> Director Leo Fischel of Lloyd's Bank believed, as all bank directors did before the war, in progress. Being a man who was good at his job, he naturally knew that it is only in things one really knows about that one can have a conviction on which one is prepared to stake anything. . . . Worn out by stocks and bonds, or whatever he was dealing with in his department, with no recreation other than an evening at the opera once a week, he believed there was such a thing as general progress, which must somehow resemble the picture of ever-increasing lucrativeness presented by his bank.[7]

A number of writers understood, or at least sensed, that the Habsburg Arcadia was an illusion. Naturally, the fact that the monarchy appeared to be bankrupt, and that it had little to offer in the sphere of more modern values such as democracy, progress, and vitality, did not allow idealizing it fully. The uniqueness of interwar idealized, nostalgic, or indeed apologetic images of the monarchy was based on a paradox: how was it possible that this doomed and backward country was actually a better place to live than the more progressive and just present? The charm of sentimentalism, and the beauty of the past it praises, is always based upon the fact that this past is fragile, and that it cannot compete with the triumphant present. Austria-Hungary suited this sentimental paradigm perfectly because it was so anachronistic when it still existed, only its inhabitants did not know it and enjoyed the pleasures it offered joyously and innocently. Seen from the a posteriori perspective, when the monarchy was no more, it seemed a strange paradox that it had appeared so stable, and prosperous, and secure. When stability, prosperity, and security are lost, however, they immediately become illusions. Hence, it demanded some mental effort to reconstruct what was lost with Austria-Hungary. In a number of interwar narratives we come across such reconstructions unexpectedly; the past is being evoked by some coincidental stimuli. In Heimitio von Doderer's *The Demons*, the narrator allows himself such reminiscence only once, walking the sunny streets of Vienna in springtime:

> In the old days, when all frontiers were open, Europe had pored through here . . . happily falling in with the polished local lifestyle, which maintained a pretty and inimitable balance between the great Empire outside and the here and now of hills, vineyards, old courtyards, and ancestral customs in the suburbs, as well as the modest gracefulness of the small townhouses of noblemen in a still and cool street in the heart of the Old City. Thus lay the here and now on the one side, which we might call the heart's side, the side of familial and social life, the little world of rounded forms; for outside lay the most variegated landscapes, climates, and costumes, lay the ice of glaciers and lowland plains, blue sea and southern vineyards, all the multilingual richness of a vast empire, full of pomp and rituals to which the individual owed certain duties inherited from fathers and forefathers. In balance between these two poles moved the nonchalance of the round-dance, the smiles of charming, worldly-wise women, the handsome men who succeeded, with an often astonishingly small application of intelligence, in being fully qualified representatives of one of the most charming cultures that ever was among the many that have vanished from our vast continent. [8]

Some of the most characteristic features of the memory of Austria-Hungary in its Austrian, or indeed Viennese form, are to be found in this passage. There are the beauty, and richness, and charm of the old times; the geographical and cultural variety of the "vast empire"; and the subtly noted traditionalism and conservatism of its citizens. Finally, there is the patriotic pride of someone who identifies himself with the legacy of this empire, tempered by his awareness of the fact that the empire had eventually fallen. Indeed, the artistic and intellectual quality, and originality, of some of the apologetic images of Austria-Hungary arises from acknowledging that the monarchy had its flaws, from the awareness of the fact that, in spite of all its splendor, it was doomed to failure. All nostalgic, and yet intelligent, descriptions of the old monarchy include it and are therefore equivocal and cautious in praising it:

they cannot avoid taking into consideration that the greatness of the empire, and all its blessings and charms, were but temporary, and that its firmness, which seemed the most attractive aspect of the Austro-Hungarian reminiscences, was illusive.

Probably the most famous literary account of this awareness, and the combination of nostalgia, pity, and sarcasm that resulted from it, is *The Man without Qualities*. Let us regard one more of Musil's brilliant characteristics of the empire he ironically called Kakania:

> There, in Kakania, the misunderstood State that has since vanished, which was in so many things a model, though all unacknowledged, there was speed too, of course; but not too much speed. . . . Of course cars drove along these roads—but not too many cars! The conquest of the air had begun here too; but not too intensively. Now and then a ship was sent off to South America or the Far East; but not too often. There was no ambition to have world markets and world power. Here one was in the center of Europe, at the focal point of the world's old axes; the words "colony" and "overseas" had the ring of something as yet utterly untried and remote. There was some display of luxury; but it was not, of course, so over-sophisticated as that of the French. One went in for sport; but not in madly Anglo-Saxon fashion. One spent tremendous sums on the army; but only just enough to assure one of remaining the second weakest of the great powers.[9]

"The misunderstood state" seems to be the key to Musil's reasoning. Obviously, there is irony involved in it, for states are not texts and they do not call for an interpretation, and yet, the irony should not be confused with mockery. Austria-Hungary, he suggests, was not as desperately anachronistic as it was popularly believed; it was not an old curiosity shop, but "a model, though all unacknowledged." A model for what, however? What follows may seem a parody of the state as it should be: modern, powerful, technologically advanced, and efficient. Austria-Hungary did not meet these criteria, but it skillfully pretended to do so. This leads us from the domain of history to metaphysics. Disappointed with history, disgusted with politics, and frustrated with the economy, many post-Austro-Hungarian writers located their lost motherland outside of these spheres, refusing to view it as an ordinary state like so many others, and imagining it as a model country, whose existence was primarily spiritual. Certainly, it could not compete with other great powers in its number of planes and cars, in wealth, colonial policies, or the arms race, but all that made it more humane and tolerable for its citizens. Actually, in numerous literary images of the monarchy its backwardness is wholeheartedly appreciated: it is presented as an undisputable advantage of Austria-Hungary. In other words, the monarchy was not only a middle-class Arcadia but also an archaic one. It represented a traditional order, which was therefore close to the natural one, or indeed to the one prescribed by God. This conviction was certainly strengthened by the fact that the monarchy symbolized the time before the Great War, before the world went mad. It was perhaps best characterized by a short, poetic, and painful comment by Joseph Roth in his *The Radetzky March:* "In the years before the Great War, at the time the events chronicled in these pages took place, it was not yet a matter of indifference whether a man lived or died. When someone was expunged from the lists of the living, someone else did not immediately step up to take his place, but a gap was left to show where he had been, and those who knew the man who had died or disappeared, well or even less well, felt silent whenever they saw the gap."[10]

It is indeed difficult to imagine better characteristics of the sorrowful difference between cruel, inhuman modernity and the idealized, semimythical past. Numerous novelists and poets of the industrial and postindustrial era attempted to render it, but few managed to grasp it as persuasively as Roth did. The fact that he had Austria-Hungary at his disposal—which he truly missed and mourned, especially as he developed his addiction to alcohol—evidently helped him: an entire country epitomized the past and passed away with it. *The Radetzky March* was a requiem for the monarchy and his masterpiece, but Roth also expressed his belief that that world had been a better place to live in a number of minor works. Those of lower artistic quality are often more explicitly sentimental, or indeed reactionary. The following narrator's declaration from the opening pages of *The Emperor's Tomb* summarizes this attitude:

> I am not a man of my time. In fact I find it hard not to declare myself its enemy. Not, as I often remark, that I fail to understand it. My comment is merely a pious one. Because I am easy-going I prefer not to be aggressive or hostile and therefore I say I do not understand those matters which I ought to say that I hate or de-

Karl Lueger, the leader of the Christian Democrats and mayor of Vienna, with Franz Joseph

spise. I have sharp ears but I pretend to be hard of hearing, finding as I do that it is more elegant to feign this handicap than to admit that I have heard some vulgar sound.[11]

As with all semimythical interpretations of the past, the one concerning Austria-Hungary emphasized the role of the so-called common people, the rural population, living in proximity to Nature and God, and innocently indifferent toward the phenomena that undermined and destroyed the monarchy: modern political life and nationalism. Having common enemies in the camp of powerful and cruel modernity, it assumed, the monarchy and the folk had to have something in common. The monarchy, epitomized by the venerable emperor Franz Joseph, suited the simple people's imagination of the natural order, engrafted in them primarily by the church. "God and the emperor are always together," concludes the illiterate Huzul (a mountaineer) from the Carpathians of eastern Galicia, the main protagonist of *Salt of the Earth* by József Wittlin. When the hero is being enrolled in the army, and takes the military oath, the narrator explains its sense half-ironically: "For the emperor Francis Joseph would never admit that man was formed out of earth. He was a believer neither in the doctrine of materialism nor in Haeckel's philosophy. He was a convinced dualist, and would not deny to the most wretched of his subjects, to the stupidest of the Huzuls, the possession of a soul"; and "In the Imperial and Royal military algebra, God was represented by an endless series of naughts added to the highest possible numeral, the Emperor."[12]

The humane character of the monarchy, and the blessings of the patriarchal rule of Franz Joseph, seemed particularly attractive for the authors who disliked nationalism. Thus, apparently, they retrospectively ascribed pro-Habsburg feelings to ethnic communities that had neither enjoyed privileges under the Habsburg rule nor profited from the dissolution of the monarchy. Joseph Roth, probably the most famous admirer of the monarchy, focused on the Jews, especially the poor Jews of eastern Galicia, whom he knew from his own childhood and youth. The Huzuls, a people living in the Carpathians, discovered by Polish intellectuals at the turn of the century when folklore became popular among the educated classes, also perfectly suited this model. Austria-Hungary, at least from the point of view of folklore admirers, seemed a protector of their traditional culture, endangered by the competing Polish and Ukrainian national movements, and the international powers of modernity. Hence, one of the most striking formulations of Habsburg loyalty, and the idealized, or ideally simplified, Habsburg political philosophy, is to be found in the monumental saga about Huzul life by Stanisław Vincenz, *Na wysokiej połoninie. Nowe czasy. Księga pierwsza: Zwada* (On the high uplands). The political credo of the emperor Franz Joseph and the interpretation of the constitution of 1867, as related by an elder of the community to his people and formulated by Vincenz, were:

> Be as you like, my people! Whether you are of God's faith, or of the human faith, the people's or the nobles', the Christian or the Jewish one, the Latin or the Uniate, the Turkish or the Bosnian—I like what you like. Don't be troubled with your faith; faith is a skin, and no one is responsible for one's skin. As an emperor, I like your skin very much. Therefore, I believe you, and politely ask you one thing: do not bring shame on me. Trust each other, that's the most ancient faith. And do good, do the best, I know you can. It will be very nice, it will please me the most: it will be the most famous constitution! Your Franz Joseph the Apostolic, or whatever you like.[13]

This folk-style political philosophy resembled a laissez-faire manifesto, and yet it was rather about *laissez-croire*. What the bourgeoisie appreciated as the liberalism of Austria-Hungary, could have, with a bit of literary imagination, been presented as patriarchal conservatism, suiting mountain shepherds and peasants. Notably, what Vincenz imagined as a political doctrine to seduce his beloved Huzuls involved more moralizing and more references to religion than a Viennese bourgeois like Zweig or Musil would find appropriate. What seemed the age of reason and progress in Vienna was still the age of faith in the Carpathians. The simple people, Vincenz suggested, did not expect the government to be efficient and up-to-date with other governments' policies. In fact, the ideal government of the simple folk did not pursue any policies at all, except for providing a humble number of jobs, preferably jobs requiring the wearing of uniforms. The writers' love for Austria-Hungary was ambivalent: in spite of all the sentimentalism and nostalgia evoked, they could not forgive the monarchy that it abandoned them by failing to pass the exam in modern history. All their enthusiastic memories were overshadowed by this painful flaw. Consequently, they conveyed this love, in its pure form, undisturbed by historical consciousness, to the so-called simple people. They were supposed to have enjoyed the life of the Habsburg subjects "with an astonishingly small application of intelligence," as Doderer put it: naïvely and straightforwardly. The backward political institutions, and the anachronistic outlook of the monarchy, did not trouble them; on the contrary, they were supposed to have believed that what was old was also authentic, sanctioned by tradition, and to have appreciated monarchical pomp and splendor.

Of course, some authors mocked such beliefs. They did not share the opinion that the Austrian bureaucracy was "the best in Europe," as Musil and so many others believed; the alleged respect it enjoyed irritated them. For example, Emil Zegadłowicz, author of one of the bitterest works of Polish anti-Habsburg literature, the novel *Zmory* (Nightmares), ironized: "The uniform expressed the subjects' love for their monarch, and simultaneously it expressed God's grace, for God, as we know, was particularly inclined toward Austriahungary." The story takes place in a Galician town, where a classical *gymnasium* is one of the most respected institutions. The *gymnasium*'s beadle berates one of its teachers, who happens to come to work pretty drunk, "It will be a disgrace! You are a state official, aren't you, Tony? You have to protect your honor, you're an imperial-royal son-of-a-bitch, don't you know?"[14] We should not be misled by the author's sarcasm, however. Actually, both fragments, and many others like it, confirm that the monarchy and its institutions enjoyed much respect among the "simple people." The author found it pitiful, but did not deny it. Such involuntary, unintended information belongs among the most precious that literary fiction can reveal to us about the past.

Moreover, some authors saw the alleged deficiencies of the Habsburg administration, such as corruption and nepotism, as its advantages, and praised them overtly. "The best bureaucracy in Europe" was, after all, an aristocratic apparatus, and its principles were far from egalitarian. Admirers of the Habsburg did not hide that—they viewed it as an indication that the monarchy was ruled intelligently and skillfully, and that the authorities perceived Habsburg subjects as human individuals rather than as abstract citizens. Joseph Roth, for example, wrote enthusiastically in *The Emperor's Tomb,* one of his most nostalgic novels:

> There existed in my vanished world of the old Monarchy those precious and priceless, unwritten, unrecognized and impenetrable rules with which the initiates were familiar and which were cast in a bronze more enduring than written rules themselves. These rules saw to it that out of every hundred petitioners just seven would see their wishes favorably, quickly and silently fulfilled. I realize that the barbarians of Absolute Justice are today still enraged by this. To this day they snarl at us: aristocrats, aesthetes. And every moment I see how they, the non-aristocrats and anti-aesthetes, have made their way straight for their brothers, the barbarians of the stupid and plebeian Injustice. Absolute Justice, too, is a sowing of a dragon's teeth.[15]

Other authors' attitudes toward Habsburg nepotism, or indeed corruption, were certainly more ambiguous. Doderer, however, did not condemn it either, viewing it as necessary to rule the monarchy efficiently. Introducing a character known for his fortune won in the offices responsible for the war supplies during World War I, he commented: "Oddly enough, the old Empire had not always disdained the services of such people. They actually performed a valuable function—until, at any rate, they had entrenched themselves well enough to set about shearing the sheep (that is, the government)."[16] Reminiscences of nepotism as an ordinary way of dealing with everyday problems are omnipresent in post-Austro-Hungarian literature; most typically, its image is rather cheerful, occasionally comical. Jan Parandowski, for example, in his *Niebo w płomieniach* (Heaven in the flames), made the father of the main protagonist, who happens to have been freshly promoted to *Hofrat,* seek protection for his child against the priest teaching religion: a canonry is to be available, for the priest who occupies it is dying. Fortunately, however, the *Hofrat's* son makes his way through the exams, and the aged canon miraculously recovers from his mortal illness.[17]

Austrian writers liked to approach such issues humorously. Moreover, it had been an important element of the Austrian auto-stereotype to emphasize that moralizing was not a part of the Austrian national character. Certainly, it had its origins in the old Prussian-Austrian dichotomy, or indeed animosity, based, most importantly, on Catholic-Protestant opposition. The vast majority of interwar Austrians considered themselves Germans, and they certainly seemed German to the others, but they eagerly emphasized how little they had in common with Prusso-Protestant accuracy, militarism, and puritanism. Supposedly, Austrian antipathy toward these values also owed a lot to snobbery in its Habsburg version: in this country every bourgeois dreamt of being an aristocrat, or at least a *gentilhomme,* and this meant a certain dose of tolerance in moral matters, and a strict obedience to the code of good manners. In public affairs, a certain disorder—*Schlamperei*—was considered an important pillar of the society, and this meant that the authorities and the people had to approach each other with some indulgence. *The Man without Qualities* may well be seen as a panorama of this attitude toward life, and a product of the subtle sense of humor it demands.

Hence, it is no wonder that Austro-Hungarian writers paid a lot of attention to the joyous side of life before the Great War; it is, after all, the best fuel for nostalgia in any circumstance. Of course, the entertainments Austrian culture had to offer did not evaporate with the monarchy completely. They tasted different, however, in the epoch of security and minimum inflation when the authors who narrated them had also been younger, which always helps enjoyment of both sinful and innocent pleasures. There were at least three institutions typical for prewar entertainment: the café, the theater, and the bordello. Recollecting his adolescence in Vienna, when he was a frequent guest to all of them, Zweig wrote, "It must be said that the Viennese café is a particular institution which is not comparable to any other in the world. As a matter of fact, it is a sort of democratic club to which admission costs a small price of a cup of coffee. Upon payment of this mite every guest can sit for hours on end, discuss, write, play cards, receive his mail, and above all, can go through an unlimited number of newspapers and magazines."[18] The word "democratic" is to be noted in this description: it was relatively cheap—incomparably cheaper than a membership in an English-style club, or a decent place in the theater—and probably the only place where one could get acquainted with respectable citizens without an invitation. This was why the café was so precious to Zweig when he was still a *gymnasium* student and dreaming with a teenage determination of meeting writers and artists. In the era before telephones, many people, including famous ones, had their *jours fixés* in their favorite café, and could have been approached relatively easily, although being invited to the table was, of course, a rare honor. The cafés, with their liberalism and endless, smoky, intellectual and artistic discussions were a symbol of Viennese culture.

This culture radiated throughout the entire Austrian—that is, Cisleithanian—part of the monarchy, whereas Transleithania copied Viennese patterns in a slightly modified Budapest version. The cultural-aesthetic snobbery, oriented toward the capital, may actually be considered a substitute of shadowy Habsburg patriotism. It was not much less passionate than nationalism, it outlived the monarchy for many decades, and it managed to coexist with nationalisms of its successor states smoothly. Fascination with Viennese cultural life and entertainments is omnipresent in post-Austro-Hungarian literature. Its center, apparently, was the opera and the theater, particularly the Burgtheater. Elias Canetti, the future Nobel Prize winner, supposed that his mother—a Jew from Bulgaria, who spent many years in England and Switzerland—worshipped this institution in a religious manner, and that her pious enthusiasm for it surpassed the respect she had for the Judaic tradition.[19] The theater and the classical German culture it promoted were her patriotism or, perhaps, her religion.

After the massive rebuilding of Vienna alongside the newly created Ringstrasse in the 1880s, the city virtually became a pattern for provincial architects, who constructed their versions of the famous opera house, the new Burgtheater and the railway stations in such local capitals as Prague, Lviv, Cracow, and Zagreb. Smaller cities could not afford such luxuries, but a Viennese-style café was to be found in any town that also had a railway station. Roth, who traveled a lot throughout the monarchy, wrote:

> All little stations in all little provincial towns looked alike throughout the old Austro-Hungarian Empire. Small and painted yellow, they were like lazy cats lying in the snow in winter and in the sun in summer, protected by the glass roof over the platform, and watched by the black double eagle on its yellow background... The one coffeehouse in Zlotogrod, the Café Habsburg, situated on the ground floor of the Hotel zum Golden Baren where I was staying, looked very much like the Café Wimmerl in the Josefstadt where I was accustomed to meet my friends in the afternoon.[20]

Despite all his nostalgia for the monarchy, however, not all of Roth's memories of it were idyllic. Born in a petit bourgeois Jewish family in the town of Brody, the last one before the Russo-Austrian frontier, which was considered the frontier of European civilization by many, he had his doubts about the splendor of the capital city. He bitterly remarked, "The brilliant variety of the Imperial Capital and Residence was quite visibly fed... by the tragic love which the Crown lands bore to Austria: tragic because forever unrequited... So much trouble and so much pain so freely offered up as though it were a matter of course and in the natural order of things, so as to ensure that the center of the Monarchy should be universally acclaimed as the home of grace, happiness and genius."[21] The provinces were, indeed, overshadowed by the imperial capital, and the more they tried to copy from it, the more it was evident how helpless their efforts were. Tadeusz Żeleński, one of the most prominent figures of the interwar literary scene in Poland, who had spent his youth in Galician Cracow, recollected that "there was some organic sadness, some, one might say, infection of sadness" in this ancient Polish capital. "The bourgeoisie," he observed "preferred the bigot Biedermeier style. If there was some 'debauchery,' it was not lively, it did not fuel business and did not provide a living for hundreds of people; it was shameful and ugly. The proximity of Vienna was disastrous: one sought any pretext to go to Vienna, rather than drink a bottle of wine in Cracow."[22]

Bigotry, however, had powerful enemies in Austria even before the Great War. In literature, it was most famously attacked by Arthur Schnitzler, who scandalized contemporary public opinion with his stories and dramas portraying adulterers, sex addicts, and prostitutes. His literary production won him the friendship of Sigmund Freud, whose theories he reciprocally supported. In the first years of the century Karl Kraus, the enfant terrible of Viennese journalism, shocked his contemporaries with his public campaign against penalizing prostitution, a ubiquitous phenomenon in big cities of the time, which, nevertheless, was ignored by the official press. Prewar sexual morality was, eventually, heavily criticized by interwar authors, including these who generally sympathized with the monarchy. Zweig devoted a lot of space in *The World of Yesterday* to this issue: the sexual emancipation of the youth following the Great War was for him an indisputable change for the better—perhaps the only one he acknowledged. He emphasized that the double, and indeed false, morality of the bourgeoisie actually enforced the popularity of prostitution, and he pitied both the prostitutes, for their poverty, and their clients, terrorized by fear of the venereal diseases.[23] Similarly, but in a slightly more pathetic manner, Zegadłowicz criticized the youth's innocence in "the most beautiful matters of the body"; he did not, however, seem to believe that the problem had been solved by the interwar time. Moreover, despite his socialist and anticlerical convictions, in his novel he described two "lyrical and idyllic" bordellos, both of them perfectly petit bourgeois: clean, orderly, and frugal. Apparently, he expressed all his anger against Austro-Hungarian sexual morality in the passages concerning the matrimonial life of the cantina owner of the local garrison. "During their numerous impregnations," his wife was supposed to have been stubbornly staring at a portrait of the emperor Franz Joseph, loyally attempting to evoke some similarity between the monarch and her future offspring.[24] Evidently, Zegadłowicz was happy to link this popular superstition with the poor woman's respect for the imperial-royal family. He would have been extremely pleased to have read a popular biography of the empress Elisabeth, Franz Joseph's wife, by his contemporary Egon Corti. Elisabeth,

Corti informed us, suffered numerous reproaches from her mother-in-law (the two empresses did not like each other, for sure) because during her pregnancy she kept a couple of parrots in her apartments, and the dowager empress was afraid that her grandchildren might inherit some of their physical features.[25] Perhaps what she unconsciously had in mind was the famous oversized Habsburg nose, which the enemies of the dynasty found proof of its genetic degeneration, resulting from the custom of marrying close relatives.

In that epoch writers frequently used sexual motifs to condemn the moral standards of their contemporaries, particularly the social condition of women, whose sexuality was still a taboo. Dostoyevsky's Sonya, the good prostitute; Tolstoy's Anna Karenina, the innocent adulteress; and Hardy's Tess, the mistreated lover, were already classics by that time. The brothels, of course, served as symbols of social inequality and oppression, and fictional characters who enjoyed some sympathy from their authors carefully avoided visiting these highly stigmatized and yet ubiquitous institutions. Astonishingly, however, some Austrian authors chose them as settings symbolizing the monarchy itself. In *The Radetzky March* the main protagonist, the young lieutenant von Trotta, experiences a sort of patriotic revelation in the salon of the brothel he visits with his colleagues from the regiment, because this profane space is decorated by the portrait of the emperor Franz Joseph, whom he admires so much. Franz Werfel made it even more straightforward. In his story *Das Trauerhaus,* the owner of a cozy bordello for the petty officials in Prague dies on the day the archduke Franz Ferdinand is murdered, and so the imminent closing up of the business becomes a metaphor for the decline of the monarchy. "Do the great powers of this world leave its stage more spectacularly? It seems to them that they are still fighting a war, but they are being dissolved and dismembered before they realize it," inquires the narrator, anticipating the fate of Austria-Hungary. However, the story does not end with this melancholic night, when all the clients and staff get drunk recollecting the past glory; it continues with the adventures of one of the employees. In the postwar era, "when the Negro saxophones were roaring" and the ladies on the streets were uncovering their bodies more shamelessly than the prewar prostitutes, she becomes a theater star and the wife of a deputy to the parliament. Her husband is known as an idealist, "for he hasn't yet been involved in any financial scandal," and he supports a bill against prostitution. "Most desirably," concludes the narrator sarcastically, "he should be promoted to a minister with the next reconstruction of the government."[26] The story is certainly not a masterpiece, and hence it clearly mirrors the ambiguity of the author's attitude toward Austria-Hungary. On the one hand, comparing it to a brothel was surely not a compliment. And still, the institution was quite more cozy and cheerful, and everyone cared about courtesy and appearances. On the other hand, it seemed quite innocent in comparison with the postwar era, when sin and corruption became shameless and fashionable. The bitter irony that Werfel had for the monarchy was tame in contrast to the furious mockery he reserved for its successors.

Waiting for the Apocalypse

Literary fiction explored the decline and fall of Austria-Hungary in its own way. Whereas historians attempted to explain it, determining its causes and imagining its alternatives, fiction focused on the individual experience. This experience was dominated by the Great War, which killed millions of Europeans and left many more shocked, disillusioned about the nature of modern civilization, and ruined. In short, the passing of the Habsburg monarchy was accompanied by a drama more tragic and spectacular than anyone could have imagined in the summer of 1914. Horrible as it was, it was also an opportunity for ambitious writers to explore the issue that everyone considered breathtaking. Millions of "ordinary people" took part in the most disastrous military conflict yet; millions of individual experiences became tragic in a way that everyone acknowledged. In short, there was a lot of work for writers, and the first stage of it—that is, attracting the attention of the public—had been completed by history. In more peaceful times, an average reader of fiction expects that something unusual will soon happen in the story; the readers of stories concerning the last years of Austria-Hungary knew it would be the apocalypse. This was, of course, a challenge for the authors; nevertheless, having well-informed readers is always an advantage. Likewise, in more peaceful times authors have to try hard to convince their readers that the events they are narrating are fascinating or terrifying. In contrast, Joseph Roth could have trusted his readers to understand, when he laconically commented on the meeting of the Austrian and Russian officers a few months before the war: "And none of the Tsar's officers, and none of the officers of His Apostolic Majesty knew then that over the glass bumpers from which they drank Death had already crossed his bony invisible hands."[27] Most probably, all of them knew an officer who had perished during the war, and most of them realized how naïvely the military had imagined, in 1914, the future conflict. The writer had only to skillfully stimulate their imagination to make his point.

Let us, however, begin chronologically. Before the war there was the crisis. In contrast to historians, novelists did not really try to link them. The inner political crisis of the monarchy went practically unnoticed for many of its citizens, and it was too abstract to be responsible for the apocalyptic experience of the war.

The Radetzky March is full of fatalism and a sense of doom from its first page to the last. Its main characters are victims of fate, and at a certain point they realize that and accept the verdict. There is only one of them who seems upset about it; moreover, he is able to conceptualize their problems and link them with the decline of the monarchy. It is Count Chojnicki, a Polish aristocrat from Galicia, void of national feelings and full of loyalty toward the monarchy. Actually, his theories are a little extravagant, and his interlocutors seem to be ignoring them, or perhaps they are unable to understand them. This makes him a perfect prophet, an Austro-Hungarian Sibyl, disgusted with both the present and the future he predicts. His analyses and his prophecies are appropriately chaotic. They are worth quoting at length:

> This empire's had it. As soon as the Emperor says good night, we'll break up into a hundred pieces. The Balkans will be more powerful than we will. All the peoples will set up their own little dirty statelets, and even the Jews will proclaim a King in Palestine. Vienna stinks the sweat of democrats, I can't stand to be on the Ringstrasse any more. Ever since they got their red flags, the workers have stopped working. The mayor of Vienna is a churchgoing janitor. The clergy's desperate to ingratiate itself with the people, you can hear the sermon in Czech if you please. In the Burgtheater they put on Jewish garbage, and they ennoble one Hungarian toilet-manufacturer a week.... This age does not want us any more! This age wants to establish autonomous nation states! People stopped believing in God. Nationalism is the new religion. People don't go

to church. They go to nationalist meetings. . . . The German Kaiser will still rule if God deserts him; by the grace of the nation, it would then be. But the Emperor of Austria-Hungary may not be deserted by God. And now God has deserted him![28]

Apparently, Roth equipped Chojnicki with some of his own anger, and the extravagant count also appears in his other novels. However, Chojnicki's fierce philippics hardly make an apology for the monarchy. His opinions may be painfully insightful, but they express mere frustration, and mirror the narrowness of the empire's social basis. The first plural, the imperial-and-royal "we" he employs, hardly refers to anyone but denationalized aristocrats like himself, and the imperial-and-royal officers, whose duty is to stay loyal. The Czechs and the Jews, the democrats and the manufacturers, the churchgoers and the nonbelievers—they are all excluded from Austro-Hungarian patriotism. The count is a paradox, for he has been portrayed as a fundamentalist who was the only one who realized the obsoleteness and inadequacy of the values he represented. He stood for Joseph Roth's helplessness, despair, and inability to explain what went wrong with his beloved monarchy—or perhaps his refusal to acknowledge its flaws.

Other authors did their best to do the same, with various results. Zweig tried to reconstruct the atmosphere of social turmoil, and the growing tension in the monarchy in the years before the war. It seems, nevertheless, that he understood it much less than "the feeling of security" of the bourgeoisie, to whom he himself belonged, which fully trusted in the stability of the Habsburg political system. For example, he claimed,

> A remarkable shifting began to prepare itself in our old sleepy Austria. The masses, which had silently and obediently permitted the liberal middle classes to retain the leadership for decades, suddenly became restless, organized themselves and demanded their rights. And it was just in the last decade that politics broke into the calm of easy living with sharp and sudden blasts. The new century wanted a new order, a new era. . . . All the underground cracks and crevices between the classes and races which the age of conciliation had so laboriously patched up, broke open once again and widened into abysses and chasms. In reality it was during the last decade preceding the new century that the war of all against all began in Austria.[29]

His reasoning is perfectly correct—and it is perfectly clear that it was written by someone who had observed the events from "the calm of easy living" and presumably refused to acknowledge the significance of the process until after the war, when it became a public secret. Zweig, in contrast to Chojnicki, was a progressive liberal, who had a lot of sympathy for "the masses" and no prejudices against what he vaguely called "a new order." He did not dare to call this new order a disorder, and yet he believed in the mysterious "age of conciliation." Historically speaking, what he probably had in mind was the age of absolutism, and the first decades after the Agreement of 1867, when German-Magyar domination in the monarchy remained unchallenged, and socialists were still considered dangerous criminals. The literary effect he achieved, however, was the juxtaposition of the "age of conciliation" with "the war of all against all," reminiscent of the time before and after the judgment of Paris, and before and after the tower of Babel.

Musil, of course, was much wittier, but not much more conclusive, even though he was the author of the melancholic-sarcastic aphorism "God withdrew his credit from Kakania."[30] *The Man without Qualities* is full of remarks on the problems troubling this twin sister of Austria-Hungary. Some of them, however, are purely humorous, some surpass reason and involve metaphysics, and some are parodies—which occasionally means a fusion of the preceding two. It also remains unclear whether he was perfidious, or careless enough to have included some false statistics concerning the prewar time, and introduced a number of ahistorical details, such as radio and streets jammed with cars. The main characters of the novel belong to the social elite of the monarchy. Among them, there is a certain Count Leinsdorf, who represents the authorities and the same social group to which Count Chojnicki belonged: the supranational aristocracy that considered Austria-Hungary its home. Still, Leinsdorf is an intended parody of an aristocrat, and although he has good manners, a lot of respect for culture, and a great deal of Habsburg patriotism, he is certainly not perspicacious; one can actually suppose that the count's intelligence is rather limited. He observes "the existence of certain 'displeasing phenomena of public nature,'" but reacts to them simply with the official optimism, "and he waited for them to disappear of their own accord."[31] One of these phenomena was the rising of national antagonisms and anti-Semitism. Still, the majority of the situations when Musil mentioned them are supposed to be comical rather than tragic. For example, the daughter of Leo Fischel, the director of Lloyd's Bank who believes in progress, falls in love with a pan-German, racist student, and becomes an enthusiast of Aryan racial purity, causing a lot of irritation and the despair of her Jewish parents. The narrator's attitude toward such problems is more than ambiguous—on the one hand, he mocks the old-fashioned worshippers of reason and progress who underestimated them; on the other hand, he seems to find them artificial and dull himself. Perhaps one conclusion drawn from *The Man without Qualities* about the crisis in Austria-Hungary could be that it was natural, since the entire elite of this country was composed of clumsy, pathetic, and childishly naïve figures.

To be sure, Musil also claimed that modernity and Austria-Hungary did not go smoothly together. But he was desperately vague about it, as if he wished to emphasize that such terms as "the new" and "change" are always relative, and they are most probably a trompe l'oeil, an illusion of the perspective. Thus, he was highly ambivalent about the "new people and new ideas," as seen in the following:

> These people and these ideas were not wicked. No, far from it. It was only that the good was adulterated with a little too much of the bad, the truth with error, and the meaning with a little too much of the spirit of accommodation. . . . a mysterious disease had consumed the earlier period's little seedling of what was going to be genius, but everything sparkles with novelty, and in the end one can no longer tell whether the world has grown worse or whether it is merely that one has grown older oneself. When that point is reached, a new time has definitely arrived.[32]

In the final analysis, we do not learn too much about "the mysterious disease" that inflicted the citizens of the monarchy. One thing Musil claimed for sure was that Kakania became obsolete and outdated because of it—but he did not find it a reason for despair; he rather seemed intrigued by this fact, and struggled intellectually with it, obtaining disputable results. A few hundred pages later he returned to this problem and explained that it was nationalism that undermined the pillars of the monarchy. As noted, nationalism did not scare him. Actually, one could add that while writing the novel he sympathetically observed the rise of the young Nazi movement, which disappointed him soon after Hitler took power. Nevertheless, it seems that Musil viewed the nationalism of the Habsburg nationalities as a sort of joke of Providence, which outwitted the old Franz Joseph, who had thought himself as its representative:

> But when God withdrew His credit from Kakania, He did something special in that He made all its nationalities realize the difficulties of civilization. They had been sitting prettily like bacteria in their culture-medium, without worrying whether the sky was as round overhead as it ought to be, or alike; but all at once they had begun to feel they were in a tight place. . . . And so it was easy for the intellectuals, after they had persuaded themselves that it would all be different if each nation within the Empire had its own way of life, to convince the Kakanian national minorities of the same thing. This was, in fact, a sort of substitute for religion, or a substitute for the dear good emperor in Vienna, or simply an explanation of the incomprehensible fact that there were seven days in the week.[33]

There are more passages like that in the novel: witty, ironic, and inconclusive. One could suppose that Musil wrote his impressive, unfinished, multivolume book about Kakania simply in order to demonstrate his distance from Austria, Austrian history, politics, and debates. Does it mean he did not care for the old Austria? He certainly considered it unique, an exception among states that deserved special attention, for some universal phenomena that are normally unnoticed can be better observable in this peculiar environment. It could apparently be compared to a sick person—Musil being a student of medicine rather than a family member.

As I noted, post-Austro-Hungarian writers hardly attempted to integrate the Great War that annihilated the monarchy into the story of its crisis. Evidently, they resembled the majority of the interwar historians of the monarchy in this respect. Most probably, such an intellectual operation would be intolerable for them, for assuming that there was a causal relation between the inner crisis of the monarchy and the war would imply blaming the authorities for its outbreak. As Zweig bitterly remarked about his generation,

> Then the people had unqualified confidence in their leaders; no one in Austria would have ventured the thought that the all-high Em-

peror Franz Joseph, in his eighty-third year, would have called his people to war unless from direct necessity, would have demanded such a sacrifice of blood unless evil, sinister and criminal foes were threatening the peace of the Empire. . . . A mighty respect for the "authorities," the ministers, the diplomats, and for their discernment and honesty still animated the simple man. If war had come, then it could only have come against the wishes of their own statesmen; they themselves were not at fault, indeed no one in the entire land was at fault.[34]

Interestingly, although Zweig openly suggested that he realized at that point that the war did not actually come against "the wishes of the statesmen," he did not see any connection to the inner troubles of the monarchy either. The writer, who briefly served in the Austrian propaganda unit during the war and then became an open pacifist and left the country, preferred to view the war as a sort of international conspiracy, or perhaps madness, of the men in power—a legitimate perspective, indeed. Moreover, he forgot to add that it was not only "the simple man" who refused to acknowledge any responsibility for the war: most intellectuals did so as well. Still, the question of why the war had to come, and who was responsible, remained unclear, and the gigantic scale of this most tragic episode in modern history certainly contributed to this state of mind. The majority of historians has not reached an agreement upon these questions even today, so there is no point in blaming authors like Zweig for their indecisiveness between their sentiments for the monarchy and the shocking effects of the war.

Heimitio von Doderer was certainly an exception among Austrian writers, for he did not avoid highly critical opinions on this subject in his novels. In his *Strudlhofsteige*, he described a discussion about the assassination of Archduke Franz Ferdinand in Sarajevo: an ex–army major recollects the bellicose and romantic mood among the Habsburg officers, who expected the war to be a noble adventure, and desired revenge on the Serbs whom they viewed "like the Trojans who captured Helena." This was the standard image of the summer of 1914, emphasizing the naïvety and innocence of the military, and thus waiving the problem of responsibility for the conflict. However, the major is opposed by a young, intelligent man, who argues that "there has never been a situation in Europe which had to cause war. It is the pathetic parlor of those who have interest in it: politicians, generals,

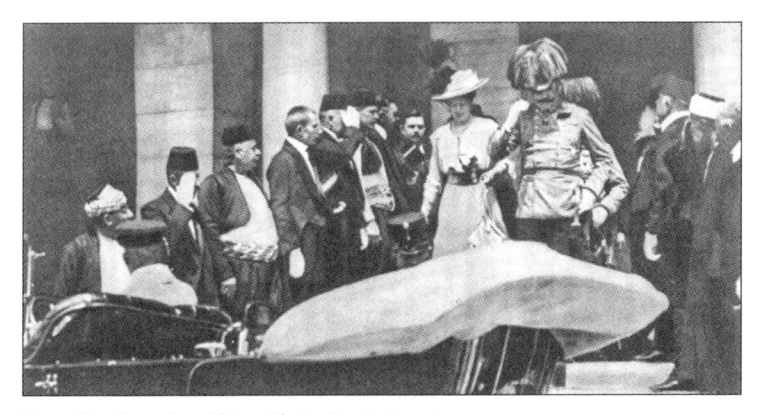

Franz Ferdinand and his wife Sophie in Sarajevo

bigheads, and historians, or those people in whose heads the newspapers' language bubbles like water in the toilet." The young man continues his reasoning, claiming that the assassination of the archduke was Austria's perfect opportunity for reconciliation with Britain.[35] Obviously, these are only the young man's opinions and it would be an overstatement to argue that they perfectly mirrored Doderer's. Still, the young man is neither an idiot nor a knave, and it seems we are being invited to like him and take his words seriously.

In *The Demons*, Doderer's most important novel, it is the narrator who bitterly comments on the question of the responsibility for the war and its consequences: "For intelligence had failed.... Intelligence had not been able to prevent the World War and its unfortunate conclusion. Intellectuals, with their gift for language, had done the talking for the inarticulate people. And they had spoken evilly, had preached madness. Afterward a general hatred for every kind of authority erupted. It manifested itself not only as rebellion but as a kind of ostentatious rowdiness."[36] Other authors preferred to suggest that the war came unexpectedly. It would be unfair, however, to claim, as I implied above, that they did so simply to avoid discussing its causes and the responsibility for its outbreak. There were, after all, enough discussions on the "war guilt question" among historians, journalists, politicians, and other "bigheads," as Doderer put it. Moreover, after four years of exhausting, bloody fighting, the dissolution of Austria-Hungary, revolutions, and the formation of the successor states, few people still cared how all had begun. The war was much more than a political issue. As Joseph Roth noted, "the Great War which is now, in my opinion, rightly called the World War, not only because the whole world was involved in it but also because, as a result of it, we each lose a world, our own world."[37] The war was, first and foremost, a cataclysm, a phenomenon escaping human understanding. This is why in *The Radetzky March* the news about the assassination of Archduke Franz Ferdinand reaches the Galician garrison during an open-air ball, interrupted by a storm. Roth chose this old, unequivocal, and telling metaphor to emphasize the supernatural character of the events, which surpassed his contemporaries' imagination. The Austro-Hungarian officers, hosted by Count Chojnicki, cannot understand the significance of the news, exactly as they cannot see the first lightning, which they mistakenly take for fireworks or "Chinese lanterns."[38] Or perhaps they simply did not want to stop dancing and start fighting? Interestingly, the same news reached Zweig in a similar setting: during a folk fest on the occasion of Saints Peter and Paul Day. There was a local orchestra and there was dancing, too; only Count Chojnicki and the fictional storm were not present. Still, Roth's fictional reconstruction and Zweig's memory of this ominous day are strikingly similar. The local folks, whom Zweig observed, were even less ready to grasp the consequences of the archduke's death than the officers from Roth's novel. And after a few moments of nervous hesitation they resumed drinking and dancing, because the weather was still perfect, and because "Franz Ferdinand lacked everything that counts for real popularity in Austria; amiability, personal charm and easy-goingness."[39]

What followed was the deterioration of Austria-Hungary, and "the end of the world" for these who considered it their motherland. Even those who had other motherlands from which to choose, however, and after 1918 eagerly identified themselves with one of the successor states, were impressed by the totality of the change. In the prologue to his *Salt of the Earth* Wittlin noted,

> The black, two-headed bird, the eagle of the triple crown, clasps in his talons a golden apple and a naked sword. Why did he loom so suddenly above our heads, darkening the sky with the stretch of his sable plumes? . . . He slipped from the red seals of the baptism, the marriage, and the death certificates. He took sudden flight from

my tattered certificate of citizenship. He disappeared from the judicial sentence, condemning me to a fine of ten crowns for willfully crossing the railway line. He escaped from the brass buttons of the postman, from the cap of the Treasury watchman, from the helmet of the gendarme. And so, bearing the sword, he hovered over our heads, like some giant airplane.[40]

Ethnic and political affiliation mattered a lot when the Great War was narrated. It left no room for those who wished to stay neutral. Some authors patriotically sympathized with the cause of the monarchy, some emphasized the horrors of the conflict, and some welcomed Austria's disaster with joy and satisfaction. Naturally, the first, like so many authors of war stories before and after, often sacrificed artistic value and psychological credibility for the sake of patriotic emotions and idealization of heroism. Adventures of young, brave men who fight desperately for their country, honor, and the attention of some beautiful ladies who share their moral code, may in the end seem kitschy for modern readers who happen to also know some of the great antiwar novels by authors of the "lost generation." What saved such narratives about the Austrian soldiers from being indisputably trite, however, was the peculiar fate of their country, the premonition of the imminent apocalypse of "their world." A perfect example of such a story is *Die Standarte* (The flag), by Alexander Lernet-Holenia. Its main protagonist is a young cavalry officer who serves in Serbia in the last days of the Great War. He is animated by unlimited and unreflective loyalty to the Habsburg dynasty, and supreme love for an aristocratic girl. He is confronted by an older officer, a German who plays the role of a Sibyl, resembling the one that Chojnicki fulfills in Roth's novels. His friend explains to him some basic facts about the ethnopsychology of Central Europe. Austrians, he claims, are pessimists in comparison to the dashing Germans, because of their experience with the "colonized" peoples of the region. Those people, "the Polish and Ukrainian peasants," do not understand that "the fate of Germany and Austria is the world's fate" and hence their loyalty to the authorities is uncertain. Accordingly, one day, when rumors about the revolutions and the armistice reach their unit, the soldiers refuse to obey orders—and this is "the end of the world," as the narrator puts it: "the visible remained still, but the invisible was undergoing a profound change, the world was reshaping inside of the people, it was deteriorating and breaking down."[41] Morally devastated, the young hero rescues his regiment's flag, and carries it back to Vienna only to find out that the imperial and royal family has just left the Schönbrunn palace. The monarchy is no more, his world is over, and he burns up the flag, symbolizing his loyalty and honor, in the fireplace of the abandoned palace.

A much more artistically successful example of post-Austro-Hungarian literature is *3 November 1918*, a drama by Franz Theodor Csokor. It is set in a sanatorium for Austro-Hungarian officers in the mountains that soon will become the Austro-Yugoslav border, during the two days when the monarchy breaks up. When the news reaches the multinational corps, the officers first cannot believe it, and then they immediately acquire their "new" national identities, their new loyalties. Their sense of comradeship and interpersonal relationships quickly deteriorates; now some of them are even enemies, no one cares for each other anymore. The commander commits suicide, the others hurry to join the newly formed national armies, following the symbolic order *Abmarsch aus Österreich-Ungarn!* The two who are left, an Austrian and a Slovene, raise arms against each other, foreseeing the future territorial conflict between their new-old motherlands.[42] The drama is simple, and yet touching: the dissolution of Austria equals the dissolution of the human community, the breakdown of a civilization. It is not a naïve apology for the Habsburgs, nor for the imperial and royal army and its virtues. The officers turn out to be weak men, driven and governed by forces they neither control nor understand. Under the Austrian rule, these forces made them cooperate—even though this meant fighting a war against people whom they neither knew nor hated; now they were supposed to hate their comrades too. If the play were not so politically engaged on the so-called wrong side, and if it were not so historically accurate, it would actually resemble the theater of the absurd in the style of Ionesco or Beckett.

Let us finally have a look at some writers who wholeheartedly hated the monarchy and rejoiced in its demise. They were, to be sure, many; however, as I claimed, most of them did not care for Austria-Hungary anymore, once it was over. The monarchy did not really fit the role of a demonic enemy: few people had feared it when it still existed, few had suffered real oppression from it, and now it was dead. Moreover, it apparently died because of its own impotence, incompetence, and lack of stamina. Nonetheless, a writer who successfully managed to demonize Austria-Hungary was certainly Jaroslav Hašek, the author of *The Good Soldier Švejk*. And yet his success was only partial: few of his readers end the book inspired by rage against the monarchy. Švejk is simply too funny for that; he is probably the most ridiculous soldier ever created, although one can suppose that many such warriors have indeed fought behind the lines of many fronts. Švejk is a caricature of a soldier, and his skillfully simulated, fantastic stupidity and straightforwardness mercilessly unmask the absurdities governing the institution he is supposed to serve: the imperial and royal army.

Nevertheless, *The Good Soldier* was intended as a bitter critique of Austria-Hungary. The book is full of spiteful remarks about all who had any sympathy or loyalty for it. Germans, Hungarians, and Jews are mocked furiously. In fact, no one who is not a Czech patriot animated by anti-Habsburg feeling is spared. Habsburg patriotism or any signs of loyalty to the monarchy are presented as a sort of mental and moral feebleness or simply as irredeemable stupidity. One such awkward character is Švejk's immediate superior, Lieutenant Lukaš, whose attitude to his national identity the author analyzed in detail: "Lieutenant Lukaš was a typical regular officer of the ramshackle Austrian monarchy. The cadet school had turned him into a kind of amphibian. He spoke German in society, wrote German, read Czech books, and when he taught in the course for one-year volunteers, all of whom were Czechs, he told them in confidence: 'Let's be Czechs, but no one need know about it. I'm a Czech too.'"[43] When Hašek mentioned someone showing any signs of Austrian war patriotism, he dismissed such a person with less than a sentence. All of them are pitiful, irritating, and ridiculous, like the rich Czech lady from the Association of Gentlewomen for the Religious Education of the Troops, who "described how she saw the religious education of a soldier. Only when he believes in God and has religious feelings can a soldier fight bravely for His Imperial Majesty and not fear death, because then he knows that paradise awaits him. She babbled on and said a few more stupid things like this."[44] Furthermore, Lieutenant Lukaš seems a relatively reasonable and amiable person in comparison to his own superiors, who are almost invariably German-Austrian, are all detestable, and occasionally earn a comment like, "Colonel Friedrich Kraus, who bore the additional title of von Zillergut after a village in the district of

Salzburg which his ancestors had already completely fleeced in the eighteenth century, was a most venerable idiot. . . . If we analyze his mental capacities, we reach the conclusion that they were not a bit better than those which had made the big-lipped Franz Joseph Hapsburg celebrated as a patent idiot."[45] Except for expressing his disgust with all things Austrian—such as aristocratism and stupidity—Hašek took delight in emphasizing the disloyalty of the Czechs. Czechs soldiers are animated by hope that Russians have already taken Budapest. Czech civilians mock the emperor and wish him to lose the war: "His Imperial Majesty won't win this war," an old Czech vagabond says. "There's no enthusiasm for it at all, because, as our schoolmaster in Strakonice says, he wouldn't have himself crowned. Now he talks as much soft soap as he likes. When you promised you'd be crowned you should have kept your word, you old bastard!"[46] This is a reference to the fact that Franz Joseph did not crown himself the King of Bohemia after the Compromise with Hungarians in 1867, fearing that the Czechs would demand similar conditions. Švejk and his Czech comrades hate Hungarians even more than they despise Austrians: the Hungarians, after all, fought this war with much enthusiasm and sacrifice. Moreover, when Švejk's unit finally arrives at the front in Galicia, they turn out to be anti-Semitic and anti-Polish as well: there is mutual distrust between them and the local population, whom they occupy rather than liberate from the Russians. The villagers do not want to give up their food to the brave Czech soldiers, but Švejk easily outsmarts and terrorizes them, performing fake preparations for the execution of the Polish "traitor." A Jew, however, cheats them and obtains a "horrific price" for his cow, "which was only skin and bones"—and so he joins the cohort of fictional Jewish characters created to be hated for their unscrupulous greed.[47] This is not to suggest that Hašek was a Czech chauvinist, nor that he made his lovable, frivolous hero a chauvinist. On the contrary, the author was actually an anarchist, who converted to communism in revolutionary Russia and served in the Red Army propaganda unit with much enthusiasm, although he was certainly also a devoted Czech patriot. Like all good writers, however, Hašek was politically incorrect, and for him all means were appropriate to ridicule and defame the Habsburg monarchy. Apparently, what irritated most Czechs about the monarchy was its being an affront to Czech national pride, and he played this card as ruthlessly as he could, employing a panoply of national prejudices, flavored with class antagonisms, obscenities, absurdities, and some jewels of military stupidity. Paradoxically, *The Good Soldier Švejk* has become an international antiwar classic in spite of its being so profoundly Czech. Furthermore, although it is probably the fiercest anti-Habsburg polemic ever written, the image of the monarchy did not suffer from it too much: many of its modern readers view it as a satire against the militant state as such; perhaps more clumsy, disorganized and laughable than other states.

Still, *The Good Soldier* aimed to discredit the monarchy in Czech eyes. Hence, it tells us virtually nothing about the non-Czech anti-Habsburg or antiwar feelings. Let us, therefore, conclude by noting that there were other literary images of "good soldiers." The Polish version, for example, was *C. K. Dezerterzy* (Imperial-and-royal deserters) by Kazimierz Sejda. In contrast to Hašek, Sejda emphasized the supranational character of the war experience. His novel is a story of a group of imperial and royal soldiers, each representing a different nationality, who flee their unit and travel through the monarchy with false documents. Lacking Švejk's genius, they nevertheless experience the same stupidity, bestiality and fanaticism of the Austro-Hungarian military, and they make parallel use of the absurdities of the war administration. The story is not so obsessively anti-Habsburg as it is full of compassion for all who suffered from the war, and a much more serious criticism of those who were giving orders from behind the lines and "bearing a brooch with the 'God, punish England' inscription, while simultaneously locating their savings in British banks."[48] Austria-Hungary in Sejda's novel is corrupted and dehumanized by the terrible, irrational and bloodthirsty war. Its horrendousness is not immanent. Neither is it a disgusting monster by definition, but only a country that could have been a tolerable place to live, if it did not demand its citizens to fight and die so pointlessly. The monarchy, in other words, is a state that chose an ugly agony for itself, and its citizens refused to participate. Sejda wrote, "One could feel the hope for the imminent, tragic end of four years of fighting in the air; one could see it on the faces of the soldiers, and of the women who were waiting in the long queues to get some bread for their children. The specter of defeat was raising its dark wings over the immense body of the Habsburg monarchy."[49] Another Polish anti-Habsburg and pacifist novel was a collection of war stories under the title *Zielona Kadra* (The green cadre), by Jerzy Kossowski.

Although the majority of its characters are Poles—some of them "the greens," that is, the deserters from the imperial and royal army, and some are soldiers forced to fight against the Italians, with whom they sympathize—it also stresses the supranational aspect of the Habsburg experience. All nations of the monarchy are presented as united in their passive resistance against the German-dominated government and the folly of the war. In one of the stories, a Polish and a Hungarian pilot who are in love with the same Slovene girl from Trieste drop the bombs from their plane over the sea instead of attacking some target in Venice, out of respect for this famous city. In fact, the only war hero in the book is a handicapped Italian policeman, who sacrifices his life for the motherland in a sort of kamikaze mission against the detested Austrians.[50]

Austro-Hungarian Fantasies

Post-Austro-Hungarian literature was exceptional also in its outstanding inclination toward political camouflage. The idea, of course, is not at all unique: political writers since Plato, including Thomas More and George Orwell, have commented on the situation in the countries they themselves created. They did so, however, because of censorship or in order to give their thoughts a more general impact, and to leave the joy or the terror of comparing the fruits of their imagination with the real situation to their readers. Interwar authors writing about Austria-Hungary did not have to fear censorship: the monarchy was no more, and everyone could insult it as he or she pleased. Still, some of them preferred not to call the monarchy by its real name, presenting it as a fantastic realm. However, Musil's Kakania, von Herzmanovsky-Orlando's Tarokania, and von Rezzori's Teskovina were neither utopias nor antiutopias; they were masquerades and everyone could recognize them easily. Their geographical location, history, and their political institutions openly mirrored those of the Austro-Hungarian monarchy, only the image was occasionally deformed, as if these fantastic countries were essentially more Austro-Hungarian than the monarchy itself. The monarchy, after all, was perfectly normal in so many aspects, it lived a boring life as did so many other countries, and it did not represent any ideal, but rather overwhelmingly monotonous reality. In replacing its name with a mask the writers were unmasking what was unique in it—and what constituted the flawed ideal that the monarchy represented.

Seeking the origins of the inclination of Austro-Hungarian writers for historical-political fantasies, one could point out the dramas of Hugo von Hofmannsthal or Alfred Kubin's pre-surrealist novel *The Other Side*, which tells a story of travelling to a country accessible exclusively through one's dreams. Nevertheless, the continuity between these works and the interwar literature on Kakania or Tarokania seems disputable. The latter, apparently, owed more to the absurdities and curiosities of the real Austria, fully revealed and elucidated by its downfall. Retrospectively, the monarchy seemed to many of its writers a grotesque imitation of a real state, a great power in the buffo style, and its decline appeared a comedy of errors. Some authors ironically claimed that these errors resulted exactly from the oversophisticated Habsburg nomenclature, pointing out the monarchy's complicated and incomprehensible political structure. Musil, having described the division of the monarchy into Hungary, officially called the Kingdom of St. Stephen, and Austria, which lacked any official name and was therefore called "The Kingdoms and Lands represented in the *Reichsrat*" (the Council of the Imperial Realm, i.e., the Austrian Parliament), argued that the monarchy "perished of its own unutterability."[51] Sandor Friedrich Rosenfeld (alias Roda Roda) found the issue so admirably irrational that he decided to discuss it at length in his "Österreichisch-ungarisches Staatsrecht" (The Austro-Hungarian constitution). In the story the political structure of the monarchy is being explained to a foreigner according to the following scheme: the entire monarchy consists of two parts, and each of them consists of two parts, which consist of two parts, and so on, notwithstanding the fact that some of the following divisions are unofficial and therefore top secret. The Triune Kingdom of Croatia, Slavonia, and Dalmatia, for example, is officially a part of the Lands of the Crown of St. Stephen (Transleithania), however, Dalmatia itself is divided into two parts, one of which belongs to Cisleithania; politically, moreover, the Kingdom falls into two parts: the city of Fiume (Rijeka) being under the direct control of Budapest, and the rest enjoying autonomy from Hungary (and Austria, of course). Later on, as the divisions continue, the author introduces some fantastic names of nonexistent lands and territorial units, until the interlocutor of the narrator goes out of his head, having imagined that he himself consists of two parts, one of them being represented in the *Reichsrat*.[52]

The main thread of *The Man without Qualities,* if this novel has a main thread, is constructed upon a similar intention to ridicule the most fundamental features of the Austro-Hungarian constitutional order and politics. In the book a group of upper-class, impassioned Austrian patriots organizes the so-called Parallel Action: a committee to celebrate the seventieth anniversary of Franz Joseph's rule in 1918, which could compete with the planned festivities to honor German emperor Wilhelm II. First, the sense of the absurd comes from the fact that neither the emperor nor his monarchy lived until the date of the planned anniversary. Second, the entire initiative is supposed to reveal the particularly Austro-Hungarian identity problem. Participants of the Parallel Action desperately attempt to challenge the Germans, who are naturally expected to celebrate their national spirit and their great power status. Needless to say, the Austrians do not have any comparable idea symbolizing or uniting their country, and hence they obsessively attempt to concoct one, referring to a number of depressingly abstract ideals. Accompanied by numerous comments on the dualist constitution, dividing the country into two parts which "matched each other like a red-white-and-green jacket and black-and-yellow trousers,"[53] the entire story may seem to be a cruel derision of the Habsburg political system. And still, it is a critique by an intellectual too fascinated with the uniqueness of this system to be considered its true enemy.

Absurdity as the distinctive feature of Austrian politics is even more openly ridiculed in the flamboyant novel *Maskenspiel der Genien,* by Fritz von Herzmanovsky-Orlando. The story takes place in a fantastic country called Tarokania, located somewhere in the borderlands of Austria, and as typically happens in the provinces, in some respects more Austrian than Austria proper. Tarokania is a name derived from a game of cards on which the pattern of the political mechanism of the Tarokanian government is based. Its kings and its officials are named after particular cards, and their positions depend on the role of the cards in the game. Still, it is ruled in the "old Austrian" bureaucratic manner that values secrecy and splendor of authority more than anything else. Visitors crossing the border of the country first experience this when all foreigners are carefully searched by the police, who are looking for the smugglers of a special kind of sausage. What makes the operation truly Tarokanian is that the name of the forbidden sausages is a state secret, and that everyone knows that it has never been found, and hence it is rightly supposed that it exists but only as a means of "inspiring fear and insecurity, and a way to demonstrate the power of the authorities." Pompous appearances are an obsession of the Tarokanians, who immediately become Austrians when abroad, so it may seem that the whole country is just a fabrication. Still, as one of the characters explains, the absurdities of Tarokania should not be judged by appearances: as a matter of fact they are perfectly transparent for its citizens and hence the country is in a way more normal than other countries: "In our country nothing happens a bit more unusually than elsewhere. The sequences of the events are simply more transparent, which can be confusing for foreigners. It is like theater that actually is the improved version of reality. The South is ridiculous with its disorder, the North with its order. We, the lucky fellows, are in the middle between the yashmak and the spiked helmet."[54] Notably, Herzmanovsky-Orlando's Austria is not only a country of the absurd, it is also a borderland of Homeric Greece, its spiritual continuation and its heir. Hence, in the novel the secret Austrian diplomatic expedition departs to Greece in search of the mythical omphalos—the hub of the universe. Literary critics call his novel Byzantine because of the atmosphere of mystery and the ostentatious, pompous formality. Moreover, it certainly is Byzantine if we assume that the Eastern Empire symbolizes perfect decadence in the eyes of Westerners. The author, however, seemed to appreciate the Greek "magic legacy" that constituted the historical mission of Austria, carried, as he claimed, with the assistance of Aphrodite. Apparently, the dilemma that troubled the participants of Musil's Parallel Action did not apply to Herzmanovsky-Orlando—for him irrationality and the sense of the absurd were the core of Austrian identity.

Another fictional country modeled after Austria-Hungary is Teskovina, in Georg von Rezzori's *Ein Hermelin in Tschernopol* (An Ermin in Tschernopol). More precisely, the country is a literary incarnation of the author's native province of Bukovina, the most eastern province of Cisleithania, inhabited predominantly by Romanians and Ukrainians (it was incorporated into Romania in 1919, and then into the Soviet Ukraine in 1945) but culturally dominated by Germans. Remarkably, Rezzori did not bother to invent a fictional name for its capital city. Teskovina is yet another, certainly more realistic, version of

Tarokania: located at the periphery of the empire, it also embodied its most essential features: the Byzantine inclination for ceremonies, secrets, and hierarchy, and the "most ossified bureaucracy in the world." The most characteristic aspect of local life is, again, the passion for paradoxes, which makes its deficiencies so easily tolerable for the population. The local administration, one of the characters of the novel explains, is not inefficient because of its being perfectly corrupted, it is because of a lack of any resistance and the ideal conformity of the population that deprive all official decrees of their actual meaning. He calls it a higher version of passive resistance and the truly baroque style, in which the passion for form and order arises from the assumption of their absurdity and farcicality.[55]

In short, in Teskovina we come across the most typical aspect of Austro-Hungarian politics as recorded by literary fiction: its irrationality, pretentiousness, absurd appearance, and miraculous inefficiency that nonetheless work. Moreover, all these shortcomings seem to make Austria, whatever her literary name, a livable place, especially in comparison with the well-organized, efficient monstrosity known as the so-called modern state. Paradoxically, while ridiculing the famous Austrian bureaucracy, of which the Austrian historians were so proud, the writers also praised it—it possessed, they suggested, the most precious feature a bureaucracy can have: it was harmless. This may be best illustrated by a scene from the short story "Wiosna" (Spring), by Galician author Bruno Schulz. Its main protagonist, Joseph N., bitterly disappointed by his beloved, intends to commit suicide. He is rescued by an officer who arrives to arrest him for his "standard Biblical dream," which has been detected by the imperial bureaucracy and declared illegal: the absurd order of the Habsburg monarchy once again paradoxically saves one of its citizens against the natural chaos of the existence.[56]

There were, to be sure, authors who did not lack fantastic imagination and still sincerely detested the Austrian political order. Emil Zegadłowicz, for example, in the prologue to his most famous novel, gave a historical account of the sociopolitical situation in the monarchy, written from the perspective of a historian from a distant future, constructing his narrative from the fragments of "ancient" texts and archeological sources. The imagined author classifies the monarchy as "the ideal militaristic and Semitic-theocratic state," in which "the privileged—i.e., those in uniforms—easily exploited the population financially and symbolically." As the narration proceeds, however, the democratic ideas of the author are challenged by his love for the grotesque:

> From age eleven, every respectable Austrian subject was raised with a love for his uniform and its glorious ideals: that the uniform of an Austrian picantropus ennobles and that the soul of the uniform is its honor: mystic and divine. And it depends, one used to say, not on the person inside of the uniform, which would eventually be understandable, but on the absurd: the buttons, the medals, the stripes and the cutting of the uniform. Credo quia absurdum est! All these irrational ingredients are fused into the irrationality of the state. The problem of uniforms is a religious problem—because it is nonsense—and it stresses the hierarchy and the splendor of the authorities, which in those remote times still originated from god.[57]

Finally, let me recall the author who created the most powerful and impressive image of Austrian bureaucracy and its methods: Franz Kafka. Kafka was neither a democrat nor an ironist. In contrast to all other authors discussed above, he did not intend to ridicule the Austrian authorities, although no other author re-created the absurdity of their actions in a comparably persuasive manner. In his two most famous novels, *The Trial* and *The Castle,* this ex–Habsburg subject described the institutions whose style strikingly resembles the one that the other authors considered typically Austro-Hungarian and mocked mercilessly. Kafka's court and Kafka's castle, representing authority as such, are also apparently irrational, and it seems that their main objective is to impress their subjects and keep them obedient, even though their expectations are ridiculously capricious in the eyes of the rational individual. Their methods also resemble those we know from other post-Habsburg literary fantasies: Byzantine pomp and obsessive secrecy, corrupted administration and the impenetrable labyrinth of hierarchies—all confusing the people rather than serving any rational purposes. The difference is that in Kafka's novels no one outsmarts the conceited and stilted officials, and the narrator himself does not unmask the absurd claims of the authorities. Taken deadly seriously, these claims are not ridiculous but horrendous. Therefore, perhaps, the abstract state that Kafka created is rarely associated with the Austria-Hungary that scarcely anyone feared, especially after its breakup. All typically Austro-Hungarian motifs he employed lose their peculiarly Habsburg character because of his pessimism, radicalism, and asceticism. Nevertheless, dark, obsessive, and terrifying as he was, he remains a literary child of the clumsy, anachronistic, and pathetic monarchy, as Adolf Hitler remains its political child.

CHAPTER FOUR

THE EMPIRE EPITOMIZED: FRANZ JOSEPH

In narratives about Austria-Hungary the person of Emperor Franz Joseph is omnipresent. Apart from his numerous biographers, he inspired political and cultural historians, essayists, authors of fiction, and memoirists. It may seem that for interwar authors, writing on any aspect of the Austro-Hungarian past without discussing his role was scarcely possible. Indeed, it appears that he symbolized his country and his time in a much more general sense than any other monarch. Such popular labels as "Napoleonic France" or "Victorian England" designate a particular period, a political tendency, or a mentality; in case of Austria-Hungary the person of Franz Joseph symbolized all of them. Eventually, for many interwar authors he simply epitomized *his* monarchy, a view shared by many of its citizens, and so his life story and his country's history became inseparable. As I shall demonstrate, his critics were all aware of this fact, and if they disapproved of some of his policies, they had to take into consideration that their criticism toward his person might easily have been confused with hostility toward the monarchy.

The special position that Franz Joseph occupied in narratives on Austria-Hungary had a number of factual reasons. First, as already mentioned, the monarchy lacked any "modern" patriotic ideology, and so the dynasty and the person of the monarch remained crucial for the ideology of its political legitimacy. After all, everybody knew that the country was a dynastic state, and that its policies were always subordinated, or at least strictly related, to the interests of the Habsburgs. Among modern historians it was A. J. P. Taylor who formulated this principle most brilliantly: "In other countries' histories the dynasties were but episodes; in the history of the Habsburg empire the nations were a complication in the history of the dynasty."[1]

Second, Franz Joseph ruled his monarchy for sixty-eight years, and at the end of his reign hardly anybody could remember any other monarch. He took care to nurture his popularity and reputation. His birthday was the most celebrated public holiday, with music, eating, and drinking for everybody throughout the realm. Portraits of the hoary, whiskered emperor were to be seen in offices, cafés, palaces, and hotels. In his later years he became so remote from reality on the one hand, and so omnipresent on the other, that he was popularly considered a semimythical figure, a symbol rather than a real person. Both Robert Musil (sarcastically) and Franz Werfel (sadly) noted that one could doubt whether Franz Joseph was still alive, or whether he had ever existed.[2] Richard von Schaukal claimed that he became "encased in his dignity like in armor" and therefore resembled a "remote star."[3] Leon Sapieha commented on the war years that "sometimes one could hear gossips, whispering that Franz Joseph had already died long ago, and that his death was kept in secret. The others, however, believed to see him soon at the front."[4]

Finally, his personal power and influence were extraordinarily strong, even by late nineteenth-century standards, partially due to his peculiar constitutional position, and partially to his "legendary" authority and ability to nominate obedient ministers. Since his youth, Franz Joseph remained a devoted autocrat: a faithful son of his mother and diligent pupil of the princes Klemens Wenzel von Metternich and Felix of Schwarzenberg, all of them devout Catholics and reactionaries. Forced to accept the agreement with Hungarians and grant the constitution in 1867, all his remaining years he carefully guarded all his prerogatives, which were many.[5] First, he fully controlled the joint Austro-Hungarian government, comprising the foreign and military affairs, and the joint ministry of finance. Second, his influence on the separate Austrian and Hungarian governments was also preponderant, especially after 1897, when the former could no longer form any parliamentary majority. Actually, also in Hungary, where the government always depended on the parliament, his prerogative was to accept the legislature, both bills voted by the parliament and those proposed by the government. Surprisingly, Franz Joseph's privileged position met with few complaints and little resistance; competing nationalities and parties preferred to seek his support and favors rather than challenge him. Interestingly, historians of the interwar period scarcely noted this phenomenon—only Joseph Redlich observed the peculiar nature of the opposition in the monarchy, which opposed governments and other parties but never the powerful monarch himself.[6]

Therefore, it does not seem astonishing that interwar authors tended to identify the person of the monarch with his country. The idea of a *unio mystica* of the monarch and the country had had a long tradition. Its most telling example was probably the Early Modern scholarly concept of *aemulatio,* a mystic similitude of two essentially different and unequal phenomena. During the Renaissance scholars used this concept to explain, or perhaps express, humanity's similarity to the gods (and the Christian God), their dependence on the stars, or their destiny as members of a particular lineage.

A number of interwar writers refer, at least rhetorically, to this concept, and suggest that Franz Joseph and *his* monarchy shared certain features and, most importantly, shared the same fate. Accordingly, with the aging of the emperor, the monarchy was weakening and declining. Karl Tschuppik, for example, claimed that "When Franz Joseph, the last link consolidating the monarchy, perished, the nationalities chose against the Habsburgs. They rendered justice to him (Sie haben ihm Recht gegeben)."[7] The former sentence can be interpreted simply as the a posteriori description, emphasizing the emperor's authority. The latter, however, openly suggests some mysterious influence of the monarch on his subjects, as if they had been waiting for his death to accomplish a plan that he would disapprove of. Leon Sapieha, who constantly mocked the monarchy, described the death of Franz Joseph with astonishing respect and a certain mysticism: "No one doubts that the last years of your rule were not cheerful at all for you, old lord. . . . You preferred to close your eyes forever, than see the legacy of your dynasty crushed."[8] Again, the developments suggested by the author are of a supernatural kind, for Franz Joseph, in contrast to his son, did not commit suicide but died of natural causes. However, the reasoning implies that Franz Joseph could not live longer than his monarchy, although if anybody chose the moment of his death, it was surely Providence. Similarly, Eugene Bagger, one of the most critical biographers of the emperor, argued that his longevity seemed intended by nature itself, who wanted to keep him alive as long as his monarchy, which "the last of the Caesars" embodied so perfectly, still existed.[9] It does not really matter whether his death was determined by the imminent fall of the monarchy, or vice versa; what was important was their mutual, supernatural, and irrational dependence. Eventually, the actual order of events precisely corresponded to the natural, supreme order, so the monarchy could not exist without Franz Joseph, and yet he, as an individual of human sensitivity, had to die *first*. In other words, as Bruno Brehm put it, "Providence spared him" the experience of the dissolution of his monarchy, "to which he devoted his whole life."[10]

The mystic kinship between Franz Joseph and Austria-Hungary in historical writing is only implied. In the literary fiction it became a phenomenon *tout court*, comprehensible for all who are able to take a close enough look. Let us, for example, regard the striking, imaginative scenes created, independently, by Franz Werfel and Józef Wittlin, of Franz Joseph signing the manifesto declaring the beginning of World War I, formulated by his ministers. Astonishingly, both authors suggested that the emperor knew that the war would be the mortal blow to his monarchy—in other words, that Providence might have spared him the view of his country's dissolution, but not the awareness of its imminent fate. Werfel put it as follows:

> The declaration of war lies on the Emperor's table. His ministers and the chief of the general staff have badgered him for days with lectures, warnings, memorials, threats. He has put them off, up to the margin of his strength. . . . He settles his horn spectacles on his nose, puts pen to the paper, and his signature, in an easy, rather elegant script, flows along beneath a text which will cost the lives of twelve million men.
>
> To sign up, to put on paper with a flourish the name of Franz Joseph—that was the essential part of his duty, through seven decades. And now he has written this last frightful signature too, knowing as no one else does, that it is a death sentence upon his empire. Then he gets up, does the Kaiser, and says, as we are told: "Well, if we must perish, at last we will do it decently and in order."[11]

An almost identical scene is to be found in the novel *Salt of the Earth*, by Józef Wittlin. Here, too, the emperor does not fully realize what sort of document he is signing, and at the same time he is the only person who understands the fatal implications of this act. Wittlin added one significant detail: after signing his first name, "Franz," the emperor cuts his finger with the pen, and a bit of royal blood drops on the document, sinking into the fresh ink.[12] Thus he emphasized the symbolic union of the monarch and his subject, the union of royal blood from the cut finger and the blood of soldiers who were to die during the war. This symbolic communion of fate is typical of the characteristics associated with Franz Joseph. Without it, suggesting that the monarch knew the fatal consequences of the decision would be absurd: why should he have accepted it, then? The only logical interpretation seems to be that Franz Joseph did not act independently but in accordance with his own and his monarchy's destiny—and that these were actually one.

Joseph Roth introduced the same motif in perhaps the most famous novel about the decline of Austria-Hungary, *The Radetzky March*. Roth overtly wrote about the hidden relation between the emperor and his monarchy, focusing on his death. What history writers only implied, in literary fiction became a certainty, realized by one of the novel's main protagonists, while he was waiting for the news from the imperial deathbed in front of Schönbrunn Palace: "His son was dead. And now the Emperor was dying. And, for the first time since Herr von Trotta had been notified of his son's death, he believed that his son had not died in vain. The Emperor cannot survive the Trottas! thought the District Commissioner. He cannot survive them! They saved his life, and he will not survive the Trottas."[13] The von Trotta family was existentially linked to Franz Joseph; the grandfather saved his life at Solferino, the son perished for him during the first weeks of the Great War. This explains why the father assumes that the emperor cannot outlive the family, consisting only of himself, an old and broken man. One could even suspect that in believing so the father finds some comfort after the death of his only son. It is, however, less clear why the son had to die. And yet Roth suggested there was still some logic in this youthful, apparently absurd, and tragic death. The most loyal and faithful of families, von Trotta may simply symbolize the monarchy, which was dying with its monarch. If the family was linked to Franz Joseph with special ties, then the youngest Trotta had to perish if his monarch was dying. Apparently, he belonged to an inner circle, which shared its emperor's fate in a fuller way than did ordinary citizens. Eventually, however, the causal relations in the novel are not very clear, as it is not a detective story but a sort of a manifesto, a "*Marseillaise* of conservatism" as Alfred Doppler has put it.[14]

Historians have frequently noted the alleged similitude between the emperor and Austria-Hungary, emphasizing that he himself, and many of his contemporaries, believed in it. Hugo Hantsch, for example, wrote: "He was by far not the only one to believe that the monarchy and his person constituted one." And he added: "He embodied the idea of a bureaucratic state [Beamtenstaat] in a most perfect and dignified manner."[15] Alfred Pribram argued similarly, "He had a deep sense of his exalted position as a ruler. To the end of his days he remained profoundly convinced that the Empire over which he ruled was *his* Empire and the peoples *his* peoples."[16] They were not simply relating some popular state of mind, as historians of the medieval ages do when they inform the reader that the people of that time believed in magic. Informing their readers about Franz Joseph's state of mind they, rather, implied that he acted as if he and his realm constituted some sort of unity, so even if this belief was not correct in terms of common sense, it nevertheless had significant impact on actual historical developments. Still, this characterization of the *communis opinio* about the emperor added a certain legendary flavor to many passages on him even in academic histories. Consciously or not, those historians acknowledged that Franz Joseph's image mattered no less than his real person.

Needless to say, novelists noticed the overwhelming symbolic significance of the person of Franz Joseph for his subjects' perception of their country. Let us, for example, regard a fragment of the best-selling novel by a Hungarian writer, Sándor Márai:

> Fifty million people found their security in the feeling that their Emperor was in bed every night before midnight and up again before five, sitting by candlelight at his desk in an American rush-bottomed chair, while everyone else who had pledged their loyalty to him was obeying the customs and the laws. . . .
>   Vienna and the monarchy made up an enormous family of the Hungarians, Germans, Moravians, Czechs, Serbs, Croats, and Ital-

Franz Joseph at Hofburg, the perfect monarch at work

ians, all of whom secretly understood that the only person who could keep order among this fantastical welter of longings, impulses, and emotions was the Emperor, in his capacity of Sergeant Major and Imperial Majesty, government clerk in sleeve protectors and Grand Seigneur, unmannerly clod and absolute ruler.[17]

Márai argued that the true significance of the emperor's person rested with his popular image. The security of the fifty million inhabitants of the monarchy, in other words, did not result from his outstanding political or diplomatic skills and achievements but from the fact that the people respected him personally—and so they acted responsibly themselves. His function, hence, seems to resemble *toutes proportions gardées*, the one ascribed to the Christian God by the enlightened philosophers. Márai notes, moreover, that the citizens of Austria-Hungary respected Franz Joseph not simply because of his imperial majesty but also because of his personal virtues, embodied in his everyday habits. And these were the virtues of a perfect bureaucrat or, if you like, an officer of middle rank: punctuality, accuracy, reliability, diligence.

Scholars also eagerly commented on apparently minor details from Franz Joseph's personal life. For a modern reader, the importance of these details may often seem enigmatic. Nevertheless, they provoked much controversy among those for whom the emperor was still a semi-legendary figure—or an ancestor of the celebrities of the pop era, if you like—and who assumed that all those details deserved a careful exegesis. First of all, the person of the monarch was supposed to perfectly embody the virtues that were also considered the pillars of his state: the bureaucratic, military, and aristocratic spirit. Almost all authors who discussed his historical role stressed that Franz Joseph spent most of his time at his desk, that he worked hard from dawn till dusk, and that he never neglected his official duties; in other words, that he was a perfect bureaucrat. Some of those eulogies may even resemble apologies for a ruler who failed, but tried so hard. On the other hand, some of them imply that the emperor undertook an almost superhuman effort to sustain his disintegrating monarchy, and that its continued existence depended solely upon his diligence, accuracy, and stubbornness.

Probably the most apologetic and detailed account of the monarch's everyday virtues is to be found in the essay "Der Herrscher, wie ich ihn gekannt," by Count Leopold Berchtold, Austria-Hungary's minister for foreign affairs, who personally composed the notorious memorandum on Serbia in July 1914. The author of another highly patriotic essay, published during the war but after Franz Joseph's death, claimed that the emperor was "permanently full of dignity, accurate, gallant and courteous, always helpful" and that in his advanced age those virtues "made him very useful in international relations."[18] The naïvety of this reasoning could seem appealing in a novel, but applied in a political essay it induced mainly sarcasm. The sarcasm, however, was of a peculiar kind, for critically disposed authors did not dismiss minor details from Franz Joseph's life as unimportant. To the contrary, they analyzed them even more carefully. According to Eugene Bagger, for example, Franz Joseph's private life proved that he was a person unable to grasp "real life," which he escaped by obsessive work. It also shows that he did not understand the true nature of his position and duties, and that he suffered from "spiritual agoraphobia."[19]

Other authors observed, a bit more precisely, that the emperor spent most of his time working on documents of minor importance, and that he exercised his power on a too-broad and detailed level, which did not allow him to concentrate on the critical issues essential for his country. For example, the author of the highly critical study *Kaiser Franz Joseph und sein Hof* analyzed the monarch's passion for the military. His knowledge of the details of his army, such as names of the commanders and their units, argued the author, "was truly impressive"; however, it brought little in the way of practical results. The emperor, he claimed, had little understanding of military strategy and his distrust of technical innovation was disastrous. Even more harmful for the military power of Austria-Hungary was his personnel policy, favoring obedient, ignorant aristocrats, such as the long-term chief of the general staff Friedrich, Count Beck. He concluded, "Such a situation among the highest military ranks is possible exclusively in an army which is supposed not to be, in its commander's eyes, a tool of militarism and imperialism, but merely a decorative and representative institution."[20] Obviously, Franz Joseph's love for the military was seen as a virtue by less-critical writers, such as Egon Corti and Hans Sokol, who emphasized on the last pages of their lengthy and yet extremely successful biography, that the emperor was "a true soldier with all his heart," and his soldiers "took their oath to him not only because of military discipline."[21] With this naïve supposition, Corti and Sokol addressed the truly paternalistic image of the monarch; for the soldiers, they claimed, he was both one of them and their emperor-father, so they swore to him—and presumably fought—not only because of army discipline but also because they did not want to disappoint the old man, so dear to them. Moreover, they again stressed (awkwardly) what Franz Joseph's subjects thought of him—or what they wished them to have thought—suggesting that they could not be fully wrong. This kind of logic, typical for legends rather than academic writing, is unfortunately present in many accounts of his life.

Authors writing about Franz Joseph could hardly avoid discussing his responsibility for his monarchy's final catastrophe, however. Austrian Prime Minister Ernest von Koerber, cited in *Franz Joseph und sein Hof,* put it in a bon mot: "Franz Joseph did harm to us twice: once with his youth, and once with his old age."[22] That the emperor's youthful policies were dramatically unsuccessful is rather obvious, although many of his biographers avoid stating it clearly. Young Franz Joseph stubbornly guarded the principles of outdated absolutism, which his mother and his mentors Metternich and Schwarzenberg had implanted in him even before he ascended to the throne, and he impetuously fought several wars against more powerful enemies. It was popularly believed, however, that after the military catastrophes of 1859 and 1866, and after the agreements and the constitution of 1867, he became wiser, more circumspect and peaceful, and that he finally learned to take into consideration his subjects' will and needs. Eventually, one did not need to read much about Franz Joseph to believe so, for his whole life story seemed so logical: ambitious and ignorant in his youth, the ruler became cautious and calm, having experienced (but learned from) a number of bitter failures. What, then, were the mistakes of his old age?

Astonishingly, most criticism regarding Franz Joseph's last years did not arise from those who believed he was responsible for the outbreak of the Great War. The opinion, so convincingly expressed in the literary accounts of Werfel and Wittlin, that he was not to blame for this decision despite his personal involvement, prevailed. Actually, historians of the interwar era had to face a large-scale debate on the so-called war guilt question, which concerned nations, rather than particular personalities. In context of this debate, the moment when Franz Joseph decided to sign the declaration of war against Serbia seemed like a little piece of the great, international puzzle, and blaming the dead emperor seemed to trivialize these great events. Only those authors who still cared for the House of Habsburg's reputation discussed the issue in detail. For example, Count Arthur Polzer-Hoditz, a close cooperator and biographer of Franz Joseph's heir, Charles, emphasized that "irresponsible advisors" were exclusively responsible for the fatal decision.[23]

When there were reproaches against the emperor they came from those who blamed him for not having properly prepared the monarchy for the war, or indeed for not having started it at some other, better chosen moment, that is, earlier than it actually happened. *Kaiser Franz Joseph und sein Hof,* for example, informs us that a perfect opportunity for crushing Serbia occurred when King Alexander and Queen Draga were assassinated in 1903, but the old emperor and his minister for foreign affairs, Count Agenor Maria Gołuchowski, did not decide to take action. This was one of the first symptoms, argued the author, of the fear against risk and decisive action, typical for the aging emperor.[24] Similar to this is the opinion of A. F. Pribram, who also suggested that Austria-Hungary missed several occasions to attack Serbia before 1914 and pointed out that the monarchy's position in the last decades before the war generally deteriorated, also because of the lack of internal reforms. He argued, "The responsibility for this fact, so fateful for the Empire and for the dynasty, rests largely with Franz Joseph, who in the last years of his reign continued to strive to preserve peace for his realm, but avoided decisive measures."[25] According to Hugo Hantsch, the aged emperor became "detached from reality," and yet somehow he remained "a realist in the political sense of the term."[26]

Liberally disposed authors also complained about the emperor's inability to take action due to his advanced age; they just meant another sort of action. Joseph Redlich, for example, a former imperial minister, claimed that Franz Joseph in his last years was simply too old to deal with the "megalomania of the Magyars" and the Austrian bureaucracy, unable to change the centralized state into a "union of national democracies."[27] The latter idea was, according to Redlich, essential for the improvement of internal relations within the monarchy. Being an Austrian patriot and a true liberal, Redlich believed that if only the nationalities had been treated more fairly they would have never rejected the Habsburgs. However, his biography of the emperor fails to explain why Franz Joseph should have shared this view, or why he should have tried to implement Redlich's ideas in his old age, if all his life he had conducted different policies. Apparently, Redlich, like many others who praised or reproached Franz Joseph, just could not imagine any other factor comparably important for the history of Austria-Hungary as the monarch's character, disposition, or will.

Franz Joseph's policies were in general poorly analyzed by interwar authors, except to explain some of his alleged mistakes as due to youthful inexperience, or the soundness of his advanced age. Obviously, during his almost seven-decades-long rule, the emperor must have had tried a number of policies, responding to the needs of the moment. And yet interwar historians preferred to discuss the fixed traits of his character and his private habits. They may have avoided analyzing his political strategies because this would lead to the question of his personal responsibility for the very results they condemned. For example, almost all Austro-German historians disapproved of the consequences of the Agreement of 1867 with the Magyars, and still Franz Joseph's personal responsibility for the agreement and its maintenance for a half century either escaped their attention entirely or was passed over without much comment. By contrast, they criticized the second party of the agreement, the Magyars, at length and with much passion, emphasizing their "megalomania," stubbornness, and chauvinism. In a sense, historical writing on Franz Joseph strangely resembled the situation that took place under his rule, when all parties bitterly fought each other and were highly critical toward the imperial government, but none of them actually dared to challenge the emperor himself. His critics mainly focused on details from his personal life, unmasking some of his virtues as a perfect bureaucrat, so intensively glorified by his admirers. They did not, however, dare to identify his mature political strategy either. A number of them solved the problem by claiming that his political genius was in having no political philosophy at all. Apparently, the idea of a political philosophy, or indeed any constant policy, guiding the emperor's actions provoked associations with modern political party life, and Franz Joseph was anything but a politician of this sort. Thus, his apologists stressed that he was not a man of "doctrines," and that he simply adjusted his policies to the needs of the moment, and that instead of a political philosophy, he had the "instincts" of a true statesman.[28] Accordingly, A. F. Pribram observed that "he was not without skill in the choice of his advisors, but had an instinctive dislike of men whom he felt to be his intellectual superiors. He also disliked men of independent character."[29]

One of the few historians who at least noted some controversial policies of the emperor was Heinrich von Srbik. Obviously, he had to refer to the personal character of Franz Joseph as well, and dismissed the accusations that the monarch was indecisive or passive, or that he manipulated nationalities' animosities against each other. Franz Joseph, argued von Srbik, embodied the Habsburg ideal of universalism, based on the assumption that the idea of a nation-state did not apply to Central European reality. Finally, the German historian attempted to explain the allegedly nonpolitical character of the emperor's rule by claiming that he did not view his role in political terms but as a mission fulfilled in the name of God.[30]

Facing the fact that the military failures of the emperor's youth had been quite insignificant in comparison with the total disaster facing the monarchy in 1918, a disaster crowning the sixty-eight years of his reign, some historians responded with an astonishing, implicitly counterfactual interpretation. For example, Hermann Gsteu, author of a textbook of Austrian history, argued that the breakdown of the monarchy was not at all Franz Joseph's fault; to the contrary, he reasoned, it was his great achievement that the monarchy survived for so long! Viktor Bibl also emphasized that one should not be surprised that the monarchy fell in 1918 but be astonished that it survived till 1918, and he labeled it "the miracle of the House of Habsburg."[31]

As noted, Franz Joseph's responsibility for starting the world war and the following breakdown of his monarchy had scarcely been discussed in interwar historiography. The reproaches were diffused, tamed by the fact that in 1914 the monarch was, by contemporary standards, a very old man, and they certainly did not correspond to the horrors of the war and the fall of the "greatest of European dynasties" and its almost five-hundred-year-old empire. For the authors who sympathized with Austria-Hungary, criticizing Franz Joseph was mentally uneasy, and emotionally risky, for he was to them a still-powerful symbol of his country. And yet, their inability to assess his rule critically, and to analyze the purposefulness and efficiency of his policies, may still seem astonishing to us.

One can only speculate on the reasons for this. One possible explanation may be found in an essay by Elias Canetti. Canetti was an exception among the authors who wrote about Austria-Hungary, for he never referred to the omnipresent figure of Franz Joseph. In the context of the discourse on Franz Joseph, his opinion on the position of rulers and conquerors in history seems remarkable:

> Even after centuries, historians are still conscientiously balancing their character traits in order to reach what they believe is a fair judgment of them. The fundamental naiveté of this activity is virtually palpable. These historians are in fact giving in to the fascination of a power that is long past. By thinking themselves into an age, they become contemporaries, and they absorb something of the fear that the real contemporaries had for the ruthlessness of the power-wielders. They fail to realize that they are *yielding* to it while honestly sifting facts. There is also a more noble motive, of which even great thinkers were not free: they cannot get themselves to admit that a huge number of persons, each containing all possibilities of mankind, were slaughtered for nothing, absolutely nothing. And so, afterwards, they hung for meaning. Since history has always gone on, an apparent meaning in its continuity can always easily be found. And historians make sure that this meaning is given a kind of dignity.[32]

Still, Franz Joseph's reputation cannot be viewed as a product of his treatment by historians. It seems that most authors writing about him simply adjusted to his popular image. This image had been shaped by Habsburg propaganda during his long rule, and by a number of peculiar circumstances. They all contributed to an archetypical ideal of the monarch.

Franz Joseph enjoyed the reputation of a kindhearted and magnanimous ruler. All his life royal audiences for citizens were regularly organized; every respectable person could attend, having waited a few months for her or his turn, and the monarch treated all of them politely. He had the appearance of a perfect patriarch and his good manners impressed many, evoking an aura of dignity and splendor. It was easy for him to please his subjects with some honor that would be remembered for the rest of their life. Leon Biliński, for example, proudly emphasized that while he served as the joint minister of finance, his wife was invited for a private dinner with the emperor in Bad Ischl—an honor because it was not at all common for ministers' wives to dine with him outside of Vienna.[33] Common people did not dream about dining with the emperor, but still many of them sincerely believed that he loved them. Let us examine just two examples of the evidence for this belief produced by Jewish authors, for his good reputation among the Jews is probably the best known, and their admiration for him was perhaps the purest.

Lydia Harnik was a Jewish girl born in Bukovina in 1909 and brought up in "the German spirit" and "the atmosphere of the Austrian state-patriotism," which included the cult of "the legendary emperor Franz Joseph, who became a mythical figure already during [his] lifetime." During the war Harnik, her family, and many other Jews escaped to Vienna, where they lived in miserable conditions. The authorities did not care too much about the refugees, and still decades later Harnik, well aware of the "legendary" reputation of Franz Joseph, recollected the rumors about his reaction when he learned about their situation. "The magnanimous, kind and humane" emperor, claimed Harnik, got very upset and exclaimed: "I possess the huge palace of Schönbrunn, and the city mayor cannot find a shelter for those poor refugees!"[34] Since the author did not mention any actual help from the authorities, we can be sure that the whole story was nothing more than the gossip of desperate people, who nevertheless kept their faith in their monarch.

Manès Sperber was a Jewish-German writer and in his youth a

communist. In spite of his political engagement, he could not stop the feelings of grief and sorrow after the death of the legendary emperor, especially when he heard of his father's despair. Sperber's father, still a religious Jew, complained, "Austria is ending with him. He was good to us, and now, nothing is certain anymore." Decades later, Sperber commented, evidently confusing his thoughts from various moments, "His death was like an end of a certain world. Among those who thought like that were many elderly people, but I did think so as well, although I was young and rebellious, especially because of the events that were to come later."[35]

This allegedly kind heart hardly made Franz Joseph an exception among rulers, which presumably tells us more about the nature of subjects, who generally tend to believe that monarchs love them. Nevertheless, Franz Joseph possessed other qualities that burnished his "legendary" status: he was lonely and unhappy. Franz Werfel observed, "The form of Franz Joseph, the last Emperor, occupies the center of the stage because it was a great figure of decline."[36] It is not coincidental that Werfel fully ignored Charles, the last emperor. Franz Joseph suited the idea of decline, and thus the image of Austria-Hungary, much better. Apparently, they shared one splendid but unfortunate destiny. One did not have to be an Austrian "state-patriot," or indeed an admirer of Franz Joseph, to view the emperor in those terms. For example, Ignacy Daszyński, the Polish socialist leader, and one of the most rebellious deputies in the Viennese parliament, characterized Franz Joseph with just two adjectives: "very mediocre, and very unhappy."[37]

There were good reasons to consider Franz Joseph an unhappy man during his lifetime. His only son committed suicide, his brother was executed by the Mexicans, and his beloved wife was assassinated by an Italian anarchist. His antipathy for Franz Ferdinand was popularly known; however, the assassination of the heir to the throne in Sarajevo was a blow for the Habsburg family, over which the emperor presided. Popular rumor reported that when the emperor learned about the assassination, he uttered, "Nothing has been spared to me." Karl Kraus, the Viennese master of mockery and irony, made this phrase the refrain of a song by the old emperor, lonely in his palace and in his dotage.[38] Considering the vacuum that surrounded him in his private life, it is no wonder that the aged Franz Joseph spent all his time fulfilling his official duties. Only Austria-Hungary was left to him, and from the a posteriori perspective it seemed, of course, that he was worried about its future and apprehended its breakdown.

Empress Elisabeth did not allow herself to be painted or photographed anymore when she turned thirty-five years old. Franz Joseph, by contrast, is invariably remembered as an old, lonely man, enduring his fate with dignity. According to Hermann Broch, as a consequence people did not feel compassion for him but considered him a symbol of the majesty as such. Broch's interpretation partially explains why so many authors confused Franz Joseph's personal fate with the one of his monarchy:

> Immense was the shell of solitude in which he lived his uncannily bureaucratic, abstractly punctual official life, no matter whether in the Vienna "castle" or in the simple Biedermeier villa at Ischl where annual hunting vacations took him, always in abstract exactness, always in solitude, always in dignity. Wilhelm I was called the first soldier of his empire, Edward VII was the first gentleman of Europe, Franz Joseph I was the abstract monarch par excellence. . . . And this did not occur because a sheer Greek-tragic excess of personal misfortune weighed upon him, neither did it occur from the awe-inspiring effect of such misfortune—this kind of awe-inspired compassion simply disappears from view when masses are not a public and therefore know no compassion—but it occurred because, perhaps even as a result of all his deficiencies, he had become capable of taking upon himself the thrilling dignity of absolute solitude.[39]

For the modern reader the interwar image of Franz Joseph may be astonishing, for his reputation surely should have owed much more than it did to what was probably his gravest sin and certainly his fatal mistake: starting the Great War that annihilated his monarchy and millions of his subjects. He was popularly considered a symbol not just of his country but also of the best aspects of "the good old days" of European peace and stability. Ironically, it would not have been possible to sustain this popular misconception without the atrocities of the war and the dissolution of Austria-Hungary. And yet it was due precisely to this enormous, fundamental change in the lives of Central Europeans that Franz Joseph was able to escape much of the criticism that is normally expressed concerning the failures of statesmen in power. Most of the "mistakes" of his youth—the wars, repressions, and awkward absolutist attempts to reform the monarchy—all were forgotten. What mattered after the Great War was that he had been a conservative protector of an idyllic past and that he struggled alone against his fate and that of cruel modernity. And if Austria-Hungary's destiny and his personal destiny were one, he had no choice but to represent it and perish with what he considered dignity.

CONCLUSION

It is time to comment again on the objectives of this book. Its purpose has been to reconstruct interwar discourse on Austria-Hungary and determine the mechanisms of its development, particularly the flow of ideas between various genres. I have intended to identify the points that make this discourse exceptional and those that are typical for historical thinking of the first half of the last century. I have not attempted to verify what interwar authors wrote on Austria-Hungary. It does not really matter for the purposes of this analysis whether they were right or wrong in their opinions on the monarchy. This book only traces how and why they arrived at these opinions.

Notably, the historical debate on the monarchy did not evolve through bringing about new facts. One of its characteristic features was that it was an immediate response to a grand-scale historical change, which rapidly transformed all earlier attitudes to Austria-Hungary and opened the floor for a completely new discussion. Its authors can scarcely be divided into well-informed and ignorant ones. Their task was not to inform but to interpret well-known facts. This refers to historians, essayists, and fiction writers alike. The only difference that matters from the point of view of this book is that the latter could color their interpretations with a great number of fictional events and characters, whereas historians had to stick to the sources. Fiction matters to my analysis only as far as it stuck to reality, as it represented and reinterpreted it.

Like all discourses of its kind, the one on Austria-Hungary was governed by a certain mechanism: it was simultaneously exclusive and responsive. It revolved around a limited number of problems and motifs, constantly reinterpreting them by absorption of new elements that fit its paradigm. Below I shall list them and discuss the ways in which they were introduced and perpetuated in the discourse on the monarchy.

Of course, right or wrong, some of the authors analyzed in this book argued more intelligently and convincingly than others. Some were slaves of group-thinking and ideological slogans of their time, and some thought more independently and rose above prejudices of their intellectual environment. Some were highly talented writers, and the majority was mediocre. As I shall demonstrate further in this chapter, the talented ones were not few but of course they were still in the minority. In order to identify characteristic aspects of the discourse it will be necessary to have a closer look at the mediocre writers, whose works have been mostly forgotten by generations since, but nevertheless significantly influenced ways in which we view the monarchy today. Only their writings allow us to determine what was typical for the interwar image of the monarchy.

Naturally, no single text analyzed in this book can be simply reduced to the sum of its aspects shared with other texts. They are all individual entities and all typologies are generalizations that unavoidably neglect their individuality. Nevertheless, they are necessary if we want to understand the discourse in its entirety, assuming that it is not an artificial construct. After all, the original recipients of the texts analyzed in this book also referred to other texts of the same kind while reading them. Understanding, and probably also the very interest in interpretations of the history of Austria-Hungary, was only possible in the context of a variety of opinions, images, and arguments. Moreover, their authors did not simply study their subject and write about it; they were aware that they were competing with other authors, and that if they wanted to impose their interpretations on their readers, they had to involve in them the points that had already been covered by their colleagues or rivals.

Let us begin with reexamining the basic points of view on the monarchy. How can they be defined and how far do they determine the attitudes of the authors whose writings we have analyzed?

Austria-Hungary and Identity

In the preface to his *The Decline and Fall of the Habsburg Empire*, which analyzes post–World War II historiography on the monarchy, Alan Sked points out that most historical discussions on Austria-Hungary in America are, more or less, counterfactual: they attempt to inquire whether the fall of the monarchy was unavoidable and what could have been done to save it. These attempts, Sked argues, evidently indicate that the majority of American historians tend to believe that it would have been simply better if the monarchy had not broken down—exactly like the authors analyzed in this book.[1] In this respect things did not change between the 1930s and at least 1979, when George Kennan stated, "The Austro-Hungarian Empire still looks better as a solution to the tangled problems of that part of the world than anything that has succeeded it."[2] Sked suggests that this tendency can be explained by the preponderant influence gained by refugees from Central Europe on American studies on the monarchy. Furthermore, he confronts it with the opinion prevailing among British historians, who tended to view the monarchy as the Habsburgs' *Hausmacht*—an imperialist dynastic power that, by definition, could not satisfy the needs of its population. In other words, a couple of decades after World War II the attitude toward Austria-Hungary was still determined by nationality or ethnic origins.

Needless to say, it was also like that in the interwar time. However, the situation was a bit more complicated. One reason for this was that immediately after the dissolution of the monarchy there was still no Austrian nation. Moreover, there were more nationless Austro-Hungarian "orphans" than just the Austro-Germans—other "Austrians" in the pre-1918 sense of the term. There were supranational aristocrats and businessmen, ex–imperial and royal officials and officers, and German-speaking Jews in all corners of what had been Austria. Thus, it is more reasonable to speak about identity than nationality or ethnicity as the basic factor determining interwar attitudes: the identity that mostly correlated with nationality was occasionally in flux, and quite often was a matter of personal choice. It was one of the rare moments in European history when a large number of people could, or indeed had to, decide whom they wanted to be, since the imperial and royal Austrian identity was quickly expiring.

Authors whose writings have been analyzed in this book can be clearly divided into several groups corresponding with their national and political self-identification. First, there was a relatively small group of these who still considered the monarchy their motherland. Or perhaps it would be more appropriate to say that after the monarchy had broken down they did not find any other motherland. They might have been German culturally, or Jewish religiously, or someone else linguistically, but ideologically they did not identify themselves with any other country—and this meant no country at all, for Austria-Hungary was no more. They remained, as Franz Werfel put it, "children of the Old Austria." They embodied the official cosmopolitanism of the monarchy and testified for it; in a way, all that was left after the "Old Austria" was them. Their number was relatively small, but their importance for the legacy of Austria-Hungary was disproportionally significant. They were the parents of the "literature of the Habsburg myth" that won them immediate popularity at home and was to dominate the image of the monarchy in the West after World War II. Apparently, their significance can be explained by the fact that in this group there was a number of highly talented authors. And yet, as I argued, it seems that the basic reason for that was more pedestrian: they simply cared the most. The monarchy was their topic, and the awareness of the fact that it was politically irredeemable motivated them to immortalize it. They were less involved in contemporary ideological disputes than others because they cared less for the present; their point of reference was located in the past. They participated in the "who is to blame?" debate, but less zealously, since, from their point of view, the dissolution of Austria-Hungary was a general loss for all its inhabitants. They were less angry about it than, say, the German or Hungarian nationalists, who viewed the monarchy as a useful tool of their respective national interests. They were, rather, astonished that it had broken down because they viewed it as serving common interests. The fact that such a good idea as the Habsburg monarchy could have gone bankrupt so easily and with so little resistance made them draw more general conclusions, about the nature of politics, history, or the human condition.

Another group is composed of those who accepted the fact that the monarchy had abandoned them and sought another motherland. This was the case of the majority of Austro-German authors, whose attitudes varied between loyalty toward the Habsburgs and the German nation. More or less sympathetic toward the monarchy, they simply accepted the fact that it was irrevocably gone. Their old imperial and royal identity expired, but this was not a tragic loss for them, for they had a spare one, which they could easily take out of their deep closets where it had been kept under the Habsburgs. Apart from being practical, this attitude also had an intellectual advantage: it was open for historicity of the sociopolitical developments. Its authors were changing their identities, and they understood that the world around them was changing too. They might have had their sentiments and regrets, their phobias and dogmas, but they knew that change was a part of the natural order. The Hungarians, for example, viewed Austria-Hungary in these terms: married to the Habsburgs with no love, they considered them a phase, an epoch in their national history. Particularly because of their trauma of Trianon, they saw dualism as an idyll, but they also remembered that the idyll had been full or reproaches and animosities. Also, many Poles from Galicia shared this approach, although 1918 brought them national liberation and was regarded as the most serene moment in their national history. But they also remembered that the fall of Austria-Hungary was a great astonishment, and many of them wondered, as József Wittlin put it, where the double-headed Habsburg eagle had flown.

Somewhere between the first and the second group were the few "true Austrians"; for example, the authors of *Die österreichische Aktion* and other worshippers of the Austrian idea. Deprived of the monarchy, they turned their hopes toward the fragile German Republic of Austria. Obviously, their situation was the most complicated, for the republic never enjoyed much popularity, nor respect, among its own citizens, who finally welcomed the Anschluss to Hitler's Germany with tremendous enthusiasm. Moreover, they themselves had little love for the republic; they only considered it a temporary home for the Austrian idea, and inferior to the monarchy by far.

Third, there were authors who approached Austria-Hungary with little emotion, foreigners for whom the monarchy was just a country like many others. Evidently, the lack of emotional engagement and prejudices that naturally follow it seems a necessary prerequisite for objectivity or at least impartiality. Interwar British or Swiss authors writing on the monarchy had the advantage that their Central European colleagues were to gain only a generation later: they were not involved in the debates concerning responsibility for any local misfortunes. They were not obsessed with the "who is to blame?" question, and therefore could afford a cold analysis of the situation, asking instead who really had interest in the monarchy's survival, and who profited from its downfall. And yet their studies on Austria-Hungary were remarkably one-sided, aside from some notable exceptions such as *Nationalgeist und Politik,* by Friedrich Hertz, which gave a more detailed view than a standard monograph. The monarchy, as they saw it, was typically an exemplification of a larger historical phenomenon, a clear-cut historical construct. Basically, it served them to discuss two such phenomena: the supranational state and the empire. Schematic as it was, this approach was fruitful. With time, Austria-Hungary has continued to appear in this context in the history of Europe; in many cases it was reduced to an example illustrating these problems.

The next group is composed of authors who considered themselves members of nations oppressed by the Habsburgs. As noted, it is a broad category, for practically all nationalities of the monarchy claimed this status. Even the Austrians and the Hungarians felt underprivileged by each other or in relation to each other. After all, the secret of the Habsburg art of governing was, according to Prime Minister Eduard Taaffe, to keep everyone equally dissatisfied. There was a difference, however, among the nationalities' levels of dissatisfaction, which corresponded with their attitudes to the monarchy varying from complaining to disloyalty. Consequently, Austrians and Hungarians viewed the dissolution of Austria-Hungary as a tragedy and the peace settlement of 1919 as a catastrophe in the history of their nations; others regarded them as a natural and desirable process leading to their national liberation. Austria-Hungary was for them a historical anomaly, a malady that ought to be cured. Obviously, their diagnoses varied: the symptoms of corruption that Czech radicals like Jaroslav Hašek observed, nepotism and German chauvinism, differed significantly from those that a pan-German historian identified: the rise of pan-Slavism and other riotous tendencies among the non-German population. Moreover, the German perspective did not mirror other nationalities' discourse of the struggle for national liberation, for it was fueled by a sense of cultural superiority and their *mission civilisatrice* in the barbaric East. Non-Germans viewed Austria-Hungary as an obstacle on their road to liberty because it was a tool of foreign domination and oppression; pan-Germans viewed it as their sacrifice on the road to national unity. All things being equal, they were both glad that the problem was over and eager to emphasize their sufferings of the past.

Finally, there was one more point of view on Austria-Hungary, which in a way combined all Austro-German attitudes with their contradictions and nuances: the Viennese. It cannot be reduced to the perspective of the Austro-Hungarian "orphans" because it did not really share their deep sense of loss, even though they were similar in their being cosmopolitan but still more German than anything else in the truly Austro-Hungarian spirit. For numerous Viennese intellectuals, such as Karl Kraus, Robert Musil, or Heimitio von Doderer, the lands of the monarchy seemed to have been the imperial and royal capital city's colonies rather than its hinterland. The monarchy provided Vienna with capital, people, energy, and topics to be discussed by political columnists—and that was basically all. It was rarely visited and hardly known to them. Certainly, when it broke down, the Viennese were shocked, impoverished, and regretful. But the city did not evaporate with its monarchy; moreover, it was still the capital, even though the German Republic of Austria demographically resembled a medieval city-state, for roughly one-third of its population lived in Vienna. Emotionally, however, the situation of the Viennese resembled that of the British after they lost their empire more than that of the Romans after they lost theirs. The Viennese perspective also overlapped with the pan-German one to an extent, for Vienna had beautiful memories of its empire, but it also had prospects of being incorporated into the united Great Germany. Finally, Vienna had the potential to dominate the posthumous image of the monarchy exactly as it had dominated it when Austria-Hungary still existed. Austria-Hungary was an exotic land for foreigners and they tended to perceive it through Vienna, whereas its citizens from remote corners of the monarchy, who were equally exotic to each other, also met and learned about each other in the capital, particularly the ambitious and talented ones. "The Habsburg myth" of post-Habsburg literature owed a lot to the Viennese perspective, from which the monarchy was scarcely visible, but strongly felt and wittily interpreted. What was mythical about it was the ahistorical image of a peaceful country of traditional order, free of the conflicts and tensions of modernity. In other words, it was like the realm of childhood—an idea that perfectly suited the minds of people who left the provinces for the capital and recollected them with the nostalgia of grown-ups, without the slightest intention to return.

To sum up: identity, mostly correlated with nationality, seems to have been the most important single factor determining attitudes toward Austria-Hungary. Ideology, experience, and imagination certainly played their roles, but turned out to be secondary when the crucial question was involved: namely, how should we evaluate the monarchy's decline and fall? There were scarcely any exceptions to this rule. Even the communist Albert Fuchs, although he eagerly quoted Stalin, was an Austrian patriot. Jaroslav Hašek, a red commissar and a witty anarchist, was full of prejudices against all things non-Czech, and all Czechs not Czech enough to meet his radical standards of patriotism. To be sure, ideology mattered when it came to details, such as Austria-Hungary's constitutional and social order. Some Austrian authors believed that its aristocratism was an obvious advantage. They associated aristocracy with honesty, temper, and good manners, and therefore claimed that even if Austria's constitution had its deficiencies it still functioned brilliantly, because the country was run by the elite. Notably, however, they did not claim the same about Hungary, even though in the lands of the Crown of St. Stephen the privileges of nobility were guaranteed by electoral census. On the other hand, only a few authors criticized the monarchy's constitution because of their democratic principles. And yet even such a democrat as Oszkár Jászi, who overtly and zealously deplored noble privileges, capitalist exploitation, national inequality, and imperialist policies, could not hide his deep regret and sorrow about Austria-Hungary's collapse. Apparently, no Hungarian author of his generation could either. Similarly, the ex-Austro-Hungarian joint minister for finance, Leon Biliński, who did not hide how enchanted he was by the personal favors of Franz Joseph for himself and his wife, could express his sympathy for the monarchy only *avant la lettre:* his Polish readers would not forgive him if he had not stressed how happy he was that the monarchy had dissolved and Poland had regained its independence.

Apparently, our conclusions are not astonishing. National loyalty seems to be a ubiquitous principle in historical writing—and not only in the first half of the twentieth century. History, after all, is not a matter of individual experience, but of a social one. It reflects the opinion of a community that produced its sources, and addresses a community of readers whom it concerns, and this usually means a national community, united by common language and the sense of a common past. Of course, good history is supposed to reinterpret common opinion, perhaps even challenge it at some vital points. However, this rarely happens in times of radical changes and crises, such as the one that occurred in 1918–1919. When Austria-Hungary fell historical writers could hardly challenge any established opinion; at least in Austria, Germany, and Hungary they were addressing a shocked and devastated audience that was sure of only one thing: something had gone terribly wrong and no one had noticed it when there was still time. In the other successor states of the monarchy the sense of triumph and relief prevailed; however, their inhabitants were also disoriented. They remembered very well that just a few years earlier Austria-Hungary had still been a great power, and that its collapse came suddenly and unexpectedly. History writers had no established interpretation of these events available to challenge; they had to establish one first. All things being equal, the collapse of Austria-Hungary came as a surprise. Like all breakdowns of empires, revolutions, and crises, it started a race for interpretation. Originality mattered less in this race than persuasiveness, and cold analysis was losing against rhetoric recalling group emotions.

And yet this race was not exactly like others. There were, to be sure, friends and enemies of the old regime, and there was the "who is to blame?" debate, more or less like in all countries that experienced a revolution. Generally speaking, however, it almost immediately became unquestionable that the monarchy was dead and would not resurrect. There were plans, or dreams, of some sort of supranational federation in Central Europe, but they never enjoyed the support of any serious political force. The opinion prevailed that the Habsburgs irrevocably belonged to the past. Certainly, this opinion was based not only on the contemporary status quo but also on the popular image of the monarchy as a state representing political principles that had been compromised and were irreconcilable with the standards of modern politics. In short, the Habsburg monarchy already seemed an antiquated idea a few years, if not months, after it had broken down. This was, perhaps, the cause why it entered the realm of fiction so smoothly and successfully. Probably no other country in the history of Europe underwent the transformation from a great power into a fantasy so quickly and spectacularly.

There is no single explanation of this phenomenon, however. We can also point to a specifically Austrian tradition of political escapism that dates back to the pre-1848 epoch that historians of culture call Biedermeier, which also coincided with the rise of the bourgeoisie and tremendous changes in everyday life caused by urbanization and industrialization. At that time Metternich's strict censorship and restrictions against all political activism led to the flourishing of culture concentrated on domestic life, the private, and the inner self. Politics and social questions became successfully eliminated from public discourse; aestheticism was preferred to activism. Ulrich Greiner called this tradition *glückbringendes Ersatzhandeln*—happy vicarious activities.[3] The turn of the century, with its cult of decadence, brought the culmination of this tendency: even though political activism was not illegal any more, the intellectual elites of Central Europe, and particularly Vienna, saw it with much suspicion. They were fascinated with "the gardens of the soul" separated from sociopolitical life by a "great wall." As Arthur Schnitzler recollected in his memoirs, in Austria "emotions and reason lived together in the human soul, but they ran separate households."[4] The dissolution of Austria-Hungary certainly traumatized Austrian writers, but many of them intuitively reacted to this catastrophe in the traditional way: retreating from the world of action into aestheticism. Robert Menasse ironically commented in his *Das Land ohne Eigenschaften: Essays zur österreichischen Identität* (Essay on the Austrian identity): "Having two catastrophes to choose [from], we always opt for the one that allows for idealization and aestheticizing. This is what we have learned from history."[5] And Greiner more seriously remarked that Austrians tended to view the inability of real action as the virtue of perfect inactivity. And yet resignation as an ideal is in fact illusive, for resignation assumes a goal that cannot be achieved, and what Austrians really lack is not the possibility for action, but its purpose. The actual ground for Austrian relativism is, therefore, the assumption that nothing develops as we plan it.[6] Indeed, such fatalism is typical for many narratives about Austria-Hungary; they are full of counterfactual scenarios indicating how the monarchy could have been saved, and at the same time infused with belief that all efforts to achieve this were in fact doomed from the beginning. Viktor Bibl formulated it when describing Franz Ferdinand's plans for reforms: in the end they all failed because of the contrarious nature of their object—*die Tücke des Objekts.*

Unintended Affinities

Bearing in mind the basic differences among narratives about the monarchy, let us now focus on what they have in common. Apparently, one could suppose that this should be the most important element of interwar discourse concerning Austria-Hungary: its core that can be considered the dominant, if not unquestionable, interpretation of the past. As a matter of fact, most readers of history intuitively assume that all historical discourses are constructed this way: they contain a number of debatable issues and controversial interpretations, and an indisputable core, which emerges in the course of these controversies as a sort of conclusion. And this assumption works also among the majority of professional historians, even though theoreticians are certainly skeptical about it, and postmodern theoreticians deny it on principle. The entire debate revolves around the fatal question: is history capable of establishing any unquestionable interpretations of the past developments and events, or does it remain a game of contradictory opinions? Needless to say, the analysis of interwar discourse on Austria-Hungary gives no satisfactory answer to this dilemma. It does, however, provide us with a picture of the mechanism of the transformation of certain hotly debated controversies into unquestionable interpretations, and the elimination of other, equally intensively discussed issues.

As noted, all authors writing about Austria-Hungary in the interwar epoch agreed on scarcely more than two things. First, they unanimously assumed that the monarchy fell because of the dissatisfaction of its nationalities. In other words, it can be said that it struggled in vain against rising nationalism—although not all interwar authors put it this way, because nationalism was, and still is, a controversial label. Second, they also shared the conviction, or perhaps the impression, that the monarchy as a dynastic power represented an antiquated political principle. Naturally, both ideas were interconnected: the basic premise for considering Austria-Hungary politically outdated was exactly the fact that it was not a nation-state, whereas nationalism was a relatively fresh ideology in Central Europe and, more importantly, it was victorious. After World War I and the unparalleled sacrifices of the combatant countries, national ideology seemed the only one that guaranteed the loyalty of the population to the state. The war was a bloody exam, and only the governments capable of mobilizing their citizens in the name of their respective ideals of national solidarity, honor, and sovereignty survived it. Certainly, the backwardness of Austria-Hungary had other sources as well: the special position of the monarch, his court and its love for the pompous rituals, and the fact that Franz Joseph, who symbolized Austria-Hungary, was himself the oldest ruler of Europe; the peculiarly post-feudal character of dualism; the Habsburgs' claims for the legacy of Charlemagne and their special relations with the papacy. As far as foreign observers were concerned, it also mattered that Austria-Hungary was a Ruritania: a country located in exotic Central Europe that bordered the Balkans and was populated by wolves, Count Dracula, Gypsies, illiterate peasants, orthodox Jews, and the notorious Polish and Hungarian nobles. However, we need to bear in mind that all of that was under control as long as Austria-Hungary existed. In the spring of 1914 Austria-Hungary was still remarkably modern in many aspects. It had excellent railways, universities, cafés, newspapers, theaters, hospitals, museums, operas, airplanes, submarines, battleships, avant-garde artists, Marxists, the first psychoanalyst, and the second metro line in Europe. Only after the dissolution of the monarchy did it turn out that Austria-Hungary had been anachronistic. Its remarkably modern-looking landscape became totally overshadowed by politics. The assumption that the monarchy had been "old," perhaps as old as Franz Joseph himself, was adopted and frequently used as an argument explaining its political decadence. Historians, essayists, and fiction writers alike called it "the old Austria," and "the old monarchy," as they called the Habsburgs "the venerable dynasty," suggesting that Austria-Hungary died of natural causes, even though, as a matter of accuracy, the Habsburg monarchy was five to seven centuries younger than the majority of European monarchies.

In other words, what the majority of interwar authors unanimously agreed upon was not necessarily the most solid, credible, and intensively discussed interpretation of Austria-Hungary's past. It was rather their first impression, their most immediate explanatory intuition after the dissolution of the monarchy. This is not to say it should be disregarded or underestimated. There were serious grounds for this intuition. The supposition that the national question would one day threaten the monarchy's existence had been in the air for decades, and it had indeed been the main concern of all Austro-Hungarian governments since the mid-1890s. In short, it was based on obvious facts and indeed it has not been questioned by any serious study since 1918, even though it remains a matter of speculation whether the monarchy could have appeased its nationalities had it not entered the Great War. Evidently, the alleged backwardness of the monarchy is more ambivalent, for backwardness as such is a relative concept. To be sure, Austria-Hungary's political constitution was anachronistic at the beginning of the twentieth century because it was neither democratic nor authoritarian, and both the efficacy of its government and its claims for legitimacy heavily depended on the personal authority of the monarch. And regardless of the personal popularity of Franz Joseph and all his other virtues, by the time he decided to start World War I he was not at all a modern man, nor did he pretend to be one.

To sum up, the discourse on Austria-Hungary had solid foundations. It was based on just two pillars: one of them was grounded in well-known facts, the other was deeply anchored in the mentality of the epoch. The idea that Austria-Hungary was an anachronism was, on the one hand, perfectly logical, given that the monarchy had collapsed. On the other hand, as already noted, World War I and the enormous changes it brought to all of Europe caused an illusion of acceleration of time, and thus it was natural for the people of the interwar epoch to regard the times before the Great War as the distant past. This is to say that interwar discourse on Austria-Hungary was highly selective, and if its authors agreed only about two ideas it was because they had good reasons to consider them unquestionable.

However, apart from these two ideas, interwar authors writing on the monarchy also disagreed upon a number of issues. Eventually, discourse on Austria-Hungary evolved predominantly from controversies. On the one hand, this fact apparently indicates that it was intellectually healthy and capable of uniting a variety of approaches and opinions. Controversies, after all, fuel the improvement of argumentation. On the other hand, it also leads to a sad conclusion: that historical debates are perpetuated by the consolidation of contradicting opinions rather than by an effort to arrive at an interpretation that would embrace them all, surpass the divisions, or synthesize the opinions that have already entered this discourse. Each time one side brings about a new argument, the other one immediately uses it for its own purposes, and hence if we read the two interpretations with the noble assumption to assess them impartially, we are often confused. Technically, these arguments, and also simple facts, lose their meaning if they are used to prove two contradicting things—like the testimonies of two people who accuse each other of attacking the other one first.

For example, let us return for a moment to the notorious problem of the monarchy's old age. As stated, for the majority of interwar authors, emphasizing that the monarchy was "old" was a rhetorical figure that was supposed to support the argument that it was anachronistic, and since it was anachronistic, it was doomed for decline. It was a metaphor derived from the organic world: the monarchy had its time, it lasted for so many centuries, and it finally passed away because of its old age. However, some admirers of the monarchy argued the opposite, employing the same argument as a metaphor derived from the world of psychology. As discussed in chapter two, for Hugo von Hofmannsthal the fact that the monarchy was old was proof of its durability and the high quality of its form of government, for which duration, as Machiavelli observed, is the best verification. Hofmannsthal's reasoning was inductive: if the monarchy had survived so many crises, it should have survived one more, and it must have been the best solution to the problems of Central Europe.

There were more unintentionally equivocal arguments like that. Let me recall just two more examples, perhaps the most striking ones. The first concerns geography (which was discussed in chapter one). For critics of the monarchy, geography was an obvious argument that the monarchy was not a coherent unit, and a factor that naturally strengthened the centrifugal forces within Austria-Hungary. For its enthusiasts, geography proved that Austria-Hungary was an economic necessity, and that its dissolution was a tragedy for the region, which was predestined for political unification. The second example concerns the private life of Franz Joseph (which was discussed in chapter four), and his attitude to his obligations as a monarch. It was well known that he used to get up and go to bed early, that he spent many hours at his desk laboriously getting through numerous detailed problems of his many subjects and particularly his army, and that he was capable of remembering thousands of people he met during his lengthy rule. Admirers of Franz Joseph considered all these facts proof of his incomparable virtues as a monarch; for his critics, the same facts indicated that he was a man of limited intellectual capacities, basically unfit for ruling his monarchy and understanding its real problems. More importantly, exhausted by discussing Franz Joseph's daily schedule, many authors omitted the problem of the assessment of his crucial political decisions. Obviously, they did not in fact quarrel whether early birds are more politically gifted than night owls; they were trapped by sentimental deduction. The petty detail became important only because it referred to Franz Joseph.

Once a controversial opinion entered the discourse, it started to live a life of its own. It provoked comments, reactions, and responses. Theoretically, it also consumed space that might have been occupied by new and independent ideas or some more original problems. It may naturally also be argued, however, that the most intensively debated problems were presumably the most important, or at least that they indicated their authors' most vital interests. Actually, the entire discourse may be compared to a net of narratives knotted by a number of concepts and ideas. Some of the knots were serious analytical questions, some were powerful symbols, and some were vague but persistent associations.

One of them was the problem of the great power status that, as discussed in chapter one, had its own logic. For a number of authors the fact that the monarchy enjoyed this status determined its immanent nature; it pursued certain policies, they argued, and undertook certain actions because it was a great power or because it had to preserve this status—and these included the suicidal decision to start the Great War. Another such idea was the concept of *Reich,* going back to the times of the Holy Roman Empire of the German Nation. According to Austrian conservatives the fact that the monarchy was or aspired to be a Reich, or epitomized this idea, also determined its nature and was used as an explanatory tool concerning its internal and external policies. Both concepts were applied not as metaphors but as categories of scholarly observation, parallel to those functioning in the mechanical and organic world.

The monarchy also evoked specific associations with other countries, particularly from classical antiquity. As noted, such parallels were natural for the authors of the first half of the twentieth century because of the eminent role that classics played in their high school education. For historians of this generation, ancient figures were no less familiar than Cromwell, Napoleon, or Metternich. Thinking about political decadence they could not avoid referring to the example of ancient Rome. Furthermore, this example was highly attractive, especially for the orphans of Austro-Hungary, but also for authors who simply wished to emphasize that the processes they narrated should be considered crucial episodes in European history. Franz Werfel wrote melancholically but immodestly that "this belonging to two worlds, this embracing of two epochs within one soul, is a highly paradoxical state, recurring seldom in history and inflicting itself upon but few of the races of mankind. There may have been, in the days when Rome fell and new states sprang up on her soil, generations like ours."[7] Similarly, Heinrich Benedikt noted that Cardinal Antonelli called the Austro-Prussian War of 1866 "casca il mondo," and commented that half a century passed before this prophecy was fulfilled, but "this fifty years brought about changes that could be compared solely to the fall of Rome."[8] Certainly, the imperial and royal symbolism of the monarchy also played its role, stimulating historians' choice of metaphors. Thus, critics of the monarchy also eagerly employed Roman analogies. Eugene Bagger, for example, called Franz Joseph "the last of the Caesars" and ironically labeled his heir Charles "Romulus Augustulus"—the last Roman emperor of the West, who ruled for less than a year when he was still a teenager.[9] In short, ancient analogies became standard for authors writing on Austria-Hungary. Even in the 1960s an Austrian essayist, Herbert Eisenreich, explained to his readers that "the uniqueness and the greatness of Austria arise from the fact that it was—as Athens had been—a great market place and melting pot of ideas."[10]

The favorite contemporary analogy of authors writing on Austria-Hungary was Britain. As noted, the analogy was evidently flattering for the monarchy, but the choice was not accidental, nor was it simply based on admiration for British political and economic might. The reasoning behind it was as follows: Austria-Hungary was famous for its peculiar, not to say bizarre, political constitution, resembling a feudal conglomerate of dependencies rather than a modern state. And yet authors who sympathized with it claimed that it should not be judged by appearances, and that in fact it was a remarkably modern and liberal country, ruled by law and spreading Western culture among the half-barbaric nations of the East. The parallel with Britain was supposed to emphasize that modernity goes nicely with traditional political institutions and a certain dose of conservatism in public affairs, and so to prove that the liberal paternalism of the Habsburgs was actually a better solution for the backward, multiethnic, and multiconfessional Central Europe than the abstract rationalism of the democrats. This parallel must have been very well-anchored in the Austrian historical imagination; for example, Hermann Broch employed it in his essay on Hofmannsthal, even though he was extremely critical toward the Habsburgs, and he wrote for an American audience, for whom analogies with Germany or Russia certainly seemed more natural.[11] Furthermore, as discussed in chapter one, it was dogma in contemporary Hungary to view English constitutional history as the only appropriate parallel to the Hungarian one, which allowed Hungarians to stress their remarkable tradition dating back to the Golden Bull of 1222—the second non-codified constitution limiting the arbitrary powers of the monarch in history after England's Magna Carta of 1215.

Finally, there was one more subject that appeared in almost all narratives on Austria-Hungary, a sort of refrain of the entire discourse concerning it: the imperial and royal bureaucracy. Pro-Habsburg historians praised it as the best public service on the planet; their less enthusiastic colleagues pointed out that, alongside the army, it was the only pan-Austrian institution, and the most important bearer of loyalty to the state. Its moral qualities were debated as hotly as those of Franz Joseph—who was actually supposed to epitomize both the bureaucratic and the military Austro-Hungarian ideals. Archetypical imperial and royal bureaucrats populated numerous interwar novels, and, as Claudio Magris observed, their figures eventually served as symbols of the ephemeral Austrian identity in the multinational monarchy.[12] Actually, not only was the bureaucrat inseparable from the memories of the monarchy, the offices themselves had the ability to evoke memories of the monarchy. For example, in Stefan Zweig's sentimental novel *Beware of Pity* a block of blank sheets of paper plays the role of Marcel Proust's madeleine: under the Habsburgs all applications had to be written on this paper, the most faithful witness of innumerable sorrows, ambitions, and everyday problems, so they easily evoke a stream of reminiscences from the time before the Great War. In his famous patriotic bon mot, Grillparzer claimed that Austria was to be found in the military camp of Marshal Radetzky, which emphasized the loyalty of the Habsburg troops and suggested that Austria, by that time still indefinable geographically, stretched as far as the conquests of its military. This idea, however, turned out to be as ephemeral as the Habsburg victories. It should rather be said that the truly Austro-Hungarian spirit was to be found in its public offices, yellow-painted railway stations, and Viennese-style cafés. A watchful observer can still sense it today in many such places throughout Central Europe.

L'empereur est mort, vive la monarchie!

As I argued, time has been generous to Austria-Hungary. Its image almost a century after its dissolution seems much more serene than in the times when people still remembered it. Its posthumous career is particularly successful in comparison with those of other European great powers. The poorest, most backward, and least powerful of them when it still existed, after its disappearance from the map it has nevertheless managed to gain a remarkably secure position in historical consciousness; in some respects its image nowadays seems brighter than those of other empires. Most importantly, Austria-Hungary does not now appear as regrettably unsuccessful a political idea as it did in the interwar time, for all European empires eventually passed causing no less relief and no more pity for their subjects than the Habsburg monarchy. And of all of them only the monarchy can claim kinship with both the Roman Empire and the European Union.

The turbulent history of the twentieth century certainly played its role in improving the monarchy's reputation. After World War I it naturally became associated with times of peace, stability, and prosperity. After World War II this image was exported to the West by refugees from Soviet-dominated Central Europe and amplified by a number of outstanding historians. The war also confirmed Austria's independence from Germany, totally discredited German nationalism, and ruined the attractiveness of nationalism in general. The gradual unification of Europe shed new light on the supranational ideals once symbolized by the monarchy. Simultaneously, its cultural heritage—symbolized by such names as Kafka, Freud, Popper, Klimt, or Wittgenstein—won international recognition. And so, politically dead, the monarchy still managed to remain an intellectual and cultural great power, additionally armed with the charm of joyful decadence.

Can we find any keys to this remarkable evolution in the interwar writings on Austria-Hungary? One was certainly the fact that the monarchy was perfectly dead as a political idea immediately after its dissolution. The German, the Russian, and the Ottoman empires also fell in consequence of the Great War, but they had heirs and continuations in their respective nation-states and the mighty Soviet Union. Neither the German Republic of Austria nor any other of the successor states aspired to such a role; indeed, Czechoslovakia, Yugoslavia, and Romania formed an alliance to make sure that the Habsburgs, who were persona non grata in Austria anyway, would never return. Its antiquated ideological façade made all hopes for its reconstructions seem unreasonable, not to say ridiculous. As demonstrated, authors who actually advocated this idea in the 1920s and 1930s were dreamers who founded their hopes on religious mysticism, and their writings definitely cannot be located in the mainstream of interwar discourse. In short, the monarchy was a political bankrupt and it constituted no potential threat to anyone.

This situation had two consequences. First, it allowed interwar authors to express pity for the monarchy. This pity was often colored with a remarkable sense of humor, but this only contributed to its popularity and attractiveness. The monarchy's anachronistic ideology, its aristocratism, its uncertain identity masked with the complicated political structure and the fantastic titles of its rulers—all this made it perfect soil for ironic and humorous imagination. Its great ambitions and its sudden deterioration made it appear a buffo-style great power. This was crucial for discourse on Austria-Hungary because it offered a chance for the tendency of those sympathetic toward the monarchy to successfully compete with those who viewed it as an oppressive force and a tool of dynastic absolutism and imperialism. In Germany *The Loyal Subject,* a cruel satire against the empire by Heinrich Mann, written in 1914, was finally published in 1918 and immediately became a best seller. Its popularity equaled the respect that the empire enjoyed before the Great War. Austria-Hungary did not provoke such outbursts of bitter resentment because it did not seem dreadful enough. Instead, Austria-Hungary attracted gifted ironists, and even the bitterest anti-Habsburg satire, *The Good Soldier Švejk,* is universally interpreted as a joke rather than as a serious critique.

Second, the situation allowed for the construction of the "Habsburg myth," which presented the monarchy as a truly archaic country, belonging to a remote epoch "before history," that is, before the political conflicts and social tensions of modernity disturbed the "natural," paternalistic order. In other words, literature of the Habsburg myth creatively adapted the actual Habsburg political ideology, which worked so awkwardly in the reality of the twentieth century, but perfectly suited the world of fantasy. Certainly, this point of view could hardly be of any use for interwar historians; and yet for some historians Austria-Hungary simultaneously belonged to the most recent past and to some remote historical epoch, closed by the grand finale of the Great War. Ubiquitously assumed antiquarianism of the monarchy on the one hand, and notorious analogies to antiquity on the other, merged into an image of the country that did not belong to the modern era. As A. F. Pribram put it, "Regrets, however, are of no avail. History has pronounced its verdict: Austria-Hungary is no more."[13] The Habsburg myth was essentially ahistorical. Still, historians have not been completely immune to its rhetorical potential: roughly speaking, half of the historians writing on the monarchy since the 1960s (especially in America) have extensively quoted Musil, Zweig, or Roth to support their analyses, or indeed instead of providing an analysis of their own. Post-Habsburg literary fiction, apart from its artistic quality, has one splendid advantage: it spectacularly demonstrates that the monarchy was the country like no other, that its problems and the ways of coping with them were unique, and that it was inhabited by truly special people. It does not simply add some aesthetic flavor to the problems related to the monarchy; it marks them with the stamp of originality.

Certainly, one of the ideas that on the one hand neutralized anti-Habsburg criticism, and on the other hand fueled belief in Austria-Hungary's uniqueness, was its supposed decadence. Decadence is an ambivalent idea, provoking both disrespect and curiosity. It dates back as far as the Greek historian Polybius and his theory of alternate periods of political and cultural growth, which found innumerable followers including Machiavelli, Voltaire, Montesquieu, and Gibbon—whose writings were fundamental for Western reflection on the problem of "the decline and fall of empires." In short, the theory assumed that, as Gibbon has put it, "prosperity ripens the principle of decay"—that states deteriorate only after they reach the peak of their internal development, when they become oversophisticated.[14] Politically, the theory was founded upon respect for the moral vigor and virtues of those who were not yet spoiled by their achievements. Obviously, the theory seemed already dead by the nineteenth century, when Western civilization believed in its endless progress. However, one of its by-products survived it: a fascination with decadence that is supposed to precede all decline. It suited the interest in Austria-Hungary perfectly, and suggested that its political deterioration must have been accompanied by outstanding cultural achievements. G. R. Marek, author of a popular history of the last Habsburgs, suggested this with one more ancient analogy, quoting Steven Runciman's *The Last Byzantine Renaissance:* "Yet was it a period of decline? In strange contrast with the political decline, the intellectual life of Byzantium never shone so brilliantly as in those two centuries [before its collapse]."[15] Of course, the "strange contrast" was not in fact strange at all: it testified to the uniqueness of the discussed phenomenon. Moreover, decadence explained Austria-Hungary's passive resistance to the forces that undermined it. If the monarchy was doomed, it was actually wise not to speed up its dissolution by destroying its fragile inner construction.

To be sure, there were authors who idealized the monarchy and authors who demonized it; but it was precisely the fact that Austria-Hungary and the political principles it represented were considered irrevocably gone in the interwar period that left some space for impartial analyses and creative generalizations. Karl Kraus called Austria-Hungary "a laboratory of modernity." Indeed, post-Habsburg authors were capable of transforming their Austro-Hungarian experience into metaphors of human condition in general. Instead of writing about Austria-Hungary they preferred creating Kakania, Tarokania, or Teskovina, which actually surpassed the monarchy in many respects. These countries were not as fantastic as their names, for they resembled Austria-Hungary so evidently that no one could have doubts where to locate them on the map of Europe. Still, it was precisely because all maps depicting Austria-Hungary suddenly became outdated that made the monarchy a perfect object of such fabrications. The monarchy's nonexistence made it a fertile soil for creative imagination and speculations.

Finally, an interesting thesis on the causes of Austria-Hungary's uniqueness has been formulated by Ernest Gellner in his *Language and Solitude: Wittgenstein, Malinowski and the Habsburg Dilemma*. In his view, Austria-Hungary in its last decades was the epicenter of the crucial conflict of modernity: the one between "the village green" and cosmopolitan, urban liberalism; or, in Max Weber's terms, between *Gemeinschaft* and *Gesellschaft*. Nowhere in Europe, he argues, was the opposition between the two principles sharper and more engaging. His observation that rising nationalism turned against the monarchy "in the name of peasant roots of community and togetherness, as against abstract rootless cosmopolitanism" does not seem too original. However, he also points out what other authors failed to emphasize: that the monarchy was not supported exclusively by its feudal elite, bureaucracy, and the army. His opinion is as follows:

> But in the end even their loyalty became doubtful. And now the center acquired a new and surprising ally: the beneficiaries of liberalism. The rickety structure, which was a survival from feudalism and baroque absolutism, somehow endeared itself to, and only to, the free-thinking liberal individualists (a strange metamorphosis indeed!) . . . An old and rigid dynasty, long linked with hierarchy, authoritarianism, and obscurantist dogmatism, did not exactly look like promising material for being the symbol of the Open Society. But, comic as it might be, the logic of the situation made it so.[16]

The logic of the situation, he claims, produced a uniquely Austro-Hungarian ideology: "pariah-liberalism," which differed from other forms of liberalism because of the pressure of nationalist, rural communitarianism, and the painful awareness of the fact that its only ally against this mighty enemy was the fading monarchy. "What wonder," he concludes, "that the most passionate, brilliant and profound paeans to liberalism in the twentieth century came from the pens of Viennese authors?" Obviously, Gellner is wrong in his supposition that the monarchy had no other enthusiasts but free-thinking, cosmopolitan liberals. As a matter of fact, when the monarchy still existed, they had relatively little love for it, and they were converting to nationalism much more frequently than to Habsburg loyalism. However, things indeed changed after the ridiculed and impotent monarchy had fallen, and nationalism (with its cult for "the village green") triumphed, showing its ugliest face in the 1930s and 1940s. From a timely distance it certainly seemed that Austria-Hungary had been the most desperate protector of individualism, cosmopolitanism, and liberalism at the turn of the centuries. Thus, Gellner's analysis appears overall correct, at least in Marxist terms of the "objective" historical forces, which Gellner himself, as one of the intellectual champions of liberalism and the idea of the open society, wholeheartedly despised. The Café Central of Vienna eventually stood against the village green and its dangerous ideology. And Gellner's argumentation clearly testifies that cosmopolitan liberals have forgiven Austria-Hungary its post-feudal obscurantism and authoritarianism and joined its more conservatively inclined admirers, making Habsburg nostalgia indeed a complex and powerful trend. This, however, was only possible because the monarchy no longer existed.

Interdiscursive Osmosis

This book has not really elucidated Austria-Hungary or the causes of its decline and fall. Nor has it attempted to do so, for one of my inspirations was the conviction that the monarchy has attracted numerous talented and insightful scholars, and that discourse on Austria-Hungary achieved intellectual and scholarly maturity a number of decades ago. This is why I have decided to take a closer look at its adolescence: the turbulent years when contradicting opinions, interpretations, and sentiments were still storming its unshaped shores. It is the advantage of historians to discover how various streams, taking their sources in dispersed impulses of the minds of the past actors, form the rivers of knowledge from which the future generations drink in blessed ignorance of their composition. However, studying the history of a discourse does not offer the bliss of certainty available to historians of the natural sciences. We are faced with a multitude of ideas that all had their grounds and their dynamics, and which can be related to specific political and social interests, although such an operation is not always sympathetic toward their authors. After all, people are free to formulate their opinions regardless of their nationality or social position, even though they are rarely capable of it. But the fact that some interpretations of the past seem more intelligent and insightful than others does not automatically make them right. Neither can we say that interpretations that can be ascribed to particular groups of interest or ideologies that are not popular anymore were wrong or shortsighted.

All we can do is sail the river of history back and trace the sources of the interpretations that we now consider acceptable and convincing.

As I argued, the posthumous image of Austria-Hungary has been disproportionally influenced by a relatively small group of authors who considered its dissolution a more or less painful loss. It is important to bear in mind, however, that the reasons for this sentiment were multifold and often contradictory. Some of these authors were political conservatives and some were liberals; some were incapable of identifying with any other country as their motherland and hence missed the supranational monarchy in spite of its numerous deficiencies; some simply discovered that life had been more stable, prosperous, and joyful before 1914, when they had been themselves young and charmingly naïve, than in the turbulent 1920s and 1930s. This is to say that the sense of loss caused by the dissolution of Austria-Hungary had no common grounds, no common ideological background, and no common logic. It had only a common dynamics, caused by the fact that Habsburg nostalgia was politically insignificant, that it was fantasy rather than an ideology. It is also important for the long-term success of this tendency, that, generally speaking, it did not idealize Austria-Hungary beyond certain limits: the monarchy it envisaged was not a utopia but a tolerable country in which to live, likable in spite of its obvious deficiencies, such as its undeniably anachronistic, and admittedly corrupt, political system. Finally, one should bear in mind that the success of this tendency has naturally been limited. Critics of the monarchy were numerous, their number involved some highly gifted authors, and they found followers in the next generations. National historiographies of the monarchy's successor states have never ceased to emphasize the Habsburgs' sins, especially concerning the oppression of their respective national movements, which Western historians have tended to underestimate—perhaps because many Western historians still believe that the monarchy, authoritarian and obscurantist as it might have been, was a Westernizing force in the world of the essentially barbarian "village greens." All things being equal, one of the grounds for the relative success of the enthusiasts of Austria-Hungary is that the most intelligent of them never denied its dark sides: their apologies of the monarchy acknowledged that its shining aspects had their shadows.

Finally, there is one more conclusion to this book. It concerns the ways in which the discourse is reproduced and perpetuated. Apparently, one of the crucial mechanisms that govern this process is the osmosis between various genres. Without taking this fascinating and still poorly-researched phenomenon into consideration, we could hardly understand the discontinuities observable within one genre. It cannot be reduced to the process known as intellectual transfer. Most importantly, the authors involved knew the monarchy from their own past, and the entire process of transforming their memories into narratives took place within the framework of the sociohistorical memory of contemporary society. Fiction writers analyzed in this book did not simply employ facts described by academic historians; historians did not borrow metaphors from artists; and essayists did not provide them with elegant formulas. The entire process was more multistage, versatile, and—awkward as it sounds—mysterious. Unfortunately, we can only see its results, and hence the actual ways in which historians, fiction writers, and essayists inspired each other must remain their secret—a secret they presumably did not fully realize themselves. However, analyzing their modes of argumentation and presentation, their rhetoric and metaphors, their values and opinions, we discover profound affinities and striking parallels. In the case of writings concerning Austria-Hungary, these affinities and parallels actually form the vascular system of the discourse. History of historiography, history of literature, and history of ideas, focusing on their own fields, fail to notice the importance of this circulation. One of the objectives of this book was to elucidate that without taking into consideration osmosis between genres where we cannot see how the historical imagination is constructed and reproduced.

NOTES

Introduction

1. Austria-Hungary is the common name of the state created by the so-called Compromise of 1867. Officially it had no common name, and as it was composed of the Austrian Empire and the Hungarian Kingdom, it was also frequently called the dual monarchy. Since in this book I mostly refer to that epoch I also employ these names. However, some of the authors I refer to or quote did not care about titular changes and employed the name Austria-Hungary for the whole period beginning with the union of the Habsburg hereditary lands (today's Austria, approximately) with the Czech and Hungarian crowns in 1526/1527, and the others called all territories ruled by the Habsburgs at any time simply Austria.

2. Actually, of those three only Marx discussed the future of Austria extensively; see Ernst Hanisch, *Der kranke Mann an der Donau: Marx und Engels über Österreich* (Vienna, 1978), 31–34 and 339–43.

3. On Wilson see, for example: Arthur Walworth, *Wilson and His Peacemakers: American Diplomacy at the Paris Peace Conference, 1919* (New York: Norton, 1986); Klaus Schwabe, *Woodrow Wilson: Ein Staatsmann zwischen Puritanertum und Liberalismus* (Göttingen: Muster-Schmidt, 1971); Jan Willem Schulte Nordholt, *Woodrow Wilson: A Life for World Peace* (Berkeley: University of California Press, 1991).

4. From the immense literature on the Paris Conference I consulted: Wolfgang Michalka, ed., *Der Erste Weltkrieg: Wirkung, Wahrnehmung, Analyse* (Munich: Piper, 1994), 28–191; Alan Sharp, *The Versailles Settlement: Peacemaking in Paris, 1919* (New York: St. Martin's, 1991), 130–59; Manfred F. Boemeke, Gerald D. Feldman, and Elisabeth Glaser, eds., *The Treaty of Versailles: A Reassessment after 75 Years* (New York: Cambridge University Press, 1998), 197–249.

5. *Hungary and Her Successors: The Treaty of Trianon and Its Consequences, 1919–1937* (London: Oxford University Press, 1937; repr., 1965), by C. A. Macartney, remains probably the best study of the subject in English.

6. A brilliant essay on interwar Austrian identity, including economic problems, is Robert Menasse, *Das Land ohne Eigenschaften: Essays zur österreichischen Identität* (Vienna: Sonderzahl, 1993). Many interesting observations may still be found in Charles Adams Gulick, *Österreich von Habsburg zu Hitler* (Vienna: Danubia, 1948), and in Mary Macdonald

Proudfoot, *The Republic of Austria, 1918–1934: A Study in the Failure of the Democratic Government* (London: Oxford University Press, 1946).

7. See Carole Fink, *Defending the Rights of Others: The Great Powers, the Jews, and International Minority Protection, 1878–1938* (Cambridge, UK: Cambridge University Press, 2004), 237–66.

8. For theoretical reconsiderations of the concept of nostalgia see the first chapter of Christopher Shaw and Malcolm Chase, *The Imagined Past: History and Nostalgia* (Manchester: Manchester University Press, 1989).

9. I owe this anecdote to the book vaguely related to the subject: Stanisław Mackiewicz, *Polityka Becka* (Paris: Instytut Literacki, 1964), 102.

10. A good example of this attitude is Jan Opočenský, *Der Untergang Österreichs und die Entstehung des tschechoslovakischen Staates* (Prague: Orbis, 1928). Although the author recalls Austria in the title of his book, he actually pays little attention to it, merely reminding his readers that it was a rotten, corrupted country, and an obstacle to the idea of the Czechoslovak state.

11. See Stephan Verosta, *Die internationale Stellung Österreichs eine Sammlung von Erklärungen und Verträgen aus den Jahren 1938 bis 1947* (Vienna: Manz, 1947).

12. For a summary of this tendency see Hans Mommsen, "Die habsburgische Nationalitätenfrage und ihre Lösungsversuche im Licht der Gegenwart," in *Nationalismus, Nationalitäten, Supranationalität: Europa nach 1945*, ed. Heinrich August Winkler and Hartmut Kaelbe (Stuttgart: Klett-Cotta, 1993), 108–22.

13. The most important of them were Henryk Wereszycki, *Pod berłem Habsburgów: Zagadnienia narodowościowe* (Cracow: Wydawnictwo Literackie, 1986) and Jòzef Chlebowczyk, *O prawie do bytu małych i młodych narodów: Kwestia narodowa i procesy narodowotwórcze we wschodniej Europie Środkowej w dobie kapitalizmu (od schyłku XVIII w. do początków XX w.)* (Warsaw: Śląski Instytut Naukowy, 1983).

Chapter 1. Austria-Hungary in Historiography

1. Henry W. Steed, *The Hapsburg Monarchy* (London: Constable & Co., 1914), xxi.

2. C. A. Macartney, *The Social Revolution in Austria* (Cambridge, UK: Cambridge University Press, 1926), 1.

3. Part of the Austro-Hungarian border was on the river Leitha; hence, from the Austrian point of view, the Austrian part of the monarchy was called Cisleithania, and the Hungarian part was called Transleithania.

4. Joseph Redlich, *Emperor Francis Joseph of Austria: A Biography* (London: Macmillan, 1929), 507. In English the Hungarian term "Magyar" is applied to denote ethnic Hungarians, whereas "Hungarian" denotes inhabitants of the Hungarian Kingdom, including national minorities. Obviously, the difference is not always clear, and authors cited in this book often mention "Magyars" to stress their nationalism.

5. Leon Biliński, *Wspomnienia i dokumenty, 1846–1922* (Warsaw: Księgarnia Hoesicka, 1925), 235–37.
6. Heinrich von Lützow, *Im diplomatischen Dienst der k. und k. Monarchie* (Munich: Oldenbourg, 1971), 269–70.
7. This is why Hungarians insisted that all common institutions of the monarchy (for example, the army) be called "imperial and royal," instead of "imperial-royal": it allowed them to pretend that the "imperial" aspect did not refer to Hungary.
8. Oszkár Jászi, *The Dissolution of the Habsburg Monarchy* (Chicago: Chicago University Press, 1929), 352.
9. Ibid., 363.
10. Wilhelm Schüssler, *Österreich und das deutsche Schicksal* (Leipzig: Quelle & Mener, 1925), 47.
11. August Fournier, *Österreich-Ungarns Neubau unter Kaiser Franz Joseph I: Eine historische Skizze* (Berlin: Ullstein, 1917), 188–96.
12. Hugo Hantsch, *Die Geschichte Österreichs* (Vienna: Styria, 1953), 399.
13. Ibid., 403, 493–95.
14. Friedrich Kleinwächter, *Von Schönbrünn bis St. Germain* (Graz: Styria, 1964), 20–21.
15. Heinrich Benedikt, *Monarchie der Gegensätze: Österreichs Weg durch die Neuzeit* (Vienna: Ullstein, 1947), 176–80.
16. Ibid., 200–201.
17. C. A. Macartney, *Hungary and Her Successors: The Treaty of Trianon and Its Consequences, 1919–1937* (London: Oxford University Press, 1965), 35–37.
18. Gergely Romsics, *Myth and Remembrance: The Dissolution of the Habsburg Empire in the Memoir Literature of the Austro-Hungarian Political Elite* (New York: Columbia University Press, 2006), 170.
19. See Péter Hanák, *Ungarn in der Donaumonarchie: Probleme der bürgerlichen Umgestaltung eines Vielvölkerstaates* (Vienna: Geschichte und Politik, 1984), 139–42.
20. Julius von Szilassy, *Der Untergang der Donau-Monarchie: Diplomatische Erinnerungen* (Berlin: Neues Vaterland, 1921), 317.
21. See Steven Béla Várdy, *Modern Hungarian Historiography* (Boulder, CO: East European Quarterly, 1976), 175–95.
22. Friedrich Hertz, *Nationalgeist und Politik*, vol. 1, *Staatstradition und Nationalismus* (Zurich: Europa, 1937), 340–41.
23. Ibid., 340, 356–57, 436.
24. Ibid., 365–68, 390–91.
25. Steinecker, "Die geschichtlichen Voraussetzungen des österreichischen Nationalitätenproblems und seine Entwicklung bis 1867," in *Das Nationalitätenrecht des alten Österreich*, ed. Karl Gottfried Hugelmann (Vienna: Braumüller, 1934), 18–29.
26. Hugelmann, ed., *Nationalitätenrecht*, 277–83.

27. Benedikt, *Monarchie,* 188–97. The citation from Alexander Pope comes from *Essay on Man,* epistle III, line 303.

28. Joseph Redlich, *Austrian War Government* (New Haven, CT: Yale University Press, 1929), 36–39.

29. Macartney, *Social Revolution,* 5–19.

30. Viktor Bibl, *Der Zerfall Österreichs,* vol. 2, *Von Revolution zu Revolution* (Vienna: Rikola, 1924), 370–80.

31. The so-called language ordinances of Prime Minister Badeni (a Polish conservative) were intended to solve the growing tension between the Czechs and the Germans of Bohemia. They obliged public offices in Bohemia, which used only German up to that time, to provide services in both languages. Since that would imply that a number of German officials would have to learn Czech, or be replaced by mostly bilingual Czechs, it caused enormous protests in parliament and on the streets of Vienna. In consequence, the government fell and no other Austrian government won parliamentary majority again.

32. Redlich, *Emperor Francis Joseph,* 448–51.

33. Heinrich von Srbik, "Erzherzog Albrecht, Benedek und die altösterreichische Soldatengeist," in *Aus Österreichs Vergangenheit: Von Prinz Eugen zu Franz Joseph* (Salzburg: Otto Müller, 1949), 132–33.

34. Schüssler, *Österreich,* 6–8.

35. Max Hildebrandt Brehm, "Krise und Ausklang," in *Das Nationalitätenrecht des alten Österreich,* ed. Karl Gottfried Hugelmann (Vienna: Braumüller, 1934), 741–44.

36. Edmund von Glaise-Horstenau, *Die Katastrophe: Die Zertrümmerung Österreich-Ungarns und das Werden der Nachfolgestaaten* (Vienna: Amalthea, 1929), 9.

37. Hugelmann, ed., *Nationalitätenrecht,* 763–70.

38. Leon Wasilewski, *Austrja Spółczesna* (Warsaw: Drukarnia Narodowa, 1907), 81–82.

39. Francis Henry Gribble, *The Life of the Emperor Francis Joseph* (London: Eveleigh Nash, 1914), 346–47.

40. Redlich, *Emperor Francis Joseph,* 368, 397.

41. Heinrich Rosenfeld, *Wilson und Österreich* (Vienna: Carl Könegen, 1919), 10.

42. Bibl, *Der Zerfall,* vol. 2, 411.

43. Benedikt, *Monarchie,* 183.

44. Alfred Francis Pribram, *Austrian Foreign Policy, 1908–1918* (London: Allen & Unwin, 1923), 13–15.

45. Ibid., 56, 19.

46. Bibl, *Der Zerfall,* vol. 2, 431.

47. Josef Schneider, ed., *Kaiser Franz Joseph I und sein Hof: Erinnerungen und Schilderungen aus den nachgelassenen Papieren eines persönlichen Ratgebers* (Vienna: Leonhardt, 1919), 17–30.

48. Redlich, *Emperor Francis Joseph*, 397.
49. They are discussed in detail in Robert A. Kann, *Erzherzog Franz Ferdinand Studien* (Munich: Oldenbourg, 1976).
50. Glaise-Horstenau, *Die Katastrophe*, 20–21; Richard Suchenwirth, *Das Tausendjährige Österreich* (Munich: Bruckmann, 1938), 250–54.
51. Schüssler, *Österreich*, 52–53.
52. Alfred Missong, "Europa: Betrachtungen über Kaisertum, Völkerreich, Völkerbund und Paneuropa," in *Die österreichische Aktion: Programmatische Studien,* ed. Ernst Karl Winter (Vienna, 1927), 44–60.
53. Bibl, *Der Zerfall*, vol. 2, 402–30.
54. Schneider, *Kaiser Franz Joseph*, 176–77.
55. Eugene Bagger, *Franz Joseph: Eine Persönlichkeits-Studie* (Vienna: Amalthea, 1927), 5.
56. Leon Sapieha, *Viribus-Unitis* (Lviv, 1920), 57.
57. Pribram, *Austrian Foreign Policy*, 63.
58. Hermann Gsteu, *Geschichte Österreichs* (Innsbruck: Universitäts-Verlag Wagner, 1937), 319.
59. Glaise-Horstenau, *Die Katastrophe*, 22–28.
60. Suchenwirth, *Das Tausendjährige*, 250–54.
61. Friedrich Funder, *Vom Gestern ins Heute: Aus dem Kaiserreich in die Republik* (Vienna: Herold, 1952), 520–21.
62. Karl Werkmann, *Der tote auf Madeira* (Munich: Kulturpolitik, 1923), 77.
63. Hantsch, *Die Geschichte,* 548–50, 558.
64. See A. F. Pollard, "Balance of Power," *Journal of the British Institute of International Affairs* 2, no. 2 (March 1923): 58.
65. Hantsch, *Die Geschichte,* 573.
66. Schüssler, *Österreich*, 25.
67. Suchenwirth, *Das Tausendjährige,* 246.
68. Heinrich Kanner, *Kaiserliche Katastrophenpolitik* (Vienna: Tal, 1922), 390–94.
69. Bagger, *Franz Joseph,* 551–56.
70. Bibl, *Der Zerfall,* vol. 2, 447.
71. Arthur Polzer-Hoditz, *Kaiser Karl: Aus der Geheimmappe seines Kabinettschefs* (Vienna: Amalthea, 1929), 31–56, 134–50.
72. Werkmann, *Der Tote auf Madeira,* 77–78.
73. Srbik, "Österreichs Schicksal im Spiegel des geflügelten Wortes," in *Aus Österreichs Vergangenheit,* 265–70.
74. Albert Fuchs, *Geistige Strömungen in Österreich, 1867–1918* (Vienna: Löcker, 1984), 85–129.
75. Ibid., 166.
76. David F. Strong, *Austria (October 1918–March 1919): Transition from Empire to Republic* (New York: Columbia University Press, 1939), 18–20.

77. See Ernst Karl Winter, "Der europäische und der österreichische Raum," in *Die österreichische Aktion* (Vienna, 1927), 24–25; Alois Rudolf Carl Jaschke, *Österreichs deutsches Erbe: Ein Europäisches Raumproblem* (Graz: Moser, 1934), 240–45.

78. See Redlich, *Emperor Francis Joseph*, 452; Hertz, *Nationalgeist*, 356–57.

Chapter 2. Austria-Hungary in Essayism and Political Theory

1. Alfred Francis Pribram, *Austrian Foreign Policy, 1908–1918* (London: Allen & Unwin, 1923), 11, 28.

2. Otto Bauer, *Die österreichische Revolution* (Vienna: Volksbuchhandlung, 1933), 101.

3. Ibid., 159.

4. Walter Kolarz, *Myths and Realities in Eastern Europe* (London: Lindsay Drummond, 1946), 42.

5. Ibid., 44.

6. See Ernst Hanisch, *Der kranke Mann an der Donau: Marx und Engels über Österreich* (Vienna: Europaverlag, 1978), 31–34.

7. Franz Martin Mayer, Raimund Friedrich Kaindl, and Hans Pirchegger, eds., *Geschichte und Kulturleben Deutschösterreichs von 1792 bis nach dem Weltkrieg* (Vienna: Braumüller, 1937), 309.

8. Oskar von Mitis, *Das Leben des Kronprinzen Rudolf: Mit Briefen und Schriften auf dessen Nachlass* (Leipzig: Insel, 1928), 155.

9. Gusztáv Gratz and Richard Schüller, *The Economic Policy of Austria-Hungary during the War in its External Relations* (New Haven, CT: Yale University Press, 1928), xxiii.

10. Ludwik Kulczycki, *Austrya a Polska* (Kraków: Centralne Biuro Wydawnictw N.K.N, 1916), 7–9.

11. Stephan Zweig, "Joseph Roth (1939)," in *Die Monotonisierung der Welt: Aufsätze und Vorträge* (Frankfurt am Main.: Surkhamp, 1976), 227.

12. Karl Gottfried Hugelmann, ed., *Das Nationalitätenrecht des alten Österreich* (Vienna: Braumüller, 1934), 277–78.

13. Heinrich Clam-Martinic, "Kaiser Franz Joseph und die Nationalitäten," in *Erinnerungen an Franz Joseph I., Kaiser von Österreich: Apostolischer König von Ungarn*, ed. Eduard Ritter von Steinitz (Berlin: Politik, 1931), 166.

14. Schüssler, *Österreich und das deutsche Schicksal* (Leipzig: Quelle & Mener, 1925), 208.

15. Friedrich Kleinwächter, *Der Untergang der österreichisch-ungarischen Monarchie* (Leipzig: Köhler, 1920), 289.

16. Alfred Rapp, *Die Habsburger: Die Tragödie eines halben Jahrtausends deutschen Geschichte* (Stuttgart: Franckh'sche Verlagshandlung, 1936), 271–73.

17. Alois Rudolf Carl Jaschke, *Österreichs deutsches Erbe: Ein Europäisches Raumproblem* (Graz: Moser, 1934), 241–54.

18. Heinrich von Srbik, "Österreichs Schicksal im Spigel des geflügelten

Wortes," in *Aus Österreichs Vergangenheit: Von Prinz Eugen zu Franz Joseph* (Salzburg: Müller, 1949), 265–70.

19. Bruno Brehm, *Die Throne stürzen: Romantrilogie* (Munich: Piper, 1959), 519–20.

20. Friedrich von Wieser, *Österreichs Ende* (Berlin, 1919), 316–18.

21. Henry W. Steed, *The Hapsburg Monarchy* (London: Constable & Co., 1914), xviii.

22. Konstanty Srokowski, *Upadek imperializmu Austryi w zwiazku z ewolucya systemu europejskiego przed wojna bałkańska i po niej* (Lviv, 1913), 56.

23. Albert von Apponyi, "Franz Joseph als König von Ungarn," in *Erinnerungen an Franz Joseph I., Kaiser von Österreich: Apostolischer König von Ungarn,* ed. Eduard Ritter von Steinitz (Berlin: Kulturpolitik, 1931), 126.

24. See Cedric Ellis Williams, *The Broken Eagle: The Politics of Austrian Literature from Empire to Anschluss* (London: Paul Elek, 1974), 113–20.

25. Viktor Suchy, "Die 'österreichische Idee' als konservative Staatsidee bei Hugo von Hofmannsthal, Richard von Schaukal und Anton Wildgans," in *Staat und Gesellschaft in der modernen österreichischen Literatur,* ed. Friedbert Aspetsberger (Vienna: Österreichisches Bundesverlag, 1977), 23.

26. Hugo von Hofmannsthal, "Die österreichische Idee," in *Österreichische Aufsätze und Reden* (Vienna: Bergland, 1956), 105–6.

27. Ibid., 107–8.

28. See Suchy, "Die 'österreichische Idee,'" 27.

29. Anton Wildgans, *Rede über Österreich* (Vienna: Speidel, 1930); see Aspetsberger, *Staat und Gesellschaft,* 28.

30. Richard von Schaukal, *Österreichische Züge* (Munich: Müller, 1918), 80–82; see Aspetsberger, *Staat und Gesellschaft,* 29–30.

31. Oskar Benda, *Die Österreichische Kulturidee im Staat und Erziehung* (Vienna: Saturn, 1936), 95.

32. W. Bauer, "Das Deutschtum der Deutschösterreichischer, 'Vergangenheit und Gegenwart,' XVII, 1927," in *Geschichte und Kulturleben Deutschösterreichs von 1792 bis nach dem Weltkrieg,* ed. Franz Martin Mayer, Raimund Friedrich Kaindl, and Hans Pirchegger (Vienna: Braumüller, 1937), 919.

33. Leopold von Andrian, *Österreich im Prisma der Idee: Katechismus der Führenden* (Graz: Schmidt-Dengler, 1937), 370–403.

34. Ibid., 337–38.

35. Ernst Karl Winter, ed., *Die österreichische Aktion: Programmatische Studien* (Vienna, 1927), 110.

36. Ibid., 32–34, 93–98.

37. Ibid., 24–36.

38. Ibid., 60–65.

39. Ibid., 90–110.

40. Ibid., 77–91.

41. Ibid., 44–60.

42. See Martin Greiffenhagen, *Das Dilemma des Konservatismus in Deutschland* (Munich: Piper, 1971), 169 ff.

43. Funder, *Vom Gestern ins Heute: Aus dem Kaiserreich in die Republik* (Vienna: Herold, 1952), 517.
44. Benda, *Die Österreichische Kulturidee,* 68.
45. See Friedbert Aspetsberger, *Literarisches Leben im Austrofaschismus: Der Staatspreis* (Königstein: Hain, 1980), 81.
46. Julius Wolf, Konrad Helig, and Hermann Görgen, *Österreich und die Reichsidee* (Vienna: Kunst und Wissenschaft, 1937), 1–34.
47. Franz Borkenau, *Austria and After* (London: Faber and Faber, 1938), 100.
48. Benda, *Die Österreichische Kulturidee,* 77.
49. Winter, *Die österreichische Aktion,* 111.
50. See Kurt Skalnik, "Auf der Suche nach der Identität: Ansätze österreichischer National-bewusstseins in der Ersten Republik," in *Das geistige Leben Wiens in der Zwischenkriegszeit,* ed. Norbert Leser (Vienna: Österreichisches Budnesverlag, 1981), 101.
51. See Friedrich Heer, *Der Kampf um die österreichische Identität* (Vienna: Böhlau, 1981), 11.
52. Felix Braun, *Anrufe des Geistes: Essays, Reden, Erinnerungen* (Graz: Styria, 1965), 137.
53. Josef Schneider, ed., *Kaiser Franz Joseph I und sein Hof: Erinnerungen und Schilderungen aus den nachgelassenen Papieren eines persönlichen Ratgebers* (Vienna: Leonhardt, 1919), 42.
54. Ignacy Daszyński, *Pamiętniki* (Warsaw: Książka i Wiedza, 1957), 99, 254, 270.
55. Joseph Bloch, *My Reminiscences* (New York: Arno Press, 1973), 27.
56. Leon Trotsky, *My Life: An Attempt at an Autobiography* (New York: Pathfinder Press, 1970), 207.
57. See Albert Fuchs, *Geistige Strömungen in Österreich, 1867–1918* (Vienna: Löcker, 1984), 274.
58. See Aspetsberger, *Literarisches Leben,* 78.
59. See Williams, *The Broken Eagle,* 277.
60. On Kraus see Edward Timms, *Karl Kraus: Apocalyptic Satirist: Culture and Catastrophe in Habsburg Vienna* (New Haven, CT: Yale University Press, 1986); Caroline Cohn, *Karl Kraus: Le polémiste et l'écrivain, défenseur des droits de l'individu* (Paris: Didier, 1962).
61. See Williams, *The Broken Eagle,* 215.
62. Robert Musil, "Politics in Austria," in *Precision and Soul: Essays and Addresses,* trans. Burton Pike and David S. Luft (Chicago: University of Chicago Press, 1978), 18–19.
63. Hermann Broch, *Hofmannsthal und seine Zeit: Eine Studie* (Frankfurt am Main: Surkhamp, 2001), 174–78.
64. Ibid., 47–54, 64–77, 183–84.
65. Ibid., 189–92.

Chapter 3. Austria-Hungary in Literary Fiction

1. Stefan Zweig, *The World of Yesterday,* trans. from the German Hallam ed. (London: Cassell, 1953), 127.
2. See Cedric Ellis Williams, *The Broken Eagle: The Politics of Austrian Literature from Empire to Anschluss* (London: Paul Elek, 1974), 87–90.
3. Ewa Wiegandt, *Austria Felix, czyli o micie Galicji we współczesnej prozie polskiej* (Poznań: Bene Nati, 1997), 33.
4. Robert Musil, *The Man without Qualities,* vol. 1, trans. Eithne Wilkins and Ernst Kaiser (New York: Coward-McCann, 1953), 32.
5. Zweig, *World of Yesterday,* 2.
6. Ibid., 196.
7. Musil, *Man without Qualities,* vol. 1, 156–57.
8. Heimitio von Doderer, *The Demons,* vol. 1, trans. Richard and Clara Winston (New York: Knopf, 1961), 353–54.
9. Musil, *Man without Qualities,* vol. 1, 31–32.
10. Joseph Roth, *The Radetzky March,* trans. Michael Hofmann (London: Granta, 2002), 120.
11. Joseph Roth, *The Emperor's Tomb,* trans. John Hoare (London: Hogarth, 1984), 7.
12. Józef Wittlin, *Salt of the Earth,* trans. Pauline de Chary (Chicago: Stackpole, 1970), 64, 100, 102.
13. Stanisław Vincenz, *Na wysokiej połoninie. Nowe czasy. Księga pierwsza: Zwada* (Warsaw: Pax, 1981), 352.
14. Emil Zegadłowicz, *Zmory: Kronika z zamierzchłej przeszłości* (Cracow: Wydawnictwo Literackie, 1984), 16 and 100. The town's name is Wołkowice, and it is supposed to be a pseudonym of the real town Wadowice, located in southern Poland, and famous mostly as the place where the future pope John Paul II was born and raised.
15. Roth, *Emperor's Tomb,* 64.
16. Doderer, *Demons,* vol. 1, 195.
17. Jan Parandowski, *Niebo w płomieniach* (Warsaw: Czytelnik, 1976), 182–83.
18. Zweig, *World of Yesterday,* 40.
19. Elias Canetti, *The Tongue Set Free: Remembrance of a European Childhood,* trans. Joachim Neugroschel (New York: Seabury, 1979), 79–83.
20. Roth, *Emperor's Tomb,* 35 and 39.
21. Ibid., 60–61.
22. Tadeusz Żeleński, *Znasz-li ten kraj? . . . Wspomnienia o Krakowie,* ed. Tomasz Weiss (Wrocław: Biblioteka Narodowa, 1983), 6–7.
23. Zweig, *World of Yesterday,* 67–91.
24. Zegadłowicz, *Zmory,* 36–37, 143, 202.
25. Egon Corti, *Elizabeth, Empress of Austria,* trans. Catherine Alison Phillips (New Haven, CT: Yale University Press, 1936).

26. Franz Werfel, "Das Trauerhas," in *Erzählungen aus zwei Welten* (Frankfurt am Main: Fischer, 1952), 232–33.
27. Roth, *Radetzky March*, 144.
28. Ibid., 148–49, 176.
29. Zweig, *World of Yesterday*, 60, 66.
30. Musil, *Man without Qualities,* vol. 2, 277.
31. Ibid., vol. 1, 241.
32. Ibid., vol. 1, 62–63.
33. Ibid., vol. 2, 278–79.
34. Zweig, *World of Yesterday*, 225.
35. Doderer, *Die Strudlhofsteige oder Melzer und die Tiefe der Jahre* (Munich: Deutscher Taschenbuchverlag, 1996), 494–95.
36. Doderer, *Demons*, vol. 1, 123.
37. Roth, *Emperor's Tomb*, 38.
38. Roth, *Radetzky March*, 319.
39. Zweig, *World of Yesterday*, 216.
40. Wittlin, *Salt of the Earth*, 7–8.
41. Alexander Lernet-Holenia, *Die Standarte* (Vienna: Zsolnay, 1996), 95–111.
42. Franz Theodor Csokor, *Dritter November 1918: Ende des Armee Österreich-Ungarns* (Vienna: Zsolnay, 1936).
43. Jaroslav Hašek, *The Good Soldier Švejk,* trans. Cecil Parrott (New York: Thomas Y. Crowell, 1974), 166.
44. Ibid., 154.
45. Ibid., 201–2.
46. Ibid., 248.
47. Ibid., 647–49.
48. Kazimierz Sejda, *C. K. Dezerterzy* (Warsaw, 1987), 197.
49. Ibid., 252–53.
50. Jerzy Kossowski, *Zielona Kadra* (Warsaw: Goebethner and Wolff, 1927).
51. Musil, *Man without Qualities,* vol. 2, 182–83.
52. Sandor Friedrich Rosenfeld (Roda Roda), *Das grosse Roda-Roda Buch* (Vienna: Zsolnay, 1988), 211–13.
53. Musil, *The Man without Qualities,* vol. 2, 182.
54. Fritz von Herzmanovsky-Orlando, *Maskenspiel der Genien* (Munich: Langen Müller, 1985), 51.
55. Georg von Rezzori, *Ein Hermelin in Tschernopol: Ein magherbinischer Roman* (Hamburg: Rowohlt, 1958).
56. Bruno Schulz, "Wiosna," *Sklepy cynamonowe: Sanatorium pod Klepsydrą* (Warsaw: Porozumienie Wydawców, 2000), 179–87.
57. Zegadłowicz, *Zmory*, 10.

Chapter 4. The Empire Epitomized: Franz Joseph

1. A. J. P. Taylor, *The Habsburg Monarchy 1809–1918: A History of the Austrian Empire and Austria-Hungary* (Chicago: University of Chicago Press, 1976), 10.

2. See: Franz Werfel, "An Essay upon the Meaning of Imperial Austria," in *The Twilight of a World*, trans. Helen T. Lowe-Porter (London: Viking, 1937), 22.

3. Richard von Schaukal, *Österreichische Züge* (Munich: Müller, 1918), 24.

4. Leon Sapieha, *Viribus-Unitis* (Lviv, 1920), 39.

5. The legal aspects of the agreement are probably best analyzed by László Peter in "Die Verfassungsentwicklung in Ungarn," in *Die Habsburgermonarchie 1848–1918*, vol. VII, *Verfassung und Parlamentarismus*, ed. Adam Wandruszka, Helmut Rumpler, and Peter Urbanitsch (Vienna: Österreichischen Akademie der Wissenschaften, 2000), 322–31.

6. Joseph Redlich, *Austrian War Government* (New Haven, CT: Yale University Press, 1929), 43–46.

7. Karl Tschuppik, *Franz Joseph I: Der Untergang eines Reiches* (Leipzig: Avalun, 1928), 8.

8. Sapieha, *Viribus-Unitis*, 40.

9. Eugene Bagger, *Franz Joseph: Eine Persönlichkeits-Studie* (Vienna: Amalthea, 1927), 7–8.

10. Bruno Brehm, *Am Ende stand Königgratz: Historischer Roman um Preussen und Österreich* (Salzburg: Styria, 1965), 556.

11. Werfel, "Essay upon the Meaning," 28–29.

12. Józef Wittlin, *Salt of the Earth*, trans. Pauline de Chary (Chicago: Stackpole, 1970), 10–15.

13. Joseph Roth, *The Radetzky March*, trans. Michael Hofmann (London: Granta, 2002), 359.

14. Alfred Doppler, *Wirklichkeit im Spiegel der Sprache: Aufsätze zur Literatur des 20. Jahrhunderts in Österreich* (Vienna: Europaverlag, 1975), 184.

15. Hugo Hantsch, *Die Geschichte Österreichs* (Vienna: Styria, 1953), 556.

16. Alfred Francis Pribram, *Austrian Foreign Policy, 1908–1918* (London: Allen & Unwin, 1923), 20.

17. Sándor Márai, *Embers*, trans. C. Brown Janeway (New York: Borzoi, 2001), 56–58.

18. August Fournier, *Österreich-Ungarns Neubau unter Kaiser Franz Joseph I: Eine historische Skizze* (Berlin: Ullstein, 1917), 208.

19. Bagger, *Franz Joseph*, 512–14.

20. Josef Schneider, ed., *Kaiser Franz Joseph I und sein Hof: Erinnerungen und Schilderungen aus den nachgelassenen Papieren eines persönlichen Ratgebers* (Vienna: Leonhardt, 1919), 31–60.

21. Egon Caesar Corti and Hans Sokol, *Kaiser Franz Joseph* (Vienna: Styria, 1960), 494.
22. Schneider, *Kaiser Franz Joseph*, 26.
23. Arthur Polzer-Hoditz, *Kaiser Karl: Aus der Geheimmappe seines Kabinettschefs* (Vienna: Amalthea, 1929), 180.
24. Schneider, *Kaiser Franz Joseph*, 20–21.
25. Pribram, *Austrian Foreign Policy*, 19.
26. Hantsch, *Die Geschichte Österreichs*, vol. II, 557.
27. Joseph Redlich, *Emperor Francis Joseph of Austria: A Biography* (London: Macmillan, 1929), 507.
28. See Hermann Gsteu, *Geschichte Österreichs* (Innsbruck: Universitäts-Verlag Wagner, 1937), 350; Friedrich Hertz, *Nationalgeist und Politik*, vol. 1, *Staatstradition und Nationalismus* (Zurich: Europa Verlag, 1937), 356–57; Heinrich Clam-Martinic, "Kaiser Franz Joseph und die Nationalitäten," in *Erinnerungen an Franz Joseph I., Kaiser von Österreich: Apostolischer König von Ungarn,* ed. Eduard Ritter von Steinitz (Berlin: Politik, 1931), 162.
29. Pribram, *Austrian Foreign Policy*, 21.
30. See Heinrich von Srbik, *Aus Österreichs Vergangenheit: Von Prinz Eugen zu Franz Joseph* (Salzburg: Otto Müller, 1949).
31. See Gsteu, *Geschichte Österreichs*, 350; Viktor Bibl, *Die Tragödie Österreichs* (Leipzig: Günther, 1937), 13. "The miracle of the House of Habsburg" refers, quite paradoxically, to the so-called miracle of the House of Brandenburg, i.e., the sudden death of the Russian emperor Peter II, which eliminated Russia from the war against Frederick II of Prussia (Brandenburg) and apparently saved the Prussian king from the imminent catastrophe.
32. Elias Canetti, "Power and Survival," in *The Conscience of Words*, trans. Joachim Neugroschel (New York: Seabury, 1979), 21–22.
33. "It may seem of minor importance, but such things matter in the monarchies: inviting my wife, the emperor evidently expressed his satisfaction with my work," explained the proud minister. See Leon Biliński, *Wspomnienia i dokumenty, 1846–1922*, vol. 1, *1846–1914* (Warsaw: Księgarnia Hoesicka 1924), 253.
34. Albert Lichtblau, ed., *"Als hätten wir dazugehört": Österreichisch-jüdische Lebensgeschichten aus der Habsburgermonarchie* (Vienna: Böhlau, 1999), 261–67.
35. Manès Sperber, *Die Wasserträger Gottes* (Vienna: Europaverlag, 1983), 88–89.
36. Werfel, "Essay upon the Meaning," 33.
37. Ignacy Daszyński, *Pamiętniki* (Warsaw: Książka i Wiedza, 1957), 252.
38. Karl Kraus, *The Last Days of Mankind,* abridged by Frederick Ungar (New York: F. Ungar, 1974), originally published as *Die letzten Tage der Menschheit* (Vienna: Die Fackel, 1919), act IV, scene 30.
39. Hermann Broch, *Hugo von Hofmannsthal and His Time,* trans. Michael P. Steinberg (Chicago: University of Chicago Press, 1984), 73–74.

Conclusion

1. Alan Sked, *The Decline and Fall of the Habsburg Empire, 1815–1918* (London: Longman, 1989), 3.
2. George Kennan, *The Decline of Bismarck's European Order: Franco-Russian Relations, 1875–1890* (Princeton, NJ: Princeton University Press, 1979), 423.
3. Ulrich Greiner, *Der Tod des Nachsommers: Aufsätze, Porträts, Kritiken zur österreichischen Gegenwartsliteratur* (Vienna: Hanser, 1979), 15.
4. Arthur Schnitzler, *Jugend in Wien: Eine Autobiographie* (Vienna: Molden, 1968), 274.
5. Robert Menasse, *Das Land ohne Eigenschaften: Essays zur österreichischen Identität* (Vienna: Sonderzahl, 1993), 23.
6. Greiner, *Der Tod*, 15, 46.
7. Franz Werfel, "An Essay upon the Meaning of Imperial Austria," in *The Twilight of a World*, trans. Helen T. Lowe-Porter (New York: Viking, 1937), 4.
8. Heinrich Benedikt, *Die Monarchie des Hauses Österreich: Ein historisches Essay* (Munich: Geschichte und Politik, 1968), 8.
9. Eugene Bagger, *Franz Joseph: Eine Persönlichkeits-Studie* (Vienna: Amalthea, 1927), 7–8.
10. See Norbert Leser, ed., *Das geistige Leben Wiens in der Zwischenkriegszeit* (Vienna: Österreichisches Budnesverlag, 1981), 103.
11. See Hermann Broch, *Hofmannsthal und seine Zeit: Eine Studie* (Frankfurt am Main: Suhrkamp, 2001), 55–57.
12. See Claudio Magris, *Der habsburgische Mythos in der österreichischen Literatur* (Salzburg: Müller, 1966), 17.
13. Alfred F. Pribram, *Austrian Foreign Policy, 1908–1918* (London: Allen & Unwin, 1923), 128.
14. Edward Gibbon, *The History of the Decline and Fall of the Roman Empire*, originally published 1776–89.
15. See George R. Marek, *The Eagles Die: Franz Joseph, Elisabeth, and Their Austria* (London: Hart-Davis MacGibbon, 1974), 460.
16. Ernest Gellner, *Language and Solitude: Wittgenstein, Malinowski and the Habsburg Dilemma* (Cambridge, UK: Cambridge University Press, 1998), 32–33.

BIBLIOGRAPHY

Primary Sources

Andrian, Leopold von. *Österreich im Prisma der Idee: Katechismus der Führenden*. Graz: Schmidt-Dengler, 1937.
Apponyi, Albert von. "Franz Joseph als König von Ungarn." In *Erinnerungen an Franz Joseph I., Kaiser von Österreich: Apostolischer König von Ungarn*, edited by Eduard Ritter von Steinitz. Berlin: Verlag für Kulturpolitik, 1931.
Bagger, Eugene. *Franz Joseph: Eine Persönlichkeits-Studie*. Vienna: Amalthea, 1927.
Bauer, Otto. *Die österreichische Revolution*. Vienna: Volksbuchhandlung, 1933.
Bauer, W. "Das Deutschtum der Deutschösterreichischer, 'Vergangenheit und Gegenwart,' XVII, 1927." In *Geschichte und Kulturleben Deutschösterreichs von 1792 bis nach dem Weltkrieg*, edited by Franz Martin Mayer, Raimund Friedrich Kaindl, and Hans Pirchegger. Vienna: Braumüller, 1937.
Benda, Oskar. *Die Österreichische Kulturidee in Staat und Erziehung*. Vienna: Saturn, 1936.
Benedikt, Heinrich. *Monarchie der Gegensätze: Österreichs Weg durch die Neuzeit*. Vienna: Verlag Ullstein, 1947.
Berchtold, Leopold. "Der Herrscher, wie ich ihn gekannt." In *Erinnerungen an Franz Joseph I., Kaiser von Österreich: Apostolischer König von Ungarn*, edited by Eduard Ritter von Steinitz. Berlin: Verlag für Kulturpolitik, 1931.
Bibl, Viktor. *Der Zerfall Österreichs*. Vol. 1, *Kaiser Franz und seine Erbe*. Vol. 2, *Von Revolution zu Revolution*. Vienna: Rikola Verlag, 1922–1924.
———. *Die Tragödie Österreichs*. Leipzig: Günther, 1937.
Biliński, Leon. *Wspomnienia i dokumenty, 1846–1922*. Warsaw: Księgarnia Hoesicka, 1925.
Bloch, Joseph. *My Reminiscences*. New York: Arno Press, 1973.
Borkenau, Franz. *Austria and After*. London: Faber and Faber, 1938.
Braun, Felix. *Anrufe des Geistes: Essays, Reden, Erinnerungen*. Graz: Styria, 1965.
Brehm, Bruno. *Am Ende stand Königgrätz: Historischer Roman um Preussen und Österreich*. Graz: Styria, 1965.
———. *Die Throne stürzen: Romantrilogie*. Munich: Piper, 1959.

Brehm, Max Hildebrandt. "Krise und Ausklang." In *Das Nationalitätenrecht des alten Österreich*, edited by Karl Gottfried Hugelmann. Vienna: Braumüller, 1934.

Broch, Hermann. *Hofmannsthal und seine Zeit: Eine Studie.* Frankfurt am Main: Suhrkamp, 2001.

———. *Hugo von Hofmannsthal and His Time: The European Imagination, 1860–1920.* Translated by Michael P. Steinberg. Chicago: University of Chicago Press, 1984.

Canetti, Elias. *The Tongue Set Free: Remembrance of a European Childhood.* Translated by Joachim Neugroschel. New York: Seabury Press, 1979.

———. "Power and Survival." In *The Conscience of Words.* Translated by Joachim Neugroschel. New York: Seabury Press, 1979.

Clam-Martinic, Heinrich. "Kaiser Franz Joseph und die Nationalitäten." In *Erinnerungen an Franz Joseph I., Kaiser von Österreich: Apostolischer König von Ungarn*, edited by Eduard Ritter von Steinitz. Berlin: Verlag für Politik, 1931.

Corti, Egon Caesar. *Elizabeth, Empress of Austria.* Translated by Catherine Alison Phillips. New Haven, CT: Yale University Press, 1936.

Corti, Egon Caesar, and Hans Sokol. *Kaiser Franz Joseph.* Vienna: Styria, 1960.

Csokor, Franz Theodor. *Dritter November 1918: Ende des Armee Österreich-Ungarns.* Vienna: Zsolnay, 1936.

Daszyński, Ignacy. *Pamiętniki.* Warsaw: Książka i Wiedza, 1957.

Doderer, Heimitio von. *The Demons.* Translated by Richard and Clara Winston. New York: Knopf, 1961.

———. *Die Strudlhofsteige oder Melzer und die Tiefe der Jahre.* Munich: Deutscher Taschenbuchverlag, 1996.

Fischhof, Adolph. *Österreich und die Burgschaften seines Bestandes: Politische Studie.* Vienna, 1869.

Fournier, August. *Österreich-Ungarns Neubau unter Kaiser Franz Joseph I: Eine historische Skizze.* Berlin: Ullstein Verlag, 1917.

Fuchs, Albert. *Geistige Strömungen in Österreich, 1867–1918.* Vienna: Löcker Verlag, 1984.

Funder, Friedrich. *Vom Gestern ins Heute: Aus dem Kaiserreich in die Republik.* Vienna: Herold, 1952.

Glaise-Horstenau, Edmund von. *Die Katastrophe: Die Zertrümmerung Österreich-Ungarns und das Werden der Nachfolgestaaten.* Vienna: Amalthea Verlag, 1929.

Gratz, Gusztáv, and Richard Schüller. *The Economic Policy of Austria-Hungary during the War in its External Relations.* New Haven, CT: Yale University Press, 1928.

Gribble, Francis Henry. *The Life of the Emperor Francis Joseph.* London: Eveleigh Nash, 1914.

Gsteu, Hermann. *Geschichte Österreichs.* Innsbruck: Universitäts-Verlag Wagner, 1937.

Hanisch, Ernst. *Der kranke Mann an der Donau: Marx und Engels über Österreich*. Vienna: Europaverlag, 1978.
Hantsch, Hugo. *Die Geschichte Österreichs*. Vienna: Styria, 1953.
Hašek, Jaroslav. *The Good Soldier Švejk*. Translated by Cecil Parrott. New York: Thomas Y. Crowell, 1974.
Hertz, Friedrich. *Nationalgeist und Politik*. Vol. 1, *Staatstradition und Nationalismus*. Zurich: Europa Verlag, 1937.
Herzmanovsky-Orlando, Fritz von. *Maskenspiel der Genien*. Munich: Langen Müller, 1985.
Hofmannsthal, Hugo von. *Österreichische Aufsätze und Reden*. Vienna: Bergland, 1956.
Hugelmann, Karl Gottfreid, ed. *Das Nationalitätenrecht des alten Österreich*. Vienna: Braumüller, 1934.
Jaschke, Alois Rudolf Carl. *Österreichs deutsches Erbe: Ein Europäisches Raumproblem*. Graz: Moser, 1934.
Jászi, Oszkár. *The Dissolution of the Habsburg Monarchy*. Chicago: University of Chicago Press, 1929.
Kafka, Franz. *The Castle*. Translated by Willa and Edwin Muir. New York: Schocken Books, 1954.
———. *The Trial*. Translated by Willa and Edwin Muir. New York: Knopf, 1957.
Kanner, Heinrich. *Kaiserliche Katastrophenpolitik*. Vienna: Tal, 1922.
Kleinwächter, Friedrich. *Der Untergang der österreichisch-ungarischen Monarchie*. Leipzig: Köhler, 1920.
———. *Von Schönbrünn bis St. Germain*. Graz: Styria, 1964.
Kolarz, Walter. *Myths and Realities in Eastern Europe*. London: Lindsay Drummond, 1946.
Kossowski, Jerzy. *Zielona Kadra*. Warsaw: Goebethner and Wolff, 1927.
Kraus, Karl. *The Last Days of Mankind*. Abridged by Frederick Ungar. New York: F. Ungar, 1974. Originally published as *Die letzten Tage der Menschheit* (Vienna: Die Fackel, 1919).
Kubin, Alfred. *The Other Side*. Translated by Denver Lindley. New York: Crown, 1967.
Kulczycki, Ludwik. *Austrya a Polska*. Cracow: Centralne Biuro Wydawnictw N.K.N, 1916.
Lernet-Holenia, Alexander. *Die Standarte*. Vienna: Zsolnay Verlag, 1996.
Lichtblau, Albert, ed. *"Als hätten wir dazugehört": Österreichisch-jüdische Lebensgeschichten aus der Habsburgermonarchie*. Vienna: Böhlau, 1999.
Lukinich, Imre. *A History of Hungary in Biographical Sketches*. London: Simpkin Marshall, 1937.
Lützow, Heinrich von. *Im diplomatischen Dienst der k. und k. Monarchie*. Munich: Oldenbourg, 1971.
Macartney, C. A. *Hungary and Her Successors: The Treaty of Trianon and Its Consequences, 1919–1937*. London: Oxford University Press, 1965. First published 1937.

———. *The Social Revolution in Austria*. Cambridge, UK: Cambridge University Press, 1926.

Mann, Heinrich. *Der untertan*. Leipzig: Wolff, 1918.

Márai, Sándor. *Embers*. Translated by C. Brown Janeway. New York: Borzoi, 2001.

Mayer, Franz Martin, Raimund Friedrich Kaindl, and Hans Pirchegger, eds. *Geschichte und Kulturleben Deutschösterreichs von 1792 bis nach dem Weltkrieg*. Vienna: Braumüller, 1937.

Missong, Alfred. "Europa: Betrachtungen über Kaisertum, Völkerreich, Völkerbund und Paneuropa." In *Die österreichische Aktion: Programmatische Studien*, edited by Ernst Karl Winter, 44–60. Vienna, 1927.

Mitis, Oskar von. *Das Leben des Kronprinzen Rudolf: Mit Briefen und Schriften auf dessen Nachlass*. Leipzig: Insel Verlag, 1928.

Musil, Robert. *The Man without Qualities*. Translated by Eithne Wilkins and Ernst Kaiser. New York: Coward-McCann, 1953.

———. "Politics in Austria." In *Precision and Soul: Essays and Addresses*. Translated by Burton Pike and David S. Luft. Chicago: University of Chicago Press, 1978.

Naumann, Friedrich. *Mitteleuropa*. Berlin: Reimer, 1915.

Opočenský, Jan. *Der Untergang Österreichs und die Entstehung des tschechoslowakischen Staates*. Prague: Orbis, 1928.

Parandowski, Jan. *Niebo w płomieniach*. Warsaw: Czytelnik, 1976.

Pollard, A. F. "Balance of Power." *Journal of the British Institute of International Affairs* 2, no. 2 (March 1923): 51–64.

Polzer-Hoditz, Arthur. *Kaiser Karl: Aus der Geheimmappe seines Kabinettschefs*. Vienna: Amalthea, 1929.

Popovici, Aurel. *Die Vereinigten Staaten von Gross-Österreich: Politische Studien zur Lösung der nationalen Fragen und staatsrechtlichen Krisen in Österreich-Ungarn*. Leipzig: Elischer, 1906.

Pribram, Alfred Francis. *Austrian Foreign Policy, 1908–1918*. London: Allen & Unwin, 1923.

Rapp, Alfred. *Die Habsburger: Die Tragödie eines halben Jahrtausends deutschen Geschichte*. Stuttgart: Franckh'sche Verlagshandlung, 1936.

Redlich, Joseph. *Austrian War Government*. New Haven, CT: Yale University Press, 1929.

———. *Emperor Francis Joseph of Austria: A Biography*. London: Macmillan, 1929.

Rezzori, Georg von. *Ein Hermelin in Tschernopol: Ein magherbinischer Roman*. Hamburg: Rowohlt, 1958.

Rosenfeld, Heinrich. *Wilson und Österreich*. Vienna: Carl Könegen, 1919.

Rosenfeld, Sandor Friedrich (Roda Roda). *Das grosse Roda-Roda Buch*. Vienna: Zsolnay, 1988.

Roth, Joseph. "The Bust of the Emperor." In *Collected Shorter Fiction of Joseph Roth*. Translated by Michael Hofmann. London: Granta Books, 2001.

———. *The Emperor's Tomb*. Translated by John Hoare. London: Hogarth Press, 1984.
———. *The Radetzky March*. Translated by Michael Hofmann. London: Granta Books, 2002.
Sapieha, Leon. *Viribus-Unitis*. Lviv, 1920.
Schaukal, Richard von. *Österreichische Züge*. Munich: Müller, 1918.
Schneider, Josef, ed. *Kaiser Franz Joseph I und sein Hof: Erinnerungen und Schilderungen aus den nachgelassenen Papieren eines persönlichen Ratgebers*. Vienna: Leonhardt, 1919.
Schnitzler, Arthur. *Jugend in Wien: Eine Autobiographie*. Vienna: Molden, 1968.
Schulz, Bruno. *The Complete Fiction of Bruno Schulz*. Translated by Celina Wieniawska. New York: Walker and Co., 1989.
———. *Sklepy cynamonowe: Sanatorium pod Klepsydrą*. Warsaw: Porozumienie Wydawców, 2000.
Schüssler, Wilhelm. *Österreich und das deutsche Schicksal*. Leipzig: Quelle & Mener, 1925.
Sejda, Kazimierz. *C. K. Dezerterzy*. Warsaw, 1987.
Seton-Watson, Robert William. *Racial Problems in Hungary*. London: Constable & Co., 1908.
Sperber, Manès. "Die Wasserträger Gottes." In *All das Vergangene*. Vienna: Europaverlag, 1983. Translated by Joachim Neugroschel as *God's Water Carriers* (New York: Holems & Meier, 1987).
Srbik, Heinrich von. *Aus Österreichs Vergangenheit: Von Prinz Eugen zu Franz Joseph*. Salzburg: Otto Müller, 1949.
Srokowski, Konstanty. *Upadek imperializmu Austryi w zwiazku z ewolucya system europejskiego przed wojna bałkańska i po niej*. Lviv: Połoniecki, 1913.
Steed, Henry W. *The Hapsburg Monarchy*. London: Constable & Co., 1914.
Steinecker, Harold. "Die geschichtlichen Voraussetzungen des österreichischen Nationalitätenproblems und seine Entwicklung bis 1867." In *Das Nationalitätenrecht des alten Österreich*, edited by Karl Gottfried Hugelmann. Vienna: Braumüller, 1934.
Steinitz, Eduard Ritter von, ed. *Erinnerungen an Franz Joseph I., Kaiser von Österreich: Apostolischer König von Ungarn*. Berlin: Verlag für Kulturpolitik, 1931.
Strong, David F. *Austria (October 1918–March 1919): Transition from Empire to Republic*. New York: Columbia University Press, 1939.
Suchenwirth, Richard. *Das Tausendjährige Österreich*. Munich: Bruckmann, 1938.
Szilassy, Julius von. *Der Untergang der Donau-Monarchie: Diplomatische Erinnerungen*. Berlin: Neues Vaterland, 1921.
Taylor, A. J. P. *The Habsburg Monarchy, 1809–1918: A History of the Austrian Empire and Austria-Hungary*. Chicago: University of Chicago Press, 1976.

Trotsky, Leon. *My Life: An Attempt at an Autobiography*. New York: Pathfinder Press, 1970.
Tschuppik, Karl. *Franz Joseph I: Der Untergang eines Reiches*. Leipzig: Avalun, 1928.
Vincenz, Stanisław. *Na wysokiej połoninie. Nowe czasy. Księga pierwsza: Zwada*. Warsaw: Pax, 1981.
———. *On the High Uplands: Sagas, Songs, Tales and Legends of the Carpathians*. Translated by H. C. Stevens. New York: Roy, 1955.
Wasilewski, Leon. *Austrja Spółczesna*. Warsaw: Drukarnia Narodowa, 1907.
Werfel, Franz. *Erzählungen aus zwei Welten*. Frankfurt am Main: Fischer Verlag, 1952.
———. "An Essay upon the Meaning of Imperial Austria." In *The Twilight of a World*. Translated by Helen T. Lowe-Porter. London: Viking Press, 1937.
Werkmann, Karl. *Der tote auf Madeira*. Munich: Verlag für Kulturpolitik, 1923.
Wieser, Friedrich von. *Österreichs Ende*. Berlin, 1919.
Wildgans, Anton. *Rede über Österreich*. Vienna: Speidel, 1930.
———. *Sämtliche Werke*. Vienna: Bellaria, 1948.
Winter, Ernst Karl, ed. *Die österreichische Aktion: Programmatische Studien*. Vienna, 1927.
Wittlin, Józef. *Salt of the Earth*. Translated by Pauline de Chary. Chicago: Stackpole Books, 1970.
Wolf, Julius, Konrad Helig, and Hermann Görgen. *Österreich und die Reichsidee*. Vienna: Verlag für Kunst und Wissenschaft, 1937.
Zegadłowicz, Emil. *Zmory: Kronika z zamierzchłej przeszłości*. Cracow: Wydawnictwo Literackie, 1984.
Żeleński, Tadeusz. *Znasz-li ten kraj? . . . Wspomnienia o Krakowie*. Edited by Tomasz Weiss. Wrocław: Biblioteka Narodowa, 1983.
Zweig, Stefan. *Beware of Pity*. Translated by Phyllis and Trevor Blewitt. New York: Harmony Books, 1982.
———. *Die Monotonisierung der Welt: Aufsätze und Vorträge*. Frankfurt am Main: Surkhamp, 1976.
———. *The World of Yesterday*. Translated from the German Hallam edition. London: Cassell, 1953.

Selected Secondary Literature

Ankersmit, Franklin. *Historical Representation*. Stanford, CA: Stanford University Press, 2001.
Aspetsberger, Friedbert. *Literarisches Leben im Austrofaschismus: Der Staatspreis*. Königstein: Hain, 1980.
———, ed. *Staat und Gesellschaft in der modernen österreichischen Literatur*. Vienna: Österreichisches Bundesverlag, 1977.
Assmann, Aleida. *Die Legitimität der Fiktion: Ein Beitrag zur Geschichte der literarischen Kommunikation*. Munich: W. Fink, 1980.

Batowski, Henryk. *Rozpad Austro-Węgier 1914–1918: Sprawy narodowościowe i działania dyplomatyczne*. Kraków: Wydawnictwo Literackie, 1982.

Benedikt, Heinrich. *Die Monarchie des Hauses Österreich: Ein historisches Essay*. Vienna: Verlag für Geschichte und Politik, 1968.

Boemeke, Manfred F., Gerald D. Feldman, and Elisabeth Glaser, eds. *The Treaty of Versailles: A Reassessment after 75 Years*. New York: Cambridge University Press, 1998.

Carr, David. *Time, Narrative and History*. Bloomington: Indiana University Press, 1986.

Chlebowczyk, Jòzef. *O prawie do bytu małych i młodych narodów: Kwestia narodowa i procesy narodowotwórcze we wschodniej Europie Środkowej w dobie kapitalizmu (od schyłku XVIII do początków XX w.)*. Warsaw: Śląski Instytut Naukowy, 1983.

Cohn, Caroline. *Karl Kraus: Le polémiste et l'écrivain, défenseur des droits de l'individu*. Paris: Didier, 1962.

Cornwall, Mark. *The Undermining of Austria-Hungary: The Battle for Hearts and Minds*. New York: St. Martin's Press, 2000.

Doppler, Alfred. *Wirklichkeit im Spiegel der Sprache: Aufsätze zur Literatur des 20. Jahrhunderts in Österreich*. Vienna: Europaverlag, 1975.

Fejtö, François. *Requiem pour un empire défunt: Histoire de la destruction de l'Autriche-Hongrie*. Paris: Lieu Commun, 1988.

Field, Frank. *The Last Days of Mankind: Karl Kraus and His Vienna*. London: Macmillan, 1967.

Fink, Carole. *Defending the Rights of Others: The Great Powers, the Jews, and International Minority Protection, 1878–1938*. Cambridge, UK: Cambridge University Press, 2004.

Gellner, Ernest. *Language and Solitude: Wittgenstein, Malinowski and the Habsburg Dilemma*. Cambridge, UK: Cambridge University Press, 1998.

Gibbon, Edward. *The History of the Decline and Fall of the Roman Empire*. London: 1776–89.

Greiffenhagen, Martin. *Das Dilemma des Konservatismus in Deutschland*. Munich: Piper, 1971.

Greiner, Ulrich. *Der Tod des Nachsommers: Aufsätze, Porträts, Kritiken zur österreichischen Gegenwartsliteratur*. Vienna: Hanser, 1979.

Gulick, Charles Adams. *Österreich von Habsburg zu Hitler*. Vienna: Danubia, 1948.

Hanák, Péter. *The Garden and the Workshop: Essays on the Cultural History of Vienna and Budapest*. Princeton, NJ: Princeton University Press, 1998.

———. *Ungarn in der Donaumonarchie: Probleme der bürgerlichen Umgestaltung eines Vielvölkerstaates*. Vienna: Verlag für Geschichte und Politik, 1984.

Hanisch, Ernst. *Der kranke Mann an der Donau: Marx und Engels über Österreich*. Vienna: Europaverlag, 1978.

Heer, Freidrich. *Der Kampf um die österreichische Identität*. Vienna: Böhlau, 1981.

Hutton, Patrick, ed. *History as an Art of Memory.* Hanover, NH: University Press of New England, 1993.
Janik, Allan, and Stephen Toulmin. *Wittgenstein's Vienna.* Chicago: Ivan R. Dee, 1973.
Jaśtal, Katarzyna. *Erzählte Zeiträume: Kindheitserinnerungen aus dem Randgebieten der Habsburgermonarchie von Manès Sperber, Elias Canetti, Gregor von Rezzori.* Kraków: Wydawnictwo Uniwersytetu Jagiellonskiego, 1998.
Johnston, William M. *The Austrian Mind: An Intellectual and Social History, 1848–1938.* Berkeley: University of California Press, 1983.
Kann, Robert A. *Erzherzog Franz Ferdinand Studien.* Munich: Oldenbourg, 1976.
———. *A History of the Habsburg Empire, 1526–1918.* Berkeley: University of California Press, 1974.
———. *The Multinational Empire: Nationalism and National Reform in the Habsburg Monarchy, 1848–1918.* New York: Columbia University Press, 1950.
Kennan, George. *The Decline of Bismarck's European Order: Franco-Russian Relations, 1875–1890.* Princeton, NJ: Princeton University Press, 1979.
Koselleck, Reinhart. *Vergangene Zukunft: Zur Semantik geschichtlicher Zeiten.* Frankfurt am Main: Surkhamp, 1979.
Leser, Norbert, ed. *Das geistige Leben Wiens in der Zwischenkriegszeit.* Vienna: Österreichisches Budnesverlag, 1981.
Lukacs, John. *Budapest 1900: A Historical Portrait of a City and Its Culture.* New York: Grove, 1988.
Macartney, C. A. *The Habsburg Empire, 1790–1918.* New York: Macmillan, 1969.
Macdonald Proudfoot, Mary. *The Republic of Austria, 1918–1934: A Study in the Failure of the Democratic Government.* London: Oxford University Press, 1946.
Mackiewicz, Stanisław. *Dunaj.* Translated by Joanna Ugniewska and Anna Osmólska-Mętrak. Warsaw: Czytelnik, 2004.
———. *Polityka Becka.* Paris: Instytut Literacki, 1964.
Magris, Claudio. *Der habsburgische Mythos in der österreichischen Literatur.* Salzburg: Müller, 1966. Originally published as *Il mito absburgico nella letteratura Austriaca moderna* (Torino: Einaudi, 1963).
Marek, George R. *The Eagles Die: Franz Joseph, Elisabeth, and Their Austria.* London: Hart-Davis MacGibbon, 1974.
Mast, Peter, ed. *Nationaler Gegensätze und Zusammenleben der Völker. Österreich-Ungarn im Spiegel der deutschsprachigen Literatur. Ein Modell für Europa?* Bonn: Kulturstiftung der Deutschen Vertreibenen, 1994.
May, Arthur James. *The Hapsburg Monarchy, 1867–1914.* Cambridge, MA: Harvard University Press, 1951.
Menasse, Robert. *Das Land ohne Eigenschaften: Essays zur österreichischen Identität.* Vienna: Sonderzahl, 1993.

Michalka, Wolfgang, ed. *Der Erste Weltkrieg: Wirkung, Wahrnehmung, Analyse*. Munich: Piper, 1994.

Mommsen, Hans. "Die habsburgische Nationalitätenfrage und ihre Lösungsversuche im Licht der Gegenwart." In *Nationalismus, Nationalitäten, Supranationalität: Europa nach 1945*, edited by Heinrich August Winkler and Hartmut Kaelble. Stuttgart: Klett-Cotta, 1993.

Nordholt, Jan Willem Schulte. *Woodrow Wilson: A Life for World Peace*. Berkeley: University of California Press, 1991.

Peter, László. "Die Verfassungsentwicklung in Ungarn." In *Die Habsburgermonarchie 1848–1918*. Vol. VII, *Verfassung und Parlamentarismus*, 322–31. Edited by Adam Wandruszka, Helmut Rumpler, and Peter Urbanitsch. Vienna: Österreichischen Akademie der Wissenschaften, 2000.

Pocock, J. G. A. "The Origins of the Study of the Past: A Comparative Approach." *Comparative Studies in Society and History* 4, no. 2 (1962): 209–46.

Romsics, Gergely. *Myth and Remembrance: The Dissolution of the Habsburg Empire in the Memoir Literature of the Austro-Hungarian Political Elite*. New York: Columbia University Press, 2006.

Rűsen, Jörn: *Geschichtsbewusstsein. Psychologische Grundlagen, Entwicklungskonzepte, empirische Befunde*. Vienna: Böhlau, 2001.

Schick, Paul. *Karl Kraus*. Reinbek bei Hamburg: Rowohlt, 1965.

Schorske, Carl E. *Fin-de-Siècle Vienna: Politics and Culture*. New York: Vintage Books, 1981.

Schwabe, Klaus. *Woodrow Wilson: Ein Staatsmann zwischen Puritanertum und Liberalismus*. Vol. 62 of *Persönlichkeit und Geschichte*. Göttingen: Muster-Schmidt, 1971.

Sharp, Alan. *The Versailles Settlement: Peacemaking in Paris, 1919*. New York: St. Martin's, 1991.

Shaw, Christopher, and Malcolm Chase. *The Imagined Past: History and Nostalgia*. Manchester: Manchester University Press, 1989.

Skalnik, Kurt. "Auf der Suche nach der Identität: Ansätze österreichischer National-bewusstseins in der Ersten Republik." In *Das geistige Leben Wiens in der Zwischenkriegszeit*, edited by Norbert Leser. Vienna: Österreichisches Budnesverlag, 1981.

Sked, Alan. *The Decline and Fall of the Habsburg Empire, 1815–1918*. London: Longman, 1989.

Straub, Jürgen, ed. *Erzählung, Identität und historisches Bewusstsein*. Frankfurt am Main: Suhrkamp, 1998.

Suchy, Viktor. "Die österreichische Idee als konservative Staatsidee bei Hugo von Hofmannsthal, Richard von Schaukal und Anton Wildgans." In *Staat und Gesellschaft in der modernen österreichischen Literatur*, edited by Friedbert Aspetsberger. Vienna: Österreichisches Bundesverlag, 1977.

Timms, Edward. *Karl Kraus, Apocalyptic Satirist: Culture and Catastrophe in Habsburg Vienna*. New Haven, CT: Yale University Press, 1986.

Topolski, Jerzy. *Jak się pisze i rozumie historię. Tajemnice narracji historycznej*. Warsaw: PWN, 1998.
Valiani, Leo. *The End of Austria-Hungary*. London: Secher & Warburg, 1973.
Várdy, Steven Béla. *Modern Hungarian Historiography*. Boulder, CO: East European Quarterly, 1976. Distributed by Columbia University Press.
Verosta, Stephan. *Die internationale Stellung Österreichs eine Sammlung von Erklärungen und Verträgen aus den Jahren 1938 bis 1947*. Vienna: Manz, 1947.
Walworth, Arthur. *Wilson and His Peacemakers: American Diplomacy at the Paris Peace Conference, 1919*. New York: Norton, 1986.
Wereszycki, Henryk. *Pod berłem Habsburgów: Zagadnienia narodowościowe*. Kraków: Wydawnictwo Literackie, 1986.
Wiegandt, Ewa. *Austria Felix, czyli o micie Galicji w polskiej prozie współczesnej*. Poznań: Bene Nati, 1997.
Williams, Cedric Ellis. *The Broken Eagle: The Politics of Austrian Literature from Empire to Anschluss*. London: Paul Elek, 1974.
Winkler, Heinrich August, and Hartmut Kaelble, eds. *Nationalismus, Nationalitäten, Supranationalität: Europa nach 1945*. Stuttgart: Klett-Cotta, 1993.

INDEX

Adler, Viktor, 101
agreement of 1867. *See* Compromise of 1867
Alexander I Karagorević of Yugoslavia, 26
Alexander I Obrenović of Serbia, 158
Alexander the Great of Macedonia, 44
America and Americans, 2, 6–7, 19, 21, 27, 35, 168, 182, 185
Andrassy, Julius, 83
Andrian, Leopold, 85, 92–93, 104
Anschluss, 8, 18, 32, 69, 72, 74, 79–80, 94, 97–98, 101, 170
anti-Semitism, 9, 37, 8, 131, 140. *See also* Jews; nationalism
Antonelli, Giacomo, 181
Apponyi, Albert, 32, 83
aristocracy, 10, 40–41, 68, 74, 94, 98–99, 102, 112, 122–23, 129, 130–31, 137, 140, 156–57, 168, 173
army, 8, 27, 30, 41, 43, 55, 68, 117, 119, 134, 138–39, 142, 156–57, 179, 182, 187; Red Army, 140

Badeni, Kazimierz Felix, 31, 38, 42, 47
Bagger, Eugene, 52, 57, 152, 156, 181
Balzac, Honoré, 48
barbarians, 14, 60, 75, 79–81, 93, 122, 171, 182, 189
Bartsch, Rudolf, 84
Bauer, Otto, 61, 71–72, 74, 79

Beck, Friedrich, 157
Benda, Oskar, 89, 98–99
Benedek, Ludwig, 42–43
Benedikt, Heinrich, 33–34, 39–41, 47, 181
Beneš, Edvard, 6
Berchtold, Leopold, 156
Bibl, Viktor, 18, 41–44, 47–48, 50–51, 57, 160, 176
Biliński, Leon, 29, 162, 173
Bismarck, Otto, 2, 42, 53, 60, 91, 97
Bloch, Joseph, 103
bordellos/brothels, 124, 126–28
Borkenau, Franz, 99
Braun, Felix, 101
Brehm, Bruno, 80, 152
Brehm, Max, 43–45
Britain and the British, 1, 6–7, 18–19, 27, 35, 39–41, 56, 72–73, 135, 141, 168, 170, 172, 181–82
Broch, Hermann, 2, 20, 106–9, 164, 182
Byzantium, 99, 145–47, 186
bureaucracy, 3, 8, 10, 36, 40–41, 52, 105, 113, 121–22, 146–47, 154–56, 159–60, 164, 182, 187
Burgtheater, 124–25, 129

café, 2, 124–25, 150, 177, 183; Café Central, 103, 188
Canetti, Elias, 2, 20, 124, 161
China, 74, 136
Charlemagne, 4, 76, 86, 99, 177

215

Charles I Habsburg, 34, 56, 58–59, 62, 102–3, 158, 163, 181
Christians, 9, 95–96, 120, 151, 155; Catholics, 40, 50, 57, 71, 92, 94–95, 97, 101, 119, 123, 130, 150
Christian Socialists, 50, 55, 98
Clam-Martinic, Heinrich, 78, 102
communists, 2, 7–9, 17–18, 21, 58, 60–61, 96, 99–100, 140, 163, 173
Compromise of 1867, 28–29, 35, 39, 47, 57, 62, 83, 96, 120, 131, 140, 150, 157, 159
Conrad von Hotzendorff, 51
conservatism and conservatives, 20, 25, 34, 39–40, 46–48, 60, 71, 83, 91–93, 97–99, 104–5, 116, 121, 154, 165, 180, 182, 188–89
Corti, Egon Caesar, 126–27, 157
Cosmopolitanism, 94, 100, 169, 172, 187–88
Coudenhove-Calergi, Richard, 19, 71, 100
counterfactuals, 5, 17, 44, 46, 49, 160, 168, 175
crisis, 29, 31, 42, 48–49, 58, 87, 129, 132–33
Croatia, the Croats, 8, 28, 43, 50, 143, 154
Czechs, 6–11, 14, 28, 30–32, 35–38, 42–43, 45, 47, 57, 64, 70, 74, 80, 84, 96, 129–30, 139–41, 154, 171, 173, 184; Bohemia, 10, 31, 42, 47, 140

Dante, Alighieri, 110
Daszyński, Ignacy, 102, 163
Deák, Ferenc, 83
decadence, 111–12, 145, 175, 177, 181, 183, 185–86
depression: economic, 8, 10, 17, 99, 110
Doderer, Heimitio, 116, 121–22, 134–35, 172
Doppler, Alfred, 154
Draga, Obrenović of Serbia, 158

Edward VII Windsor, 164
Eisenreich, Herbert, 181
Elisabeth of Austria, 1, 85, 126–27, 164
Engels, Friedrich, 38, 73–74

fatalism, 16, 48, 129, 153, 158, 175–76
feudalism, 14, 41, 45, 58, 63, 177, 181, 187–88
Fischhof, Adolf, 49
France, the French, 1, 6–9, 27, 35, 56, 69, 80, 88, 97, 112, 117, 149; French Revolution, 45
Franz Ferdinand Habsburg d'Este, 17, 25, 49–51, 75, 88, 127, 134–36, 163, 176
Franz Joseph I Habsburg, 1, 5, 9, 13, 29–31, 37–41, 46–50, 52–53, 55–57, 59–62, 64–65, 85–108, 119–20, 126–27, 133–34, 140, 144, 149–65, 173, 177–82
Freud, Sigmund, 20, 126, 183
Fuchs, Albert, 60–1, 65, 173
Funder, Friedrich, 55–6, 98

Galicia, 6, 8–9, 19, 21, 29, 68, 73, 78, 82, 111, 119–21, 125, 129, 136, 140, 170
Gellner, Ernest, 186–88
Germany, 2, 4, 6, 8–9, 12, 18–19, 33–34, 58–60, 64, 68–69, 72, 74–75, 79–80, 90–91, 94–97, 104, 137, 174, 182–84; German Empire, 14, 33, 52, 56, 58, 60, 83, 91, 95–97; Great Germany, 31, 172; Nazi Germany, 10, 80, 98, 170 (*see also* Nazis); Sudeten Germans, 10
Gibbon, Eward, 15, 45, 185
Ginzkey, Franz, 84
Glaise-Horstenau, Edmund, 18, 43, 50, 55
Gołuchowski, Agenor Maria, 38, 158
Gratz, Gusztáv, 36, 76–77
Greiner, Ulrich, 175

Gribble, Francis, 46
Grillparzer, Franz, 42, 182
Gsteu, Hermann, 54, 160

Habsburg myth, 20, 110–11, 169, 172, 185; Habsburg patriotism, 11–14, 68, 71, 77–78, 81, 83, 92–94, 120, 131, 139, 187
Habsburg, Otto, 93
Halecki, Oskar, 38
Hanák, Peter, 21, 35
Hantsch, Hugo, 32, 56–57, 154, 159
Hašek, Jaroslav, 2, 112, 139–41, 171, 173
Hertz, Friedrich, 37–38, 64, 171
Herzmannovsky-Orlando, Fritz, 111, 142, 144–45
Hitler, Adolf, 10–11, 17–18, 35, 74, 100, 133, 148, 170
Hofmannsthal, Hugo, 85–88, 98, 104, 107, 112, 143, 179, 182
Hohenzollern dynasty, 58, 79, 91
honor, 54–56, 122, 124, 137–38, 147, 162, 177
Horthy, Miklós, 9
Hugelmann, Karl Gottfried, 38–39, 78

internationalism, 21–22, 71–72, 74, 96, 103, 120

Jaschke, Alois, 79–80
Jászi, Oszkár, 30, 47, 62–63, 65, 173
Jews, 8–9, 32–33, 35–36, 38, 41, 68, 78, 95–97, 99–100, 103, 115, 120, 124–25, 129–30, 132, 139–40, 162–63, 168–69, 177
Johnston, William, 20
Joseph II Habsburg, 14, 94

Kafka, Franz, 2, 20, 109, 147, 183
Kauner, Heinrich, 57, 65
Kleinwächter, Friedrich, 32, 79
Koerber, Ernest, 157

Kolarz, Walter, 172–73
Kossowski, Jerzy, 142
Kraus, Karl, 84, 104–5, 107, 126, 139, 163, 172, 186
Kubin, Alfred, 143

Lenin, Valdimir, 17
Lernet-Holenia, Alexander, 137
liberalism and liberals, 10, 17, 25, 30, 42, 46, 61–62, 75, 77, 94–96, 99–100, 103, 107, 121, 124, 130–31, 159, 181–82, 187–89
Lueger, Karl, 119
Lukacs, John, 21
Luther, Martin, 95–6
Lützow, Heinrich, 29

Macartney, Carlile A., 20, 27, 34–35, 41
Machiavell,i Nicolò, 86, 112, 179, 185
Magris, Claudio, 20, 110, 182
Mann, Heinrich, 104
Mann, Thomas, 113
Márai, Sándor, 154–55
Marek, George, 186
Mars, Melke, 102
Marx, Karl, 4, 38, 73–74, 191
Masaryk, Tomáš Garrigue, 10, 35, 45
Maupassant, Guy, 48
memory, 3–4, 34, 53, 109, 116, 136, 190
Menasse, Robert, 175
Metternich, Klemens, 97, 107, 150, 157, 175, 181
Mickieiwcz, Adam, 4
Missong, Alfred, 50, 94, 96–97, 99
Mitis, Oskar, 75
Mommsen, Theodor, 15, 45
Musil, Robert, 2, 20, 106, 109–17, 121, 131–33, 142–43, 145, 150, 172, 185
Mussolini, Benito, 9, 17, 93, 98

Napoleon I Bonaparte, 4, 58, 87, 181
nationalism and nationalists, 4, 11–12, 18, 25, 28, 30–35, 37, 40, 42,

INDEX   217

47–48, 50, 54–55, 60–64, 71–72, 74–75, 81, 87–88, 90–91, 96–97, 99–100, 130, 169, 187
Nazis, 9–10, 18, 32, 42, 44, 50, 55, 60, 79–80, 93–94, 100, 132
nostalgia, 11, 15, 21, 28, 42–43, 78, 105, 110–12, 114, 117, 121, 123, 125, 173, 188–89

opera, 1, 106, 115, 124–25, 177
Otto I the Great, 76
Ottoman Empire, 14, 82, 184

Papacy, 13, 97, 177
Palačky, František, 14, 32
Palmerston, Henry, 76
Parandowski, Jan, 123
Paris Peace Conference 1919, 6–7, 32; Treaty of Trianon, 7, 35–36, 170; Treaty of St. Germain, 8, 68, 94
Piłsudski, Józef, 9–10
Poland and Poles, 1, 6, 8–11, 21, 28–29, 38, 43, 57, 62, 70, 77–78, 92, 125, 142, 170, 173
Polzer-Hoditz, Arthur, 58, 158
Pope, Alexander, 39
Popovici, Aurel, 25–26, 98
Pribram, Alfred Francis, 48–49, 54–55, 67, 154, 158, 160, 185
Protić, Stojan, 57

Radetzky, Joseph, 183
Radl, Emmanuel, 38
Rapp, Alfred, 79
Redlich, Joseph, 28, 40, 42, 47, 49, 64, 151, 159
Renner, Karl, 61
Rezzori, Gregor, 142, 145
Rilke, Reiner Maria, 84
Romania and the Romanians, 1, 6–9, 11, 25, 28, 32–34, 46, 50, 63, 68–69, 73, 84, 145, 184
Romanov dynasty, 14, 69, 74
Rosenfeld, Heinrich, 47

Rosenfeld, Sandor Friedrich (Roda Roda), 143
Roth, Joseph, 78, 118, 120, 122, 125, 128, 130, 136–37, 153, 163, 185
Runciman, Steven, 186
Russia and the Russians, 4, 6, 9, 14, 17, 37–38, 49, 53, 63, 71, 73–78, 80, 103, 112, 129, 140, 182, 184

Sapieha, Leon, 53, 150–51
Schaukal, Richard, 89, 150
Schneider, Josef, 48
Schnitzler, Arthur, 126, 175
Schorske, Carl, 20
Schüller, Richard, 76–77
Schulz, Bruno, 146
Schuschnigg, Kurt, 11–12, 92–93, 98, 100
Schüssler, Wilhelm, 21, 43, 50, 57, 79
Schwarzenberg, Felix, 150, 157
Seidler, Ernst, 102
Sejda, Kazimierz, 141
Serbia and the Serbs, 1, 3, 6, 8, 17, 19, 32–34, 43, 48–50, 54, 56–57, 63, 65, 84, 134, 137, 154, 156, 158
Seton-Watson, Robert, 35
Sked, Alan, 168
Slovakia and the Slovaks, 6, 8, 32, 43, 50, 73, 80
Slovenia and Slovenes, 8, 28, 43, 73, 80, 138, 142
Smolka, Franciszek, 38
Social Democrats, 25, 50, 60–61, 71–72, 74, 93, 98, 101, 103. *See also* socialists, and leftists
Socialists, and leftists, 61, 71, 73–74, 81, 87, 102–3, 105, 126, 131, 163
Sokol, Hans, 157
Spengler, Oswald, 17
Sperber, Manès, 162–63
Srbik, Heinrich, 18, 42–43, 60, 80, 160
Stalin, Joseph, 17, 35, 103, 173
Steed, Henry, 27, 81

St. Germain, Treaty of. *See* Paris
 Peace Conference
Strong, David, 62–63, 65
Suchenwirth, Richard, 50, 55, 57
Szekfű, Gyula, 36
Szilassy, Joseph, 36

Taaffe, Eduard, 42, 171
Taylor, Alan J.P., 19, 150
Thucydides, 15, 37
Tisza, István, 33
Toynbee, Arnold, 17
Trianon, Treaty of. *See* Paris Peace
 Conference
Trotsky, Leon, 103
Tschuppik, Karl, 151

Ukraine and the Ukrainians, 8–9,
 19, 28, 32, 43, 73, 78, 84, 120, 137,
 145

Vincenz, Stanisław, 120–21

Wandruszka, Adam, 21
Werfel, Franz, 111, 127–28, 150, 152,
 158, 163, 169, 181
Werkmann, Karl, 56, 58–59
Wiegandt, Ewa, 111
Weiser, Friedrich, 80
Wildgans, Anton, 88–89
Wilhelm I Hohenzollern, 164
Wilhelm II Hohenzollern, 59, 144
Wilson, Woodrow, 6–7
Winter, Ernst Karl, 95–96
Wittlin, Józef, 119, 136, 152–53, 158,
 170

Zegadłowicz, Emil, 121, 126, 146
Żeleński, Tadeusz (Boy), 125
Zessner-Spitzenberg, Hans Karl, 96
Zweig, Stefan, 78, 84–85, 109, 111–15,
 121, 124, 126, 130–31, 133–34, 136,
 182, 185